Child Abuse
Professional practice and public policy

Child Abuse

Professional practice and public policy

EDITED BY
OLIVE STEVENSON
Professor of Social Work Studies,
University of Nottingham

HARVESTER WHEATSHEAF
NEW YORK LONDON TORONTO SYDNEY TOKYO

First published 1989 by
Harvester Wheatsheaf,
66 Wood Lane End, Hemel Hempstead,
Hertfordshire, HP2 4RG
A division of
Simon & Schuster International Group

Printed and bound in Great Britain by Billings and Sons Ltd,
Worcester

British Library Cataloguing in Publication Data
Stevenson, Olive
    Child abuse: professional practice and public
    policy.
    1. Children. Abuse by adults
    I. Title
    362.7'044

    ISBN 0-7450-0500-4
    ISBN 0-7450-0612-4 Pbk

---

1 2 3 4 5   93 92 91 90 89

CONTENTS

FIGURES

TABLES

PREFACE

There seem to be indications that the informed public has now a somewhat greater understanding of the difficulties of child-protection work than a decade ago. However, few who are not involved have any idea of the complexity of the intellectual problems which have to be addressed if we are to understand the extent and nature of child abuse and reactions to it. Two authors, Liz Birchall and Robert Dingwall, tackle this head-on in their discussion of 'frequency' and 'prediction'. Their chapters are not easy reading; the subject matter is conceptually tough. They bring little comfort to those who hope that research will clear a path for action for policy-makers and practitioners, but the chapters should clear away some of the tangled brushwood – misconceptions and muddles about the state of research. Christine and Nigel Parton in Chapter 3, and Jim Christopherson in Chapter 4, move us into those areas in which social trends affect policies at national and local level, which in turn affect practice. They remind us that child-protection work cannot be separated from the prevailing culture and preoccupations of a given society at a given time. Packman and Randall (Chapter 5) take us into the worlds of the families, the children and their social workers. This is important, not only in terms of its content, but as an acknowledgement that it is here that the painful dramas are played out. Here the speculations of academics and the deliberations of policy-makers have to be converted, urgently, into action.

Christine Hallett's chapter on inquiries serves another purpose.

For more than a decade, inquiries into the deaths of children have cast their long shadows over social workers and other professionals in this work. This chapter, by its systematic discussion of their purposes and processes, helps to demystify these instruments of public policy. For those who have taken part, it may even exorcise the demons.

My two chapters on social-work practice and multi-disciplinary work are an attempt to identify the underlying issues with which managers, practitioners and educators will have to grapple in the next decade. I hope that the location of some of these in the context of child-welfare work generally, past as well as present, will have a steadying influence in these turbulent times.

The authors of this book all respect the commitment and integrity with which all but a few managers and practitioners approach their work. We have a keen awareness of the stress and pain which this work causes. We hope that parts of the book will helpfully illuminate grey and complex areas and that the critique of aspects of policy and practice will be received as a positive contribution to the improvement of child-protection work.

OLIVE STEVENSON

CHAPTER 1

THE FREQUENCY OF CHILD ABUSE – WHAT DO WE REALLY KNOW?

ELIZABETH BIRCHALL
Research Associate, University of Stirling

The National Society for the Prevention of Cruelty to Children (NSPCC) estimated that about 16,000 children were abused in 1986 (Creighton 1987a). The president of the Association of Directors of Social Services (ADSS) told the Cleveland Inquiry: 'We don't know! There are no firm statistics available . . .' (Roycroft 1987). Child abuse is undoubtedly an issue which causes great public and media concern and has dominated social services priority scales since the death of Maria Colwell (Colwell 1974). The prevalence of sexual abuse and the accuracy of diagnostic techniques were hotly disputed in Cleveland, and extensively reported, in 1987–8, and the Parents Against Injustice (PAIN) movement pressed for a similar inquiry in Leeds (*The Guardian* 11 April 1988).

Deaths from child abuse are rare. NSPCC registers covering 10 per cent of the country have recorded death figures fluctuating between 3 and 9 per cent annually since 1974 (Creighton and Owtram 1977; Creighton 1984–7) and Greenland's international study confirms this view (Greenland 1987). Creighton's careful analysis of the official child mortality statistics draws the conclusion that abusive deaths probably number 156 per annum (Creighton 1985–6). Yet 8,602 children died last year and 358 were killed on the roads (OPCS 1987). It is evidently not the volume of the problem which excites such powerful concern, though fears are often expressed in terms of a widespread or increasing incidence.

Does it matter whether we know the figures?

That a parent should kill or injure a child is so shocking that in one sense it is irrelevant to quantify the issue. Society evaluates the issue morally much as it responds to saving individual lives from dramatic hazards or to the pursuit of murderers – without regard to cost. Greenland (1987) uses Rutstein *et al.*'s term 'sentinel event' for such self-evidently important issues, but also includes the dimension that they are 'preventable and signal a failure in the . . . system'.

There is a crucial difference between the rigorous treatment of a problem *post hoc*, be it a mountain rescue, a murder hunt or an inquiry into a child-abuse death, and organising a system which prevents such tragedies. It often seems that the latter expectation is laid on the child-abuse management system when, in ignorance of the whole spectrum of abuse, public opinion cries scandal about the rare tragedies. We are also well aware, particularly after Cleveland, of an opposite public pressure, not to identify and intervene too strongly in 'too many' cases.

If we are to respond professionally to such ambivalent and powerful pressures, we need to be clear in our minds and publicly assertive on two fronts. Is it technically feasible to predict the serious or fatal abuse cases in the total population at risk? If so, what resources of time, money and skill are needed for an effective preventive programme? While these topics are not the concern of this chapter, one foundation stone of the answer to those questions must be a knowledge of the size of the problem.

A discussion of data sources

This chapter therefore attempts to draw together and evaluate a range of literature which casts light on the frequency of abuse; a time-limited contract and the relative accessibility of sources defined the limits of the review. To a considerable extent, I have had to rely on secondary rather than very diffuse original sources. 'Incidence' refers to the number of events or cases per annum while 'prevalence' refers to the frequency of an experience in a given population. In the absence of total population censuses, there are three main sources of information. These are as follows:

1. Sample surveys of victimisation in the general population.
2. Extrapolations of child-abuse register data.
3. Extrapolations of clinical and agency samples.

Figures from all these sources have been in circulation over the years in both the USA and the UK and, despite their inconsistencies, have been used and reused uncritically in much of the professional literature and in public discourse. Before presenting figures, then, it seems worthwhile to discuss briefly some of the dilemmas of measurement.

Defining child abuse

If something is to be identified and quantified, it needs unambiguous definition. While we habitually speak of the social problem of child abuse and have adopted national procedures for its management, we know the term is unduly vague. The everyday members of case conferences discuss the interpretation of minor injuries; parents dispute the boundaries of physical punishment; agency managements consider whether they can accommodate emotional abuse or neglect; sociologists investigate public perceptions of acceptable parenting standards and confront us with the concept of societal abuse arising from structural inequalities.

The story is familiar of the widening concept of child abuse from Kempe's 'rediscovery' of cruelty and origination of the term 'battered child syndrome' (Kempe *et al.* 1962) through 'the wide range of behaviours, clinical features and assumptions' (Parton 1979) to the 'last taboo', sexual abuse. Inevitably, the changing concepts fundamentally influence numbers identified.

Registers therefore reveal more about changing professional perceptions than about real incidence, and are probably useful mainly for monitoring the investigative and administrative workloads of the various agencies. They tell us about 'normative' and 'expressed' need, as currently perceived by experts and referral agencies, and nothing about 'comparative' need, as between known and unknown populations (Bradshaw 1972).

A rational discussion of incidence, which could connect with aetiology, subjective needs and service planning, must rest not only on clear definitions of the various phenomena to be counted but must disaggregate 'the child-abuse register'. Richards recognised this as long ago as 1974, when he objected to the term 'NAI syndrome' (nonaccidental injury syndrome).

> . . . because it may suggest . . . a uniformity and similarity between cases which is not found in practice. What is common in all cases is that somebody in a professional position has decided that a child has received injuries deliberately. But this situation may have arisen in a multitude of different ways (and from a multitude of causal factors). (Richards 1974, p.5)

However, much everyday professional discourse still appears to oscillate uneasily between perceptions of child-abuse work as extremely risk-laden or as a rather arbitrary slice of commonplace suffering. Our registers and our discourse need to be stratified by type of abuse and by severity.

DHSS Circulars (1974–86) have developed along the first dimension, but are internally inconsistent in their use or omission of concepts of 'severity' or 'persistence' (see Table 1.1). Moreover these rubrics are not mandatory and are not uniformly adopted by all authorities.

As there is no collation of national register statistics, the only consistent source of information on registration patterns comes from the NSPCC-administered areas. It is therefore worth noting that their register criteria are not identical with, but have largely influenced, the DHSS rubrics. Moreover, the NSPCC do make severity distinctions in their Physical Injury category:

> *Fatal:*   all cases which result in death.
> *Serious:*   all fractures, head injuries, internal injuries, severe burns and ingestion of toxic substances.
> *Moderate:* all soft tissue injuries of a superficial nature.
>
> (Creighton 1987a)

The list is limited in sensitivity, as approximately 90 per cent of the cases fall into the moderate category. As considerable unease arises around the registration 'threshold', particularly on matters of corporal punishment, it would seem helpful to grade trivial injuries separately – even though cumulatively in any one case they may indeed give grounds for serious concern (Lynch 1978).

Table 1.1: Official criteria for registration of child abuse

1970 The Battered Baby	1974 Non-accidental injury to children: LASSL(74)13; CMO(74)8	1976 Non-accidental injury to children: LASSL(76)2; CMO(76)2; CND(76)3	1980 Child abuse: central register systems: LASSL(80)4; HN(80)20	1986 Child Abuse: Working Together draft	1988 Working Together
This publication seeks to heighten professional awareness of this socio-medical problem. It contains no definitions.	Circular firmly recommending all LAs to establish NAI registers and inter-agency procedures. It contains no definitions but points out 'older children are not immune.'	Circular stating registers should include 'injured children up to . . . 16'. There is a caution against overloading the system by including 'at risk' cases.	'Previous guidance (covered) NAI, that is, physical injury and the extremes of deprivation and neglect. (T)he same requirements should apply to . . . severe mental or emotional abuse. This memorandum therefore refers throughout to child abuse.' All children under 17.	'Parents or carers (i.e. persons who while not parents have actual custody of a child) can harm children either by direct acts, or by a failure to provide proper care, or both.' These include:	'The following categories are not exhaustive nor . . . mutually exclusive. Professional staff need to consider systematically whether all or some of these categories are present (and) the degree (for) each child in the household. Children may be harmed by a parent, sibling or other relative, a carer (with) actual custody such as a foster parent or a staff member in a residential home, an acquaintance or a stranger. The harm may be the result of a direct act or by a failure to act to provide proper care, or both.'

Table 1.1 (cont.)

1970 The Battered Baby	1974	1976	1980 Child abuse: central register systems: LASSL(80)4; HN(80)20	1986 Child Abuse: Working Together draft	1988 Working Together
	Non-accidental injury to children: LASSL(74)13; CMO(74)8	Non-accidental injury to children: LASSL(76)2; CMO(76)2; CND(76)3			
			PHYSICAL INJURY 'Where . . . not consistent with the account of how it occurred, or where there is definite knowledge or a reasonable suspicion that the injury was inflicted or knowingly not prevented by any person having custody, charge or care of the child. This includes . . . suspected poisonous substances.'	PHYSICAL INJURY 'Any form including deliberate poisoning where there is definite knowledge or a reasonable suspicion that the injury was inflicted or knowingly not prevented by any person having custody of the child.'	PHYSICAL ABUSE 'Any form including deliberate poisoning where there is definite knowledge or a reasonable suspicion that the injury was inflicted or knowingly not prevented.'
			PHYSICAL NEGLECT 'Persistently or severely neglected physically for example by exposure to dangers of different kinds,	NEGLECT 'Persistent or severe neglect for example exposure to any kind of danger including cold and starvation, which results in	NEGLECT 'Persistent or severe neglect (for example exposure to any kind of danger including cold and starvation) which results in serious

including cold and starvation.'

FAILURE TO THRIVE AND EMOTIONAL ABUSE
'Where medically diagnosed as . . . severe non-organic failure to thrive or . . . behaviour and emotional development have been severely affected; where medical and social assessments find . . . persistent or severe neglect or rejection.'

serious impairment of the child's health and development.'

EMOTIONAL ILL-TREATMENT
'The severe and adverse effect upon behaviour and emotional development caused either by persistent or severe neglect or rejection on the part of the parent or carer.'

SEXUAL ABUSE
'The involvement of dependent, developmentally immature children and adolescents in sexual activities they do not truly comprehend, to which they are unable to give informed consent, or that violate the social taboos of family roles or are against the law.'

impairment of the child's health or development including non-organic failure to thrive.'

EMOTIONAL ABUSE
'The severe adverse effect on behaviour and emotional development . . . caused by persistent or severe emotional ill-treatment or rejection. All abuse involves some emotional ill-treatment; this category should be used where it is the main or sole form of abuse.'

SEXUAL ABUSE
'The involvement of dependent, developmentally immature children and adolescents in sexual activities they do not truly comprehend, to which they are unable to give informed consent, or that violate the social taboos of family roles.'

Table 1.1 (cont.)

1970 *The Battered Baby*	1974	1976	1980	1986 *Child Abuse: Working Together* draft	1988 *Working Together*
	Non-accidental injury to children: LASSL(74)13; CMO(74)8	Non-accidental injury to children: LASSL(76)2; CMO(76)2; CND(76)3	Child abuse: central register systems: LASSL(80)4; HN(80)20		
			CHILDREN LIVING IN A HOUSEHOLD 'With . . . or . . . . regularly visited by a parent or another person who has abused a child and . . . . considered at risk of abuse.' Author's note: The 1978 draft included 'Babies with a history and prognosis suggesting high risk' and other categories covering 'deliberate genital injury' and other forms of abuse (involving equal) physical, mental or emotional abuse. However these criteria were omitted from the substantive 1980 circular.	POTENTIAL ABUSE 'Where social and medical assessments indicate a high degree of risk that the child might be abused in future including situations where another child in the household had been harmed or the household contains a known abuser. These categories . . . are not necessarily exhaustive or mutually exclusive. And all of them may result in a FAILURE TO THRIVE. Professional staff need to consider whether all or some of these categories of abuse are present, as well as the degree (for) each child in the household.'	GRAVE CONCERN 'Children whose situations do not currently fit the above categories but where social and medical assessments indicate that they are at significant risk of abuse. These could include situations where another child has been harmed or the household contains a known abuser.'

So far, only the official and mainstream definitions and their inherent difficulties have been introduced. Before looking at the quantitative data from register sources, other issues need consideration.

Sociological critiques

The whole process of registering cases presupposes identifiable personal or intrafamilial pathologies which can be treated and perhaps even predicted or prevented. Gelles reviewed a number of such studies which identified 19 personality characteristics, of which only 4 were cited by 2 or more authors. He commented: 'In some of the current essays . . . I find profiles of my students, my neighbours, my wife, myself, my son' (Gelles 1979a, p.135).

As Parton and Parton discuss (in Chapter 3), Greenland (1987) is the latest to draw a high-risk profile from case studies but does not indicate how common that profile would be in the general population. Identified abusers are usually poor but the majority of poor people do not batter their children. Many people, including reputable teachers and care staff, punish children to the point of mild injury (Gil 1979b). Many people can imagine injuring their children at times of stress and the reasons why most do not are as multifarious as the interactions which lead to abuse. Parton comments on our very limited understanding of the complex network and directions of forces which create abusive circumstances and acts. Thus we do '. . . not . . . know [why], when, how often, with what degree of certainty and with what implications for the child' (Parton 1985a, p.139) a particular incident may occur.

Nagi (1977) argues that to achieve a 95 per cent identification of abuse and neglect, 54 per cent 'false positive' reports would have to be accepted, screened and excluded, but that seems a surprisingly efficient ratio. Parton (1985a) points out that where, as in matters of violence, prediction criteria are intrinsically weak and the phenomena infrequent, false positive findings can outweigh real cases. Thus if 1 per cent of the population act violently, even if prediction could be 90 per cent accurate, then 100 people per 1,000 would be falsely labelled in the process of identifying 9 out of 10 actual perpetrators.

At 90 per cent accuracy, the correct identifications would outweigh the false positives only when real incidence of the phenomenon exceeded 10 per cent. Roycroft (1987) reports that English authorities investigate approximately 4 times as many cases as are registered. Mary Pride in the USA complains that the 1,000,000 parents 'hotlined' annually overwhelmingly outnumber the 'thousands' who actually maltreat their children seriously (Ball, the *Daily Telegraph* 1987). Such criticisms imply that the difficulty of identifying appropriate high-risk families makes registers both doomed to statistical invalidity and operationally worthless or even damaging.

In contrast, much procedural and therapeutic literature stresses the value of identifying and intervening with registered families. Creighton (1984a) contends that tight management has significantly reduced the recurrence and incidence of serious abuse, though the 1985 and 1986 figures have markedly reversed this trend (see Table 1.4 below).

A second line of attack is epitomised by Gil, who sees the labelling and pathologising of individuals as a diversion from 'societal abuse'.

Every child . . . is to be considered of equal intrinsic worth and . . . entitled to . . . fully realise his inherent potential and share equally in life, liberty and happiness . . . In accordance with these value premises then, any act of commission or omission by individuals, institutions or society as a whole, and any conditions resulting . . . which deprive children of equal rights and liberties and/or interfere with their optimal development, constitute by definition, abusive or neglectful acts or conditions. (Gil 1979a, p.4)

Such a formulation is profoundly challenging to any practitioner in social administration. Concrete deficits, for instance in health and education and access to material goods, are thoroughly documented (e.g. Townsend 1979, Townsend and Davidson 1982) – but recent changes in social security provisions are worsening the poverty of the poorest. Should that 'avoidable suffering' be recorded by child-abuse registrars, as a prelude to appropriate social interventions? Greenland comments: ' . . . it should by now be obvious that little progress can be made in reducing [these] deaths until the problem of poverty afflicting some 35 million Americans, mostly women and children, is effectively dealt with' (1987, p.10).

A third critique focuses on the intrinsic indefinability of abuse criteria. No legal or professional or public consensus exists on 'unacceptable' standards. Giavannoni and Becerra (1979) discuss the failure of most American statutes to define such concepts as 'neglect' or 'a reasonable degree of interest . . . as to a child's welfare'. They find professional criteria equally problematic. The same criticisms could be levelled at the UK statute wording: 'proper development is being avoidably prevented or neglected', etc.

I have already commented on difficulties in register criteria. Nagi makes similar points and comments that in any continuum a doubtful middle area will exist. He argues that this is:

> . . . especially large in relation to cases of child abuse and neglect. At the heart of the problem lies the question of when or in what forms maltreatment is to be considered disciplinary, excessive or abusive. Much has been written [but] the numerous statements have neither significantly clarified the criteria nor narrowed the range of doubtful cases . . . (Nagi 1977, p.20).

In this country we have institutionalised the case conference and the court to define limits, but in practice 'street level bureaucrats' (Lipsky 1971) make decisions at many points between the initial observer and the ultimate registrar. Giavannoni and Becerra (1979) quote Gelles' discovery of the 'wide discrepancy in professional responses' to the same case vignettes. Nagi (1977) makes similar points and found that 'the most skilled were the least confident' about the values of intervention. For such reasons, Goldstein et al. (1973) reject the idea of legal intrusion into 'emotional neglect'.

Wolock and Horowitz (1984) however, attack the prevailing definitions and systems precisely for their inattention to the more extensive and damaging issue of serious neglect. Various American sources suggest the incidence of neglect to NAI is at least 3:1 and perhaps 10:1. Yet there are great difficulties in defining thresholds. Apart from volume problems, these threshold problems appear to inhibit British registration practices (see below).

Giavannoni and Becerra note the conflicting requirements of a service system, which offers broad definitions and invites people to receive help, and a legalistic system which must have clear criteria to justify intrusive interventions and also to avoid stigmatising false positive cases. For such reasons, the Dutch have favoured their inclusive and confidential doctor system (Baneke 1983) (see Christopherson, Chapter 4).

Lastly, there is overwhelming evidence that socioeconomically deprived groups constitute the bulk of registered cases (e.g. Creighton 1984a; Greenland 1987). It is also recognised that the poor are subjected to a greater official surveillance, so that the class discrepancy in real incidence may be exaggerated (Parton 1985a; Gelles 1979b; Dingwall *et al.* 1983). Newberger and Hyde (1979) note the obverse, that private medical practitioners see many more affluent cases than they report.

For all these reasons, some efforts have been made to discover rates of victimisation through population surveys in the USA and, to a limited extent in the field of sexual abuse, in the UK.

Surveys

There have been several American surveys bearing on child abuse incidence. Gil and Noble (1979) devised an interesting research programme, investigating a nationwide random sample of adults. Over 58 per cent thought 'anybody could' injure a child; 22 per cent thought they themselves could; 3 per cent said they personally knew of a physical injury case in the preceding year; 0.4 per cent actually admitted to abusing a child themselves.

Gil and Noble derived from the 3 per cent figure an incidence of 2.5 – 4 million physical injuries per annum, a rate of 13–21 per 1,000 children. They compared this estimate with national register totals, then averaging 6,300 per annum. Even allowing for the probability that registers will miss the more minor injuries, this discrepancy is staggering!

Prescott (1979) explored prevalence from a radically different angle. He examined the 'violence-inducing' factors in a variety of cultures, and linked American values to an 'unwanted infant' rate of 20 per cent. By inductive reasoning, he estimated 0.5 – 1.5 million infants alone would be abused.

Straus has twice sampled American parents and found that 14 per cent admitted 'punching, kicking, biting, hitting with an object, beating up, threatening or using a knife or gun' in 1975, while only 10.7 per cent confessed to similar behaviour in 1985. He recognises that a cultural change may have affected the admission rate, but believes it has also altered the real incidence of parental violence (Gelles and Straus 1987). In commenting on the Straus studies, Schene (1987) notes that still only 1 in 7 physically injured children appears to be officially identified, despite a 188 per cent increase in reporting rates in the decade.

The types of discipline and threat (over 3 per cent picked up guns at some time in their children's lives) employed by American parents seem more extreme than anything described in the Newsons' Nottingham Studies. Although straps, sticks and slippers were used on 26 per cent of boys and 18 per cent of girls aged 7 of all classes, and slaps were commonplace at ages 4 and 7, the use of other implements was too rare to score (Newson 1978).

The US data from surveys and registers are summarised and compared in Table 1.2.

Table 1.2 shows the limitations and ambiguities in American data despite a variety of research approaches. The British data is even more limited and, apart from the NSPCC series, arbitrary.

The only UK survey on general child abuse that I know of was undertaken by the BBC Childwatch team in 1986, but it can give no perspective on incidence even though many people were involved. 3,000 people responded via a questionnaire but they were self-selected volunteers, obviously highly motivated by a broadcast. 2,500 responses were analysed and they were found to be geographically and socioeconomically representative, but predominantly of young adults.

The respondents were classified as having experienced:

Sexual abuse	90 per cent
Physical violence	56 per cent
Sexual abuse and physical violence	<50 per cent
Neglect	38 per cent

'In all, nine tenths were victims of abuse within the family' (BBC 1986a).

Whether this distribution of cases reflects real incidence cannot be deduced, but it is probable that the current atmosphere would increase the response rate from sexual-abuse victims. It appears that the BBC extrapolate from this survey prevalence figures of 4 million adults and 1.5 million children victimised by some form of abuse (BBC 1986b).

Table 1.2: A comparison of US sources on child-abuse incidence

Date	Author	Definition	Database	National incidence estimated		My source
				No.	Rate per 1,000	
1968	Gil	Physical force used . . . to hurt, injure or destroy a child	National Registers	6,600	Not given	Newberger & Hyde 1979 Creighton 1984c
1971	Mulford		Massachusetts Physicians & Hospitals	200,000	Not given	Newberger & Hyde 1979
1971	Kempe	Child abuse	Live births	Not given	6	Lystad 1979
1971	Kempe	a. Severe abuse and neglect b. In need of protection by society	Not known	Not given	a. 0.12 b. 0.38	Creighton 1984c
1971	Zalba	a. May have been badly hurt b. Need protective services	Not known	30,000 2–250,000	Not given	Lystad 1979
1973	Kempe	Not known	Not known	60,000	Not given	Creighton 1984c

Date	Author	Definition	Method	Figure	Rate	Source
1975	Straus, Gelles and Steinmetz	Parents' admissions of violent behaviour and threats: punching, kicking, biting, hitting with an object, beating up, threatening or using a knife or gun	Random sample	1.5m	140	Gelles & Straus 1987
1979	Gershenson	a. Abuse b. Neglect c. Deaths	Not known	300,000 650,000 2,000	Not given	Gershenson 1979
1979	Gelles	Abuse by caretakers		0.5–1m	Not given	Gelles 1979b
1979	Prescott	Violence – factors in society correlated with ratio of unwanted infants	An inductive reasoning process	0.5–1.5m infants	Not given	Prescott 1979
1979	Gil & Noble	Physical injury	a. National random sample b. Register study	2.5–4m 6,000	13–21 0–0.31	Gil & Noble 1979
1985	Straus	As 1975	Random sample	795,000	107	Gelles & Straus 1987
1986	Department of Health and Human Services	a. Demonstrable harm from physical, sexual, emotional abuse and neglect b. Endangered through abusive or neglectful treatment	Known to agencies	1,025,900 558,800	Not given Not given	The Guardian 4.7.1988

Table 1.3: A comparison of UK sources on child-abuse incidence (excluding sexual abuse and excluding the NSPCC register series)

Date	Author	Definition	Database	No.	Rate per 1,000	My source
				National incidence estimated		
1952	Chesser	"At some time in their life . . . require the help of the NSPCC"	Not given	Not given	Prevalence 60–70	Smith 1975
1971	Kempe	a. Significant injury b. Serious deprivation	New babies (0.5m p.a.)	a. 1,500 b. 1,500	0.85 0.85	Smith 1975
1974	Oliver et al.	Severe and recurring injuries	38 victims under 4 in NE Wilts, 1965–71	3,000 300 deaths	1	Oliver et al. 1974
1975	Hall	Not given	29 cases in Emergency Dept. Preston R. I. 1970–72	4,400 757 deaths	Not given	Franklin 1975
1976	Select Committee on Child Health Services	a. Undefined NAI b. Deaths c. Brain damage d. Visual impairment	Evidence from limited local studies	a. 5,000 b. 350 c. 11% of victims d. 5% of victims	Not given	Court Report 1976
1977	Select Committee on Violence in the Family: Session 1976–77	NAI or abuse	a. Routine hospital medical practice, particularly children under 2 b. Severely injured children c. Visually impaired children d. Mental handicap hospital survey	a. 15% of all patients b. 25% of a. c. 10% of a. d. 2.5% of patients = 400	Not given	Select Committee Report 1977
1985	Creighton	Deaths caused by parents or caregivers	Analysis of Registrar General's figures.	156	Not given	Creighton 1985b

| 1986 | BBC Childwatch | Self-reported experiences of abuse. | 3,000 self-selected respondents to TV feature. 2,500 responses analysed. | Prevalence 4m adults 1.5m children | Not given | BBC 1986a BBC 1986b |

Table 1.4: Types and severities of child abuse on NSPCC registers 1977–86

Type	1977	1978	1979	1980	1981	1982	1983	1984	1985	1986
Physical injury:										
Fatal		6	8	7	8	3	3	3	6	6
Serious	112	106	76	84	83	64	54	56	93	81
Moderate	573	603	599	683	716	594	615	648	807	850
Failure to thrive	27	26	17	15	30	21	15	34	28	46
Fatal FTT										1
Neglect	No returns sought	No returns sought	3	15	30	44	62	50	71	124
Emotional abuse	No returns sought	No returns sought			4	17	31	18	22	41
SUB TOTAL:	716	741	713	819	871	743	780	809	1,027	1,149
At risk	274	317	360	293	278	288	278	208	337	462
SUB TOTAL:	990	1,058	1,073	1,112	1,149	1,031	1,058	1,017	1,364	1,611
Sex abuse	7	8	8	11	27	40	51	98	222	527
GRAND TOTAL:	997	1,066	1,081	1,123	1,176	1,071	1,109	1,115	1,586	2,138

NB. There are small discrepancies between my totals and NSPCC originals as I have omitted 1–6 cases described as 'accidental'
Sources: Creighton and Owtram (1977)
Creighton (all listed titles)

Table 1.3 summarises a variety of authoritative and/or much quoted sources.

Perhaps the most obvious observation on this material is that the incidence inferences vary widely. The evidence underlying the estimates is slender or not easily accessible and the populations differ and make direct comparisons impossible. That hospital-based studies are overweighted with severe cases is self-evident and amply confirmed by Greenland's (1987) extensive comparisons of death rates in different cohorts. It is surprising to find national incidence rates extrapolated, and widely used at the time, from such small specific studies as Oliver *et al.* (1974) and Hall (in Franklin 1975). Creighton (1987a) quotes Adelstein's statistical observation on Oliver's national estimate of 300 fatalities. The margin of error in extrapolating from such a small sample is such that actual deaths could lie anywhere between 31 and 526 per annum.

Child-abuse registers

Is it possible after all that registers are our most reliable source, despite their weaknesses? Even though all local authorities now administer or participate in register systems, no national figures have been regularly collated. Recent initiatives by the ADSS, NSPCC and Government to start collating regular national figures must be welcome. The Scottish authorities began a series of reports in 1986 (ADSW 1988). The NSPCC rightly claim that their register research is 'the largest continuous study of child abuse . . . in this country' (Creighton 1987a). 9–10 per cent of the child population live in areas covered by their registers, and they have been analysing their data since 1975.

In 1974, the DHSS compiled responses from 97 authorities covering 90 per cent of the population and a 9-month period. Although registration criteria were not then at all explicit, it may be reasonable to extrapolate a national incidence figure for registered NAI of 8,360 in that year.

The gross register totals held by the NSPCC rose slowly but fairly steadily between 1977 and 1984, from 1,000 to 1,116 cases. They then shot up in 1985 and 1986 by 42 per cent and 36 per cent respectively, so that those registers are now more than double the 1984 figure. Scottish estimates rose from 2,235 to 2,970 children on register between January and December 1987 (ADSW 1988). As already discussed, gross figures reveal little more than huge increases in the investigative workload.

It is more interesting to look at the trends in different classes and degrees of abuse (see Table 1.4).

Looking at Table 1.4 as a whole, the absorption of extra categories is evident as DHSS advice developed, and the recent explosive acceleration of awareness of sexual abuse masks the much smaller increments in other categories. Fatal cases are such a minute proportion and so subject to idiosyncratic fluctuations that no trends or national inferences can be drawn (Creighton 1985b).

If fatal and serious injury cases are considered together, as Creighton (1984a) now recommends, we see an impressive, steady decline in absolute numbers between 1977 and 1984. Had this trend continued, alongside the increases in all other categories which suggest heightened register awareness among professionals, two inferences would be tempting. Have early professional interventions improved, and pre-empted family disasters as much of the therapeutic literature describes? Has there been a cultural shift away from parental violence, as Gelles and Straus (1987) argue? However, the sharp rise in 1985 and 1986 precludes easy inferences.

The neglect and emotional abuse figures do not appear to bear any relation to real incidence. Do they reflect professional inability to define cases appropriately and/or an organisational appraisal that the child-abuse management system cannot absorb the potential volume? Do they indicate a growing recognition that much neglect is rooted in structural poverty and cannot be helped by the register system?

DHSS advice about registering 'at risk' cases has been contradictory, so the consistency of this category in NSPCC figures would appear to reflect the stability of their own rubrics and thus would not be likely to be replicated nationwide. The Scottish figures vary between 0 and 50 per cent of different authorities' register totals (ADSW 1988).

Table 1.4 summarises much of what we know about registered cases. Is it possible to extrapolate national figures from this source? Clearly not in the small categories. Creighton does infer a national registration rate for physical injury, grown from 6,816 in 1982 to 9,590 in 1986. She suggests sexual abuse registrations would be 2,932 and 6,330 in 1985 and 1986 (1987b). One could thus infer from her 10 per cent survey gross national figures of 10,000 in 1977, reasonably in line with the 1974 estimate above. However, simple multiplication in the last 2 years would not show the same consistency, resulting in far smaller numbers than Roycroft found in his recent survey. He quotes a national regist-ration rate of 25,000 and 30,000 for the same 2 years (Roycroft 1987). It is possible that the NSPCC operates a more consistent and more stringent registration standard than other local authorities.

However, we have no means of knowing. Gough (1988) found variations of 10 times magnitude in registration rates between administrative sub-areas of Glasgow and Motherwell alone. Even wider ranges appear in the categorisation of cases by different authorities (ADSW 1988). The earliest NSPCC reports (Creighton and Owtram undated; Creighton undated) gave separate details for each participating area which showed wide variations in the profile of cases. A mean rate of 20.3 per cent for serious injury reports concealed a range from 15.3 per cent to 35.8 per cent. Similarly, registration rates varied from 1 to 2.7 per 1,000 under 5s. No explanation is apparent for such marked divergences in incidence between 3 fairly similar large northern cities. Now that NSPCC registers cover many more and varied areas it is possible that local variations are even wider. Alternatively, experience may have reduced anomalous practices. It is a pity no information is now given on the scatter in their figures, not least because the degree of inter-area consistency must affect the feasibility of estimating national registration patterns.

Sexual abuse

This category has suddenly emerged as numerous and of serious concern to professionals and public alike. Because of its topicality and because the data sources in the UK are more varied than for other abuses, I have left it for separate consideration. However, similar problems of definition and divergent figures arise. Assertions that '1 in 3 girls have been victimised' and 'sexual abuse is profoundly damaging' clash with 'we don't have any idea' and 'serious sexual abuse is rare'.

Some of the statistical confusion arises because victim studies include extrafamilial encounters of an occasional and non-invasive nature such as meeting a 'flasher'. Yet we take it for granted that sexual abuse as material for registration and professional intervention is intrafamilial.

The English legal concept of incest is 'sexual intercourse between a man and his daughter, granddaughter, sister (half sister) or mother, or between a woman, 16 or over, and her grandfather, father, brother (half brother) or son. The child cannot give consent.' (Cleveland Report 1988 p.5)

This definition is an unhelpful basis for interpreting the data because England and Scotland and various States of the USA have discrepant statutes. Vander Mey and Neff claim that most researchers adopt the term 'incest' for 'all forms of erotic action' which 'result in victimisation of a child' and have been 'initiated by any adult who is related by family ties or surrogate family ties' (Vander Mey and Neff 1982, p.719–29).

Such a usage is similar to the Kempe (1980) formula which forms the recommended UK register criterion (see Table 1.1 above). If, furthermore, 'most sexual victimisation of children is incestuous' as Finkelhor (1986) concludes, then research data and our professional concerns might coincide fairly closely. Unfortunately such coterminosity of interest is elusive. Peters, Wyatt and Finkelhor (Wyatt and Peters 1986; Finkelhor 1986) found a confounding inconsistency of definitions when they examined 19 American studies. These inconsistencies compounded problems arising from sample discrepancies, and rates of abuse varied between 6 and 62 per cent for girls and 3 and 20 per cent for boys. As 300 per cent variations remained after they had standardised the data as much as possible, they drew no conclusion about incidence but recommended more rigorous research. They summarily dismissed American register figures, which are variously quoted between 100,000 and 300,000 per annum (Radbill 1978; Vander, Mey and Neff 1982; Regan 1986).

Another front is opened up by the feminist view of sexual abuse as a common and unwelcome expression of male power. The London Incest Survivors Group would like the incest law to

Table 1.5: UK surveys of child sexual abuse

Date	Authors	Population	Definition	Gross prevalence or incidence findings	Detailed findings re victims' experiences	Any national extrapolation offered	My remarks	My source
1978	Mrazek, Lynch & Bentovim	1,599 medical personnel; 1,072 cases	i. Battered children – injuries primarily in genital areas ii. Intercourse or other inappropriate genital contact iii. Inappropriate involvement with adult in sexual activities	41% of respondents had seen CSA at some time. Range: From GPs 16% to Police Surgeons 56%.	i. 4% ii. 69% iii. 16% 74% perpetrators were known to the child; 43% intrafamilial mainly father figures, but c 2% of total example were mothers. Ratio: c 6 girls: 1 boy. 39% were under 11, and 13% (all girls) were under 6.	Prevalence 0.3%	Given the method of sampling, the 'heavy end' would predominate. This prevalence is now widely accepted as an underestimate.	Original 1983 Markowe 1988 La Fontaine 1988
1982	Nash & West	Young women a. 223 patients on a GP list b. 92 students.	i. Verbal ii. Flasher iii. Sexual kiss iv. Sexual fondling v. Attempted sex vi. Intercourse	a. 42% b. 54% Mean 48%	(i-ii) c 50% (v-vi) 6.5% 19% were single experiences.		I have slightly collapsed their list of behaviours. No correlations are offered between nature of experience(s) and perpetrator.	Original 1985 Markowe 1988 La Fontaine 1988

Year	Study	Sample	Definition	%	Findings	Estimates	Notes	References
1983	Baker: *19* magazine questionnaire	3000+ self-selected readers: 1/130 of total circulation	Experiences of SA angled towards intrafamilial	36%	47% perpetrators were strangers. 8% were father figures. 34% were under 11 at first contact. Half of these were intrafamilial		Fairly divergent perpetrator details between 2 samples but I have averaged them. My correction of his percentages. My estimate.	CIBA 1984 Markowe 1988
1984	MORI/ Channel 4: interview survey	2,019 respondents = 87% response rate. Random sample of constituencies and quota sample of individuals.	Any activity which the other expects to lead to their sexual arousal.	12% girls 8% boys	7% full sexual intercourse; 69% non-contact; 72% non-contact; 13% intrafamilial; 62% one-off; 22% repeats by one person; 13% repeats by a number of people.	Prevalence 1.117m. Intrafamilial sexual abuses at age under 15 143,000. Only 1% of population suffer lasting harm.	But that is c ½m individuals.	Original 1984 Baker & Duncan 1985 La Fontaine 1988 Markowe 1988 Jay & Doganis 1987 Aitchison 1987

Table 1.5 (cont.)

Date	Authors	Population	Definition	Gross prevalence or incidence findings	Detailed findings re victims' experiences	Any national extrapolation offered	My remarks	My source
1986	BBC Childwatch questionnaire	3,000 self-selected respondents: 93% women 64% under 35	Adult sexual interference: a. touching private parts b. some form of sexual intercourse c. pornographic.	a. 83% b. 56% c. 15%	90% intrafamilial. c 50% displaying multiple psychological distress.		Clearly, self-selection will attract positive cases and perhaps the more distressed. But contrast with *19 Guardian* survey.	Sarah Caplin, Producer, in letter to *The Guardian* 14.8.87 Markowe 1988 La Fontaine 1988
1986	BBC Childwatch interview survey	2,041 adults, probability sample of areas, and quota sample of individuals.	Sexual activities for the abusers' gratification: might be intercourse or exposure, or pornographic.	4% girls 1% boys = 3% prevalence No. of cases found was 82 women and 20 men.	32% full or attempted sexual intercourse; 62% sexual kiss or touch; 23% made to do something sexual; 27% other/ unstated. 10% perpetrator a stranger; 30% unstated. 60% girls; 1st incident at age under 10. 45% boys, 1st incident at age under 10.			Markowe 1988 La Fontaine 1988

encompass any 'sexual molestation by any older person perceived as a figure of trust' (Nelson 1982). Campbell (1987) asks whether sexual abuse is '. . . martyrdom en masse . . . a million little girls and perhaps a million little boys too being sexually exploited in their own families and neighbourhoods by respectable ordinary men' (p.10). Such questions are sharply relevant both to professionals and public in the light of the Cleveland dispute, but what do we know of figures?

The UK survey data consists of 6 studies since 1978, shown in Table 1.5, but as La Fontaine remarks: 'The common use of the label CSA conceals the different meanings which may be attached to it' (La Fontaine 1988, p.2).

Reported prevalences ranged from 0.3 per cent to 83 per cent and reflect more light on the construction of the studies than on actual prevalences. Mrazek, Lynch and Bentovim were early in the field, when public and professional awareness was much lower; moreover, they sought data mainly from second- or third-line professionals who would only see a minority of cases concentrated on the severe end of the spectrum. In total contrast, the Childwatch questionnaire was completed by self-selected and highly-motivated respondents to a popular BBC programme which was vigorously campaigning for attention to the problem of sexual abuse. It is reasonable to assume that few people would seek out a postal questionnaire to report 'no experience'. That those who responded reported a high rate (50 per cent) of multiple psychological distresses would also seem likely to reflect bias in the sample.

The three studies that sampled a normal population are Nash and West's (1985) small studies in a particular locality and the two TV-sponsored interview surveys which took similar national sampling frames (see Table 1.6) (Childwatch unpublished MS 1987; MORI 1984; Baker and Duncan 1985). The gross results are very divergent, ranging from 48 per cent to 3 per cent prevalence. On comparing some cardinal details of the available data, however, the indications of prevalence of the most serious forms of abuse appear to be more convergent.

In reviewing this data, Markowe (1988) criticises the methodological shortcomings and concludes that 'This makes estimating a figure for the national prevalence of child sexual abuse an unsatisfactory exercise'. La Fontaine (1988, p.3) also points out method-

Table 1.6: UK surveys on prevalence of child sexual abuse

Total population rates	Nash & West 1982	MORI/C4 1984	BBC interview survey 1986
All SA as defined by research project	48% girls	12% girls 8% boys	4% girls 1% boys
Sexual intercourse } Attempted SI }	3.3%	0.5%	1%
'Contact'	22%	4.4%	2%

ological limitations, but concludes from 'evidence of considerable under-reporting' in the 2 TV surveys and from American findings that 'a 10 per cent prevalence rate for sexual abuse involving physical contact is quite likely' (p. 3).

Most survey data suggests that incidence has been fairly unchanging through generations (Finkelhor 1986), though the British surveys give contradictory results (Markowe 1988).

Sexual-abuse registrations are increasing exponentially in the UK (see Table 1.4 above). The most recent national estimate was 6,330 (Creighton 1987a). In addition to Cleveland, though less dramatically, many authorities were reporting 'almost double', 'treble', 'a staggering increase', etc. in the professional journals last year. The Leeds paediatricians, Hobbes and Wynne, whose clinical example was followed in Cleveland, have reported identification rates rising from 0 in the 1970s to about 500 in the first half of 1987. Moreover, they now identify 1 victimised boy to 2.2 girls, whereas in 1984 the ratio was 1:14 (Jay and Doganis 1987; Campbell 1987; Hobbes and Wynne 1987).

'Childline' (1987) is a new source of information about expressed need. Of their 22,000 callers in the first year, almost 6,000 complained of sexual abuse. They imply that 15,000 children could be attempting to divulge abuse. As 81 per cent of their children have 'never told anyone before', these figures are suggestive of a very large additional population of actively distressed children.

It cannot be doubted that the real problem far outweighs the numbers known to any register or service agency.

The fragmented mosaic revealed here cannot give a clear and

compelling picture of the human pain which it suggests. However, surveys and agency data from both the UK and USA do indicate strongly that sexual abuse is very predominantly perpetrated by men on girls, though boys are increasingly identified as victims. Serious persistent abuse generally appears to begin in primary school years, though some clinical series include over a third of pre-school age. It seems obvious that most persistent and severe abuse takes place within the familial network, although the surveys give markedly different results as to the amount of minor or single-incident abuse that children meet on the street. Although the data is not consistently cross-correlated, it seems a reasonable hypothesis that father figures, the most numerous group, are the chief abusers of small children who only come to light when seriously abused, as well as of the distressed children who ring Childline themselves, and of the adults who have belatedly revealed their bitter stories.

Since sexual abuse is not confined to the socioeconomically deprived classes, professional services and public opinion will find it difficult to acknowledge the quantity or the quality of the problem now being discovered.

Conclusion

This chapter has attempted to summarise basic numerical information about child abuse in our society. It ends up endorsing Roycroft's observation that 'we don't know!'. Yet perhaps it has clarified what it is that we do not know, and why.

Given the high level of concern caused by these 'sentinel' events, it is strange that we really know so little of either the anatomy or epidemiology of child abuse. Fundamental research into defining the problem, with contributions from victims and the general public as well as professionals, seems essential. Incidence data must also be sought from carefully-designed and adequately-sized sample surveys of the general population.

CHAPTER 2

SOME PROBLEMS ABOUT PREDICTING CHILD ABUSE AND NEGLECT

ROBERT DINGWALL

Research Fellow, Wolfson College and Centre for Socio-Legal Studies, University of Oxford

> Research designed to refine the techniques for predicting accurately those children who will continue to be at risk is urgently required, and we recommend that such research should be carried out by medical sociologists.
>
> Louis Blom-Cooper, *A Child in Trust* (1985, p. 289)

In the 1980s it is rare to find such testimonials to the potential contribution of sociological research to social betterment. As a result, it may seem churlish to quibble with the suggestion even if, as with the rest of the learned counsel's recommendations, the DHSS has shown no conspicuous desire to adopt it. On the other hand, it might also be argued, with some justice, that part of the current disillusionment with sociology reflects the uncritical enthusiasm with which such suggestions have been accepted in the past and the consequent overselling of the possible achievements of the discipline. As with all confidence tricks, the victims are likely to see through the deception in the end and to feel a proper degree of bitterness and betrayal. This chapter, then, has two principal objectives. One is to examine Blom-Cooper's proposal in the terms in which it was put. What do we know about child abuse and to what extent can its occurrence be predicted? The other is to suggest that the proposal itself might be treated as a topic for inquiry. What does the obsession with prediction tell us about our own time?

What do we know about child abuse?

It is now more than 25 years since C. Henry Kempe and his colleagues in Denver published their celebrated paper, 'The battered child syndrome' (1962), which drew public attention to a phenomenon which had been puzzling paediatric radiologists in the USA since the Second World War. Many infants with subdural haematoma, a pooling of blood at the base of the skull, were found to have fresh, healing or healed long-bone fractures. Such injuries could not plausibly have been caused by the child's own actions and there was no apparent explanation in terms of natural disease processes. During the 1940s and 1950s, the radiological world gradually came round to the view that these children were the victims of maltreatment by adult caretakers. These ideas aroused the interest of the American Humane Association (AHA), a voluntary organization with a tradition of support for child protection research and training, and the Children's Bureau (CB) of the Federal Government. In 1954 the AHA had appointed a new Director, Vincent de Francis, for its Children's Division. He was looking for new issues to mark his tenure. The Children's Bureau was a backwater of the Federal bureaucracy, which was underworked and needed a new cause to protect its budget. The joint activities of the AHA and the CB led first to the funding of Kempe's work and then to its active promotion.[1]

In the process, the battered child syndrome has undergone considerable 'diagnostic inflation'. The original concern of both radiologists and paediatricians was with young children, under 3 years of age, who had suffered severe traumatic injury. These children might, secondarily, also manifest indications of neglect. Such indications might prompt an investigation of the child's radiologic status but were not, in themselves, matters for medical concern. Occasionally, parental assaults might take the form of the forced ingestion of some toxic substance rather than direct physical trauma. The growth of the literature reflects the transformation of the original concerns to embrace virtually any problem which may have an adverse impact on a child and can possibly be attributed to some act of commission or omission by an adult. Recent examples include the administration of cannabis by teenage babysitters (Schwartz *et al.* 1986), the keeping of household pets where a child has asthma (Franklin *et al.* 1987), child labour in Nigeria (Asogwa 1986) and mistaken diagnoses of abuse (Kirschner and Stein 1985). This shift reflects both the politics of research funding and publication and, more importantly, the way in which child abuse has been used symbolically in debates over the future of state welfare on both sides of the Atlantic. Scientific research is not a neutral activity: child abuse was launched as a public issue out of a variety of private interests and its subsequent development has continued to reflect those and other influences.

Since 1962, the literature has expanded rapidly. In 1978, Kalisch published an annotated bibliography of more than 2,000 items, while Costa and Nelson (1978) claimed that the 'core knowledge' was contained in 1,600 items listed in their bibliography. *Index Medicus*, which only provides partial coverage of this field, lists some 20 or 30 references every month. It would obviously be impossible to review this literature exhaustively in the space available here.[2] Rather than dealing selectively with past studies, it seems more helpful to discuss the general principles by which research reports might be evaluated by anyone investigating the literature for themselves. The course adopted has been to take examples of each of the major types of study commonly found in child-abuse research – case series, case/control, casework models and intervention studies – from the output of one of the major British research groups, at the Park Hospital in Oxford.[3] Each type will be discussed and assessed in relation to its prospects of contributing to 'refining the techniques for prediction'.

Case studies

Many discoveries in medicine have resulted from someone noticing a series of cases with common features and proposing a hypothesis about their causes.[4] Case studies, on their own, are unable to show that these common factors are of any genuine significance in explaining the event. This is because they cannot establish that the distribution of the factors in the cases is different from that in a normal population. It may, however, be possible to compare this with a distribution known from other studies to exist in a normal population, providing a kind of control group. If differences exist, then these factors may be relevant. However, it is still necessary to rule out the possibility that they have occurred simply because of the way the series has been compiled. Perhaps the process by which cases are referred has introduced some bias. Even if this is eliminated, case studies cannot prove that a causal relationship exists between the common factors and the outcome. Some other factor may be independently related to both, causing each separately. Where a theory is well-articulated, though, case studies may contribute to its testing and modification, in the manner of critical experiments which attempt to disprove aspects of the theory under defined conditions (Mitchell 1983).

The earliest publications from the Park (by Ounsted *et al.* 1974, 1975) were based on a case series of 'approximately 86 families' which seems to have been collected during the late 1960s or early 1970s. The authors appear properly cautious about the manipulation of the data: 'Precise statistics cannot be had and we think that statistical treatment of data is likely to mislead more than to clarify . . .' (Ounsted *et al.* 1975, p.32). Nevertheless, a second series of 24 cases, selected by the team from among those referred to the Park who had received out-patient treatment, was subjected to statistical analysis. In both series, the process by which the data were collected is rather obscure. There is, for instance, no indication whether standardised questions were used or whether all the material comes from the records of clinical interviews.

The 24 families in the second series had been referred by their GPs as 'at risk' of battering, although only 8 of them had actually admitted to hitting their children 'too hard and too often'. 54 factors were examined and grouped into 4 larger categories – parental characteristics, parental relationships, probands' histories and state at referral – although it is not clear what the rationale for selecting these factors was.[5]

What emerged? Parents were reported as having distorted biographies with 15 mothers having had unhappy, emotionally deprived childhoods – it is not stated whether this was their assessment or the investigators'. The sample had a low tolerance of pain or frustration and poor health: 16 mothers reported experiencing severe migraine and 19 parents suffered from Besnier's syndrome (asthma/eczema). Of the parents analysed, 10 fathers and 19 mothers were classified as having immature and dependent personalities. They were said to be lonely and isolated with few friends: none of the mothers worked. The median age of the mothers at the case child's birth was slightly younger than the average for the Oxford Region at the time: 24 compared with 26 years of age. Parental relationships were considered to be poor: 4 mothers had had children by men other than their spouse and 6 had conceived pre-nuptially. A quarter of the sample reported housing and work difficulties, two-thirds of the mothers complained of their husbands' lack of understanding and 80 per cent said there were sexual difficulties in the marriage. The families were said to have shown disturbed mother/child interaction from the birth. Two-thirds of the mothers had been treated for puerperal depression. The children also displayed a range of health and behaviour problems: 8 vomited frequently, 10 displayed tics or displacement activities, 11 were affected by asthma and 16 were reported to have sleep difficulties, crying or irritability. At the point of referral, 16 mothers complained about the child's lack of affection and 12 of the children displayed selective speech retardation.

Five general observations can be added to the various passing comments about the methodological opacity of these papers. The most important is the lack of any operational definition of maltreatment. Although the papers claim to describe the 'psychopathology . . . of families of battered children' (Ounsted *et al.* 1974, p.447), no evidence is presented that all of the original 86 families were established batterers and all we know of the 24 in the out-patient series is that 8 parents had admitted striking a child 'too hard and too often'. While hitting children might be distasteful to many professionals, it is not intrinsically unlawful when done by parents and, indeed, still commands a substantial measure of public approval. Without explicit criteria of acceptable severity and frequency, these parents cannot be called *abusers*.

But, secondly, it is not even clear that these samples are representative of the families referred to the Park. No indication is given for the first series and the second is avowedly 'selected'. On what criteria? The authors refer to there being 48 parents, which establishes that none of the 24 families was headed by a single parent. It also appears from the wording of the text that these were all, at least nominally, legitimate marital relationships. Were one-parent families or cohabitations excluded? In the absence of any discussion, we cannot determine whether or not the results are the product of the process by which cases were selected for the study.

Thirdly, with the exception of the mother's age at the birth, there is no attempt to compare this sample with any data on the general population. What proportion of the Oxfordshire population had unhappy childhoods, for instance? Unless we know that, we do not know whether 15/24 mothers is higher or lower than the normal rate.

Fourthly, there is no real attempt to consider the way in which these factors might interact or be influenced by other, extraneous factors. If the median age at birth is lower for women in this sample than for the region as a whole, does this tell us that younger mothers are more likely to be referred as at risk or does it tell us that mothers from ethnic or social groups which tend to have babies at a younger age are more likely to be referred?

Finally, it is necessary to know whether any systematic biases are being introduced by the referral system itself. Two-thirds of the mothers had been treated for puerperal depression. Are women who have already been labelled as psychiatrically disordered more likely to be considered dangerous to their children and referred for any given intensity of concern on the part of a GP?

These are not purely academic questions. In the absence of answers, these studies become merely descriptions of the psychopathology of a group of families who happen to have been referred to the Park Hospital for rather vague reasons along undefined routes and whose differences from the general population of Oxfordshire are obscure. Case studies can be valuable instruments for generating hypotheses but their value in developing predictive tools is negligible. Their basic limitations are worth labouring for two reasons. First, because studies of this kind are still common and it is essential to understand what claims can validly be made from them. Second, because they have exercised a fascination for practitioners and policy-makers, which is quite disproportionate to their scientific validity. As a result, they may lead us to ask why certain types of study have proved attractive and to examine the factors influencing the sponsorship and reception of social research.

Case/control studies

The normal development from case series is to carry out case/control studies. These involve the comparison of 2 groups which are as alike as possible in all respects except for the factors being investigated. By comparing these 2 groups, it should be possible to determine which of these factors occur more frequently in the case group than in a 'normal' population. As a result, we might have some confidence that they are real differences rather than just chance features of a series of cases. For this reason, conclusions from case/control studies would normally be given more weight than conclusions from case series. On the other hand, as we shall see, it may still not be clear how differences should be explained.

The next phase of the Park's research (Lynch and Roberts 1977) set up a case/control study by matching a series of 50 children referred to the unit with the live birth recorded next after each of them in the local maternity hospital. But a major problem with this study, as with its predecessor, is its loose definition of the cases. Although the Park sample is described throughout as 'abused', only 23 of the children had definitely suffered some kind of physical maltreatment: 3 had 'probably' been abused, 6 had been neglected and 18 were thought to be at risk. This is not an homogenous group of children who have all shared a common experience which might distinguish them from a normal population. All they have in common is their referral to the Park so that it is still very difficult to distinguish between factors associated with abuse and factors associated with referral.

It was found that there were 5 statistically significant differences between cases and controls: more of the cases had mothers under 20, evidence of emotionally disturbed behaviour in hospital, referrals to the hospital social worker, admissions to the special care baby unit and concern recorded in the midwifery notes over the mother's ability to care for the child. Despite the limitations of the case sample, this might look like the beginnings of a predictive tool. However, the question is, 'predictive of what?'.

It is by no means obvious that these various factors are independent, in that mothers under 20 may be more likely to be defined as incompetent and emotionally disturbed and referred for social work. Having once acquired a social work record, they may then be more likely to experience further referrals. Some support for this view can be obtained by considering the socio-economic aspects of the Park sample. Compared with the maternity hospital population, social classes 4 and 5 are over-represented among the cases. But in another study (Lynch *et al.* 1976), the 29 cases from this series which were referred to the maternity hospital's social work department were compared with another control group of every 20th referral to the same department over the same period. The social work department was shown to deal with a younger and lower-class population than the hospital as a whole. But there is an anomaly in the age distribution of these 2 samples. The Park social work mothers had a lower median age than the social work controls and a greater proportion of them were under 25. But this is actually the result of a bulge in the 20–25 age group. The control group has 20 per cent of mothers under 20 compared with 15 per cent of the cases. The importance of this is that the cases have an identical social class distribution to the social work controls, which removes the intervening effect of social class on age at parity.[6] The cases actually tend to be older than the controls, when social class is held constant. If it is correct to suggest that younger mothers are more vulnerable to being labelled as incompetent or disturbed, so that these factors are only statistically significant because of that association, and it has now been shown that the statistical significance of youthful motherhood might simply reflect the socio-economic composition of the Park series, when compared with the whole maternity hospital population, the predictive validity of these indicators becomes more questionable.[7] Are they really doing any more than telling us that mothers from social classes 4 and 5 are more likely to be considered troublesome by health professionals and subjected to various levels of intervention, including referral to the Park?

The social work department study (Lynch *et al.* 1976) attempted to identify predictive factors in the 29 cases which had been referred to them originally. Did their reappearance at the Park mean that the social workers ought to have spotted the risk earlier or that their intervention had been ineffective? There was a substantial difference between the two series in that 37 of the controls and none of the Park cases had what the investigators called 'defined' social work problems, while 15 cases and 26 controls had 'diffuse' problems. 'Defined' problems were those judged to have clear limits, isolated events in otherwise stable families. 'Diffuse' problems were 'inter-locked and long-term difficulties which beset the whole family'. The authors state, however, that these problems were not always apparent at referral but emerged during work on the case. This leaves open the question of whether the nature of the problems might actually reflect the nature of the work which had been done on them. Most 'defined' problems could be made 'diffuse' with sufficient investigation. Caseload pressures often mean that social workers have to select cases on the basis of a rough initial assessment and determine whether to deal with them on the basis of a simple presenting problem or whether to look for underlying problems.

Case/control studies can be quite difficult to carry out in child abuse. A typical design might seek to compare 2 groups matched for maternal age, parity and social class to see if there were anything distinctive about styles of parent/child interaction among the group of abuse cases as opposed to the controls. However, this sort of design only works successfully when the problem is common enough to match cases and controls relatively easily and there are reliable outcome criteria. As Lynch and Roberts (1982, p.5) acknowledged later, this is hard to achieve in child abuse. The rarity of cases makes it difficult to get homogenous and well-matched groups. Even if we did, the lack of a reliable, independent test for abuse might simply mean that the control group was composed of undiagnosed cases. None the less, retro-spective case/control studies are a useful step forward from case series. Although the interpretation of the results is not always straightforward, they could be used to identify the elements of a model of the process leading to abuse which might then help to guide professionals in designing services for prediction, prevention or targeted intervention.

Casework models

Social work is full of models for practitioners which purport to explain the causes of some problem or propose a method of working towards its resolution. Many of them, however, are founded on little more than theorising from some set of assumptions about human behaviour illustrated by anecdotes from clinical experience (Dingwall 1986b). Such a model may have considerable value in giving a direction to practice or suggesting research questions, but it should never be confused with a well-grounded theory that links a set of substantial research findings into a coherent narrative. It is always essential to look critically at the quality of the evidence that is produced by an author in order to establish the weight that should be placed on their proposals.

This sort of model-building was the objective of a cluster of papers (Lynch 1976, Ounsted and Lynch 1976, Lynch and Roberts 1978) which develop the Park team's notion of the 'critical path' and the sequence of 'open warnings' which practitioners should recognise. They theorise that poor childhood experiences cause a low threshold of stress which leaves parents unable to cope with any special accumulation of problems such as poor health, inadequate housing or marital instability. People presenting with such problems should be screened as possible abusers.

Many families face such problems and only a very few will abuse their child. However, such factors can act as valuable warnings in families where parents' biographies and social pressures increase the potential for abuse. All the factors considered bring the family into contact with medical or social services providing an opportunity for mutual recognition of potential child-rearing problems. (Lynch and Roberts 1978, p.36)

The key to identifying these 'very few' is the way in which their disordered biography manifests itself in interaction with others.

Abusing parents can come from any socioeconomic group . . . certain characteristics, however, are shared. They are frequently isolated both physically and emotionally . . . They choose wherever possible to live in houses cut off from the rest of society; few have a telephone and when they do the number is ex-directory. Initial approaches from neighbours, social workers and doctors are rejected. 'We keep ourselves to ourselves.' (Lynch 1978, p. 57)

It is not entirely clear how far these statements are justified by the case/control studies, although the first quotation might be derived from the social work department research and the contrast between defined and diffuse problems and the second from the social isolation reported in the 1974 and 1975 papers. The main evidence in these papers seems to be clinical experience and case histories. Nevertheless, they provide a structure for the team's work and generate ideas for further testing and practice development. Thinking of this kind is an essential precursor to the construction of valid predictors.

Intervention studies

A prospective study would normally command greater respect than one done retrospectively, because both the participants and the investigators would be unaware of the outcome. The difficulty is in ensuring that the right variables are identified at the beginning so that the right data can be collected in a systematic and rigorous form. Where the study involves examining the effects of some kind of intervention, there is also a need to prevent other influences from clouding the picture.

One example is the Park team's prospective study of the effects of intervention in the maternity hospital (Ounsted *et al.* 1982). This begins by proclaiming the prevention of child abuse as a goal for perinatal medicine. On the basis of their research and theoretical model, Ounsted and his colleagues claim that they can predict the 6 children in every 1,000 liveborn who are likely to be abused by their third birthday.[8] Their initiative rested mainly on Lynch and Roberts's (1977) findings of an association between midwives' recorded concern and subsequent maltreatment. A ward round was instituted at the maternity hospital to pick up referrals from the midwives and mobilise preventive action. In a 12-month period, 20.5 per 1,000 liveborn children (109 cases) were referred. The main reasons given were doubts about parenting; psychiatric history; diffuse problems; marital problems; previous abuse, including suspicions and self-reports from parents about anxiety over their potential for abuse; mother's illness or handicap; and 'general social problems'.

About two-thirds of the cases were dealt with by onward referral to the primary care team while the remainder saw a consultant at the Park with 15 entering longer-term therapy and 5 being admitted for in-patient treatment. At 1 year, 2 cases were untraceable and 2 children had been adopted. There had been 1 cot death.

In 1 case the primary care workers refused to supply further information. There were 2 children in voluntary care and 2 were living with grandparents. The remainder were with their own mothers. In 74 cases there was no further concern for the child's well-being, 12 children were on at-risk registers but not causing active concern and 20 were still the subject of concern, although it is not clear whether all of them were registered.

The first point to make in evaluating this study is that the midwives' grounds for referral are not independent of the Park's previous research. Indeed, the authors stress the importance of systematic and repeated briefings of the hospital staff on the factors that they had come to regard as predictive. Thus, these reasons are not simply midwives' concerns but reflect the particular training that they had received. If the study confirms anything, it is less the predictive value of the ordinary midwives' judgement of 1975 than of the assessment by midwives who had been briefed by the Park team of the likelihood of the cases being admitted by the Park.

Secondly, the paper does not break down the cases between those receiving Park intervention and those referred to primary care teams so that we can determine whether they have different effects. In this respect it does not make the case for a specialised facility. More importantly, as Lealman *et al.* (1983) observe, 7 cases of recognised abuse occurred in the population defined as 'not at risk'. Ounsted *et al.* attach some importance to the decline in serious injuries referred to the Park. In the 18 months before the intervention began, 6 such cases had been referred to them: after 18 months of the scheme, only 1 serious case had been referred,[9] although there had been no change in the overall referral rate, which they attribute to an earlier response to less serious injuries. Lealman *et al.* point out that, in the absence of a control group who were defined as being at risk but did not receive the intervention, this cannot be unequivocally explained by the effects of the preventive work.

There are, then, some nagging questions about these findings. Arguably the 75 per cent of the children about whom there was no real concern were false positives who had been wrongly stigmatised. Perhaps the 25 per cent who were still on at-risk registers were there purely because the original referral had altered the threshold of concern in their cases rather than because there was any independent evidence. Indeed, the original investigators tacitly seem to admit this by reformulating their predictors to take account of the hospital records of the false negatives, i.e. those cases which had been defined as not at risk and then been abused. Of the 7 mothers, 5 had recorded disturbances on the ward and 3 had taken their own discharge. The new criteria emphasise non-compliance and resistance to clinical authority. These, however, have been shown elsewhere (Dingwall *et al.* 1983) to be associated with the readiness to interpret a child's condition as the result of maltreatment. In other words, there may be a simple circularity here: the record of non-compliance predicts future non-compliance which is likely to precipitate the labelling of a child as abused, but which has no established relationship to the actual treatment of the child.

This study can, however, also be used to reinforce the necessity of understanding the social context in which cases are generated. The reported change in case-mix, for instance, is equally consistent with a shift in referral patterns. Perhaps some completely extraneous change had occurred, which meant that referral agents were no longer sending the same mix of cases to the Park. Data on this are available for the period October 1978–March 1979 from another study in the same catchment area. These chronicle both respect for the Park's work with behavioural problems in children and a growing crisis in relations over its response to child-abuse cases. The Park's interventions were seen, particularly by social services, as heavy-handed, generating a level of panic, especially among other doctors and the police, which led to case-management decisions that were not in the best long-term interests of the child. Many community-based agencies, like social services, health visiting and child guidance, felt that the Park were insensitive to the child's social environment and unwilling to liaise effectively with them.

As more formal procedures for dealing with child abuse were set up, which gave a central role to the social services department, the Park were increasingly marginalised. By the end of this period, it seemed as if the main use of the team was purely strategic. This extract from a case discussion between a social services area director and a social worker is typical of local views early in 1979:

AD: I get involved quite a lot. A case conference at the [General

Hospital] can be difficult. I'm not so worried about SW going because she is pretty good at sticking up for herself. But you do have to be pretty tough sometimes. You get [Park Director] down there saying, 'if you don't remove this child it will be dead by Saturday'.

sw: He's an awful man . . .

ad: He is quite perceptive on his good days. He is very good in court as well because when he comes out with this sort of thing you can often get an order when your evidence isn't very good. But he can be very bullying at a case conference.

By the end of this study, the Park's main value to the local child-protection system was in less serious cases where they could be relied upon to make the most forceful use of the available evidence in a court hearing.

One way in which some of these methodological problems could be overcome is by the use of data from a large longitudinal study of a birth cohort, as Lynch and Roberts (1982, p. 5) have noted. This call has recently been repeated by Markowe (1988). Cohort studies are normally time-consuming and expensive to carry out. The UK, however, is uniquely fortunate in possessing 3 such birth cohorts, from 1946, 1958 and 1970, which are all still regularly surveyed.[10] It is a matter of some regret that none of them have so far shown any interest in using their data to explore questions relating to child abuse. Even this, of course, would not be entirely straightforward, since it would be necessary to establish an appropriate operational definition of abuse or risk confounding the analysis with the factors that lead to its identification by health or social services. With the older cohorts, however, it would now be possible to ask their members directly about childhood experiences, which would certainly make the task considerably more practical.[11] This might be particularly helpful in relation to sexual abuse where abusive behaviours could be more precisely specified. These self-reports could be linked to the recorded medical, social and educational history of the cohorts in an effort to identify possible predictors.

The reader may, by now, have concluded that the design of most research studies could be made problematic with the investment of sufficient time and ingenuity. This is, indeed, true, and the Park studies are far from being the worst-designed research in the field of child abuse. However, the ability to make such judgements and to value a study at its true worth is a critical skill in a reflective practitioner. When one looks at a large number of studies it is easy to get confused by what Gelles (1980, p. 880), following Potts and Herzberger (1979), has called the 'Woozle Effect'. This error, which will be familiar to readers of Winnie-the-Pooh, is of assuming that because one observation whose validity is uncertain confirms a second, both must be true. A derivation from this is the fallacy of concluding that because a similar association is reported from a large number of studies, it must be a strong one. In fact, strong associations between individual factors or groups of factors and maltreatment have been very hard to establish.

What is probably the most tightly constructed case/control study to date (Starr 1982) found that the number of statistically significant differences between the two groups was virtually that which would be expected as a chance outcome of the large number of statistical analyses performed. (The analyses themselves constitute a sample which must be expected to throw up a certain number of significant results purely by chance.) He concluded that the two groups were, overall, more alike than they were different. Previous attempts to differentiate between them were not unlike the investigation of differences between Indian and African elephants. If you just looked at ears or tails or trunks, you could find some measurable differences; but if you looked at the whole beast in equal detail, it became clear that these were of minor importance compared with their similarities.

The limited progress which has been made so far in the search for predictors of child abuse reflects the pervasive influence of two methodological fallacies. The *definitional* fallacy is the confusion of social and scientific problems and the failure to construct persuasive operational definitions of abuse or neglect. The *statistical* fallacy is the failure to recognise that, when one is dealing with a phenomenon which has a low rate of prevalence, even the best predictors yield a high and probably unacceptable level of errors.

The definitional fallacy

Research on child abuse and neglect is unlikely to progress until it recognises the distinction between the social problem of child maltreatment and the scientific problem of accounting for the incidence of particular forms of adult/child interaction. The philosophical arguments may be complex but the point is simple. Adult/child interaction is a natural phenomenon which has no intrinsic moral significance. Child abuse and neglect are terms which we apply to a particular class of interactions to define them as deviant and worthy of moral outrage.

In nature the death, starvation or rape of a child is no different from the culling of a primate band by a new dominant male. In human society, these acts are likely to be considered unacceptable. But the exact boundaries of acceptability are not fixed. When the Dinka of the Southern Sudan kill handicapped infants by placing them in the River Nile, this is not seen as an act of murder but of kindness: these children are 'really' baby hippopotamuses who happen to have been born to humans by mistake and can now find their proper home. In certain parts of the USA, a girl cannot lawfully consent to sexual intercourse until she is 18. In the UK we define sexual intercourse with a girl under 16 as a criminal offence, even if it takes place with her consent. This age limit was raised from 14 only in 1885 and has been maintained despite the falling age of menarche and earlier biological maturity of girls since that time. Throughout much of the Muslim world, the age of marriage remains at 12 or 13.

The fact that such definitions are relative does not compel us to treat them all with equal tolerance. We may still want to erect standards and to judge other individuals or cultures against them. However, it does direct us to put that exercise in its proper light. Definitions of acceptable and unacceptable behaviour forms part of the culture of a society and need to be studied in that context. The struggle to change those definitions or to replace one set by another is a conflict which is fundamentally linked to the core values of the society and their implications for the way members should behave towards each other. The outcome of that struggle reflects the distribution of cultural power. In this sense at least, child maltreatment is always a political question to be studied like any other with the interpretive tools of the social sciences. At the same time, this does not stand in the way of child development or adult/child interaction studies which attempt to map certain sorts of events independently of their social definition. We may, for example, seek to describe the prevalence of long bone or skull fractures in a child population and to develop a picture of their social or geographical distribution which could be used to predict where they were most likely to occur.[12] But we would be in error if we were to treat this as a map of the prevalence of maltreatment. That definition reflects a social inquiry into the causes of the injury and the judgement that these are unlikely either to be natural or accidental. If a parent hits a child, for example, the consequences are not necessarily proportionate to the intention. I might throw a child at a brick fireplace with the object of causing it severe pain or I might be playing a chasing game with a child who slips on a toy and bangs its head on the same fireplace. Either way, the result may be a fractured skull. In the nature of these things there are unlikely to be any independent witnesses. How is a casualty officer or a social worker to decide whether to prefer my story of the game or the alternative of a violent assault? Yet the physical consequences are potentially identical.

The greatest progress in this line is reflected in the work of Straus, Gelles and their associates. Essentially, what they have sought to do is to measure the exposure of children to acts of violence capable of causing serious injury. Although the range of acts selected has been criticised, it does have the merit of giving a clear operational definition of the circumstances in which a child may be put at risk by an adult's behaviour. As the authors stress, this does not provide a base rate for child abuse but it does help to establish the base rate upon which operate the definitional processes involved in applying that label. Finkelhor's (1986) review of research on child sexual abuse points in a similar direction when he stresses the need to disaggregate the phenomenon: peer-coerced sexual experimentation in young teenagers is a different kind of behaviour to the buggery of a 3-year-old by an adult. The more closely one can define a behaviour, the more likely it is that one can get a worthwhile estimate of its prevalence. Even here, as the events in Cleveland remind us, one must still be wary of leaping from describing the distribution of a sign to the conclusion that one has thereby defined the distribution of abuse.

As one tightens definitions, however, the incidence and prevalence figures decrease sharply. Finkelhor demonstrates very clearly, for instance, that the high rates sometimes reported for child sexual abuse are only achieved by lumping together a wide range of occurrences, from indecent exposure or access to pornographic materials to violent penetrative assaults. The former may be distasteful but they are surely qualitatively different problems requiring different types of social action by agencies other than health or social services. The estimates from the most convincing studies reviewed by Finkelhor seem to indicate a true prevalence in the range of 10 to 20 per cent of girls under 16 who have ever suffered some kind of unwanted and unpleasant sexual experience. If we disaggregate this, however, in an attempt to identify those acts which can reasonably be considered appropriate to the intervention of health or social welfare agencies, the amount of violent or degrading sexual behaviour in a domestic or child-care setting seems likely to be very much smaller. The picture for boys is less well-defined but might support an estimate of one-third to one-fifth as many boys as girls being abused. These estimates are of the same order as those produced by La Fontaine (1988) from her review of the very limited British research. The result would point to an incidence rate, i.e. new cases each year, of around 1 per cent.

The Gelles and Straus (Straus *et al.* 1980; Gelles and Straus 1987) studies discussed by Birchall (in Chapter 1) suggest that between 1.5 and 4 per cent of American children are exposed to the risk of serious physical assault in the USA each year, with some suggestion of a declining trend. This figure is consistent with the Newsons' (1970, pp. 440–1) incidence rate for frequent smacking or use of an implement to punish 4-year-olds in Nottingham during the early 1960s, which remains the best source on English family discipline. On their more liberal definition, they came up with a rate of about 7 per cent. Baldwin and Oliver (1975) estimated that about 1 child in every 1,000 under 4 in England was severely abused each year, although their study does make the mistake of sliding from a very clear and restrictive operational definition of severe injuries in children to equating them with abuse.

These issues are explored in more detail in Birchall's chapter. For the present, it should be sufficient to establish that child abuse, whether physical or sexual, is a rare event. The importance of this is what it means for the statistical prospects of achieving useful levels of prediction.

The statistical fallacy

When one is dealing with rare events, their prediction becomes subject to the statistician's version of the problem of finding a needle in a haystack. The validity of a screening instrument depends upon its sensitivity and its specificity. The *sensitivity* of a test refers to the extent to which it detects all the cases of the condition in a given population – in other words, what proportion of cases are wrongly excluded (false negatives). The *specificity* of a test refers to the extent to which it wrongly includes 'normals' in the case population (false positives). These dimensions are inversely related to each other, so that as sensitivity increases, specificity decreases and vice versa. The cut off between them is determined by the decision as to whether it is more important to avoid false negatives or false positives. Are we more concerned here to ensure that every case of child abuse is identified or that no parent is ever wrongly indicted?

But things are not quite so simple, because the predictive value of a test, the likelihood of the result being correct in any particular case, also reflects the prevalence of the condition in the population.[13] Even when a test seems to be quite promising because a high level of specificity has been achieved with little loss of sensitivity, the predictive value can be quite low if the condition is rare because the small proportion of the normal population who are incorrectly identified – the false positives – greatly outnumber the high proportion of the case population who are correctly identified – the true positives. These true positives form a very small proportion of the total population identified as positive. An example may help to clarify this. Table 2.1 summarises a study of the relationship between possible predictors on maternity records and child-abuse registration for non-Asian births in Bradford in 1979.

At first sight this looks quite promising. Two-thirds of the registrations occurred within the 18 per cent of the population predicted as being at risk on the basis of maternity records. However, the predictive value in any particular case is only 3 per

Table 2.1: Prediction of child-abuse registration in Bradford from screening of maternity records (after Lealman *et al.* 1983)

| | | On Child-Abuse Register | | Total |
		Yes	No	
Predicted from birth records	Yes	17	483	511
	No	11	2280	2291
Total		28	2763	2802

Sensitivity: 61%
Specificity: 82%
Predictive value: 3%

cent. *There are 28 false positives for every true one.* Such a rate of error might be acceptable if the test were identifying a potentially serious but socially respectable medical condition, so that the errors did not have a harmful impact on the false positives. Even then it might well be judged uneconomic. But it does not seem likely that such a rate of error would ever be acceptable in cases of physical or sexual abuse where even a false allegation may devastate the lives of both parents and children.

More refined screening instruments will make only the most marginal impact on the argument. The most successful claim a sensitivity and specificity of around 75 per cent (Starr forthcoming). Figure 2.1 plots the results of a hypothetical test which is set at 96 per cent specificity on the assumption that it is essential to minimise the number of false positives. As the sensitivity rises, the predictive value increases but, even on the high assumption of 5 per cent prevalence, never goes much above 50 per cent. In other words, half the predictions will always be wrong, even with a more accurate test than anything presently available. At 75 per cent sensitivity and specificity, the predictive value of a test at 3 per cent prevalence would be less than 30 per cent.

This conventional application of orthodox statistical reasoning demonstrates that to respond to Blom-Cooper's call would be a futile misdirection of scientific effort. This is not to say that it is not worth trying to get good maps of the social distribution of behaviours or events believed to be indicative of child abuse, which may help to focus resources and preventive efforts on particular sections of the population. But it is essential to recog-

Figure 2.1: Predictive value of child abuse and neglect screening

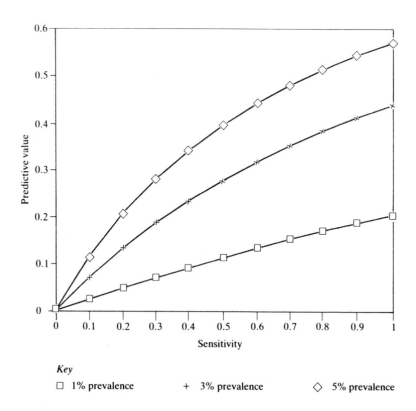

Key

□ 1% prevalence   + 3% prevalence   ◇ 5% prevalence

nise that these initiatives are not focused on a population of abusers so much as on a population of 'respectable' families who happen to include a small number of abusers. It is equally important to acknowledge that a proportion of abusers will lie outside that population.

The obsession with prediction

This chapter is not an essay in the sociology of science. Yet that literature must remind us that science itself is a social product, driven and shaped by social interests which define its problems and legitimate its methods. Within this, certain types of investigation may develop a measure of autonomy and the ability to determine their programme in ways which reflect principles of methodology which are not directly beholden to any specific sectional interest. They may be evaluated as good or bad in ways which are independent of the conclusions which they reach. Child-abuse research, however, has many of the characteristics of a pseudo-science, 'a kind of wish-fulfilment, enabling people to discover what they would like to believe' (Blum 1978, p.156). Feminists discover that it is all an expression of patriarchy; utopian socialists that it is a perversion of capitalism; conservatives that it is a symptom of moral decay. We must, then, understand the meaning of calls for research into prevention in the context in which they are made.

At one level, the attempt to predict child abuse can be seen in simple humanitarian terms. Would it not be better if we could prevent children from ever being harmed? It is, however, far from clear that a free society would ever tolerate the sort of surveillance that would be necessary to provide such a guarantee. More to the point, we have seen that our tools can never be refined sufficiently to achieve this goal. In policy terms, this means that we can only consider in what ways the welfare of a large group of children could be enhanced in the hope that some beneficial effect would trickle down to potential victims. Indeed, given the limited value of the tools available to us in defining the population which includes most of the potential abusers, we are necessarily talking about the nature of national policy for the welfare of all children. Alongside this, we must also consider the creation of an acceptable technology of surveillance for the whole child population in order to identify those particular homes where abuse is occurring.

It is the political and economic implications of this that warp both research and policy and sustain the pseudo-science of child-abuse research. Blom-Cooper's call for predictive instruments comes out of the authoritarian thrust of the Jasmine Beckford Report. The basic issues are explored more comprehensively by the Partons (Chapter 3) but, as they point out, the emphasis on dividing populations into those who shall be saved and those who shall be cast into the pit reflects the whole way in which the welfare state has been reorganised in the last 20 years. Prediction can also be a means of rolling back the frontiers of the state, of minimising the number of families to be surveyed. This retrenchment limits the range of private troubles which can be discovered and made into collective, public issues. At the same time, it also reduces the claims that can be made on the state in exchange for participation in the system of surveillance. Predicted abusers can be made into social outcasts, so beyond the pale as to obscure the extent to which a whole society or class shares many of their problems of housing, income, education and human relations.

Conclusion

It would, though, be a mistake to leave the reflective practitioner reading this chapter with the impression that nothing could be done short of utopian reform. Many of the resources and instruments for an acceptable and effective child protection policy already exist. The problem is one of a loss of professional confidence and a reluctance to defend achievements or state opportunity costs. One conspicuous example is the collapse of the public health tradition in both health and social services, with its emphasis on the positive search for unmet need and its recognition that any 'missed case' is a cause for collective concern.

The first task for any child-protection system is to devise an effective method of case-finding, which involves the careful and repeated screening of the current condition of the entire child population. There is no substitute for examining the entire population because no screening instrument can be sufficiently precise to identify risk groups. The survey must be repeated because no predictive tool is powerful enough to forecast which individual children will be maltreated. Children must, then, be assessed with sufficient frequency for physical damage or deterioration to be identified at an early stage. This may not enable every incident of maltreatment to be prevented: a child may be well one day and acutely at risk from its mother's new cohabitee the next. But it does give both children and the preventive system a chance. For such a mass programme to be acceptable, however, it must also be seen to deliver other benefits in terms of access to resources for families with other needs which are identified in the survey. Its comprehensiveness is also a guarantee against stigmatisation.

This programme is, of course, that which has traditionally been executed by health visitors. As they have become influenced by other fashions and the demands of other client groups, their enthusiasm for this mission seems to have waned. It may be that social workers should be considering whether this work might be more effectively carried out within social services departments as an agency more committed to the advocacy of children's interests and with access to a more relevant range of resources. Might a social worker with paramedical training do better than a nurse with some social work skills?

In terms of Blom-Cooper's challenge, though, this paper must come to a bleak conclusion. The amount of scientifically-validated research on child abuse and neglect is vanishingly small. The value of any self-styled predictive checklist is negligible. Indeed such tools probably do more harm than good because of the way they further undervalue and undermine professional judgement. Child-abuse research will not progress until the scientific and the social problems are clearly distinguished. The former are a topic for the mainstream of investigations into child development, family interaction and aggression within a variety of social sciences from sociology and anthropology through psychology to ethology. The latter are perhaps more distinctively the concern of the sociologist, the political scientist and the social historian.

Notes

1. This story is told in more detail through the work of Parton (1985a, pp. 48–54), Pfohl (1977), Nelson (1978, 1986), Steiner (1976).
2. Useful discussions can be found in Gelles (1980), Cohn (1983), Graham et al (1985), Finkelhor (1986) and Starr (1987).
3. The Park Hospital in Oxford is a small unit opened in 1958 to deal with neurological and psychiatric disorders in children. In the late 1960s and early 1970s it attracted a wave of referrals for child abuse. The work first came to prominence at the inaugural meeting of the Tunbridge Wells Study Group in 1973 and was specifically commended by the Parliamentary Select Committee on Violence in the Family in its first report (1977) and by the then government in its response (1978). It was also cited by the

DHSS in Draft Circular LA/C396/23D *Child Abuse: The Register System* (1978). The Unit is now staffed by a different team and publications since 1982 will not be considered in this chapter.

4. For a recent example, see Shilts's (1988, p.66) account of the first perception of AIDS by an alert technician at the Centers for Disease Control in Atlanta.

5. The selection of factors appears to reflect the influence of an aetiological model proposed by Steele and Pollock (1968) from Denver. This proposed the hypothesis that battering was not the result of some homogeneous psychopathology but stemmed from parents' inability to judge children's needs because of their own lack of adequate mothering. As an approach, it is an orthodox extension of mainstream US psychiatric theory of the period with its neo-Freudian emphasis on the importance of childhood experience as the starting point for explaining the origins of disordered adult behaviour. The Park group later equated this with the ethological notion of faulty 'bonding', perhaps reflecting the more biological orientation of British psychiatry.

6. An intervening variable is one which is independently associated with two or more others so that they appear to show similar trends, although they are not, in fact, causally related. So A and B may both increase at the same rate only because they are both related to C, rather than because they are related to each other. In this case, young motherhood and events precipitating referral to the Park may be independently related to social class, rather than having any direct association. (Women from social classes 4 and 5 are known to have their babies at a younger age than women in other social classes.)

7. It may be possible to account for the apparent excess of admissions to the special care baby unit by a similar argument. Lynch and Roberts state that there were no statistically significant differences in complications of pregnancy or labour which might account for this. On the other hand one would expect a more working-class group to have a higher rate of neonatal complications. Social factors may also exercise an influence at the margin on admission decisions. If a mother is regarded as less competent or reliable, then a prudent medical policy might produce more admissions for any given condition of the infant.

8. This figure is taken from Mitchell (1975, p. 642) who gives no source for it and describes it as a 'rough guide'.

9. This statement is repeated in Lynch and Roberts (1982, p. 11).

10. For details see Obstetrics (1948), Fogelman (1983) and Osborn *et al.* (1984).

11. Although as Straus, Gelles and their associates have shown in the USA, it is less difficult than might be imagined to ask parents directly about acts of violence towards their children.

12. See, for example, Baldwin and Oliver (1975).

13. For present purposes, prevalence and incidence can be treated as identical, since what we are interested in is the proportion of the child population abused in a given time period, whose detection is likely to be an objective for health and social services, rather than the proportion of the child population ever abused.

CHAPTER 3

CHILD PROTECTION, THE LAW AND DANGEROUSNESS

CHRISTINE PARTON
Social Worker, Calderdale Social Services

NIGEL PARTON
Principal Lecturer in Social Work, Huddersfield Polytechnic

Introduction

In this chapter we reflect on the nature and implications of recent recommendations about the best way of responding to the problem of child abuse in policy and practice. In particular we summarise and critically analyse some of what we see as the central tenets and underlying assumptions informing the major public inquiries and DHSS statements as to what constitutes good policy and practice. The tragic death in 1973 of Maria Colwell and subsequent public inquiry signalled the beginning in the UK of modern political, public and professional interest in the issue of child abuse. Developments since the mid 1980s suggest not only a revival of interest and concern but a reframing of some of the issues and a changing social context within which they are located. Throughout both periods, however, concern about child abuse has been closely interrelated with debates about the practice, attitudes and priorities of a variety of health and welfare professionals – social workers in particular. Hence our analysis will inevitably touch upon issues at the heart of social work practice and the way it may be changing in the late 1980s. During the 1970s the main priority in child-abuse policy was to encourage professionals to identify abuse where previously they might not have done and to improve and formalise inter-agency and inter-professional work through the development of area review committees, case conferences and registers. The public inquiries related to children who had usually died at the hands of their parents or caretakers from severe physical abuse and neglect and in which professionals, particularly social workers, failed to intervene. These were again significant themes in the recent reports into the deaths of Jasmine Beckford (Beckford 1985), Tyra Henry (Henry 1987) and Kimberley Carlile (Carlile 1987).

The issues addressed by the most recent report concerning events in Cleveland (1988), however, seem very different. The central concern has shifted to criticisms of unwarrantable interventions into families where the evidence for abuse, primarily sexual, appeared to be limited and where children may have been removed from their natural families inappropriately. Not only was the practice of social workers and social services departments subjected to criticism but also the diagnostic techniques and interventions of two consultant paediatricians. Superficially it seems that health and welfare professionals are caught in a political and public crossfire in which they cannot win, between, on the one hand, respecting the privacy of the family and the rights of parents and, on the other, ensuring that no child suffers serious harm from the behaviour of those same parents or guardians. These apparently contradictory concerns have become more explicit than at any time previously.

Similarly the growing concern about sexual abuse during the 1980s reflects the broadening conception of the problem of child abuse ever since the early 1970s. The problem referred to as 'battered babies' in 1970, and as 'non-accidental injury to children' in 1974, was officially termed 'child abuse' for the first time in 1980 and was to include not just physical injury but neglect, failure to thrive and emotional abuse. It is only since 1988 that sexual abuse has been included, together with the category of 'grave concern'.

Not only has the definition of the problem broadened but public awareness in recent years has heightened considerably. Most significantly, this was prompted by, and reflected in, the launch of Childline (the first free national helpline for children in trouble or danger which counselled over 22,000 children in its first year) in October 1986. Referrals to statutory agencies, particularly social services departments have increased dramatically. The NSPCC figures for 1986 showed an increase of 136 per cent in their recorded instances of sexual abuse in the previous year (Creighton

1987a); the Association of Directors of Social Services figures show that the number of children on registers rose by 22 per cent in 1985–6 – the sharpest increase in relation to sexual abuse (*The Guardian* 31 August 1987).

Recent interest and concern about child abuse therefore seems to be characterised by factors not evident in the earlier phase. There is a growth in public concern, a broadening conception of the problem, particularly in the area of sexual abuse, and much more explicit arguments about the need to intervene as opposed to the need to avoid unwarrantable intrusion in family life. In particular, we seek in this chapter to concentrate attention on the significance of the term 'child protection' which has emerged as a new way of describing work in child-abuse situations and which, we suggest, is symbolic of a changing emphasis and approach to the problem.

Recent public inquiries

As one of us has suggested previously (Parton, 1986) the Beckford Report (1985) marked something of a watershed in thinking about, and responses to, child abuse in Britain. The Report had a wider focus than the circumstances surrounding the death of one particular child and makes fundamental comments about the attitudes, responsibilities and priorities of managers and practitioners – particularly social workers – together with the nature of the problem – child abuse – to which we should be responding. In many respects this Report seems to have set the tone for the subsequent inquiries, though clearly the detail and the balance of recommendations varies. (Christine Hallett in Chapter 6 analyses the nature, role and implications of child abuse inquiries.) Underpinning the recommendations is an explicit attempt to define social work policy and practice in its statutory context. It is argued that the crucial element which provides modern social work with its rationale and legitimacy is its relationship with the law. 'We are strongly of the view that social work can in fact be defined ONLY in terms of the functions required of it by their [social workers] employing agency operating within a statutory framework.' (p. 12)

Social work, then, can not only be understood within its legal framework but, in effect, social work activity is the functioning of the law in practice. Because social workers fail to recognise this they do not appreciate their proper role and functions and hence the full significance of their responsibilities. This is a theme confirmed in the Kimberley Carlile (1987) and Tyra Henry (1987) Reports and has been recently echoed in the CCETSW Report on law teaching on CQSW courses (Ball *et al.* 1988). Thus it is argued that not only are social workers unaware of the areas of the law which impinge on their practice but that they fail to recognise that the law is central to understanding the nature of modern social work. The reports suggest that social workers' lack of confidence, particularly when working with and confronting parents, stems in large measure from their uncertainty about the legal powers and the authority that are vested in them in the statutes. This is reinforced by too much respect for parental rights and a failure to see the child as having needs and interests separate from, and independent of, the parents. This can lead to inaction, to 'drift' and a failure to take difficult decisions.

In effect, we are being asked to rethink that old social work issue of the relationship between care and control, reframed in a fuller knowledge of social work's relationship with the law. The Tyra Henry Report explicitly refers to this as 'policing' (p. 116–17). It is argued that 'policing' is central to this kind of work and should not be 'fudged' either with clients or social workers; it should provide a focus of attention for supervisors to ensure that practitioners have a 'well-developed professional scepticism' (Carlile, p. 123) and do not collude with parents. The law, therefore, far from simply providing the context of social work is at the core of social work's *raison d'être*. As Norman Fowler, then Secretary of State, commented in his covering letter with the draft DHSS guidelines (1986) following the Beckford Report, it is important to ensure 'that all staff are fully aware of the legal framework in this area and how it affects the responsibilities which they bear'.

This failure to recognise the significance of the law can have different consequences, some of which may lead to inappropriate and heavy-handed interventions, for example via an over-reliance on Place of Safety Orders as suggested in the Cleveland Report. The new emphasis is valuable because it demonstrates that the law is the crucial vehicle for negotiating the boundaries, in individual cases, between the rights and responsibilities of the state and those of the family (and hence parents), which is still recognised as the primary institution for rearing most children. Social workers are often centrally concerned with these boundary negotiations and thus, increasingly, influenced and circumscribed by the law. However, if social work has no identity separate from the law, social workers simply become state agents. This is certainly the image conjured up by 'policing'. Every social worker knows that the values and everyday practice of social work in local authority and other statutory settings are epitomised by the tension between respecting the needs and wishes of the client and acting as a state agent. Yet, in putting so much emphasis on the latter such an approach denies the legitimate dilemmas experienced by social workers and hence misunderstands the nature and essence of social work itself (Horne 1987).

Both the Kimberley Carlile and Tyra Henry Reports stated clearly what they saw as their primary tasks, very much reflecting these current concerns and priorities. The former said that 'in short, the Inquiry is about protecting the lives of children at risk' (p. 6); the latter stated it was concerned with 'an appraisal of the roles of all those people and institutions in whose hands our society places what is perhaps the most important and the most difficult of all tasks, the protection of children at risk' (p. 4).

The phrases 'child protection' and 'children at risk' seem central to understanding current attempts to develop policy and practice. They need to be understood in relation to each other. The Beckford Report contended at numerous points that certain children in the population are subject to situations of 'high risk' and that it is the primary task of practitioners to identify such high risk. In order to do so it is therefore crucial that they be familiar with these risk factors so that when they come across them in their practice they are able to intervene appropriately. Certain characteristics of families identify them as such and allow them to be separated from the rest or 'low risk' situations.

For example, in the Beckford Report the characteristics of the Beckford family were identified as consistent with research findings on what constitutes a high-risk family. Similarly the Kimberley Carlile Report referred to the 'psychopathology of the Carlile family' (p. 106) and to the 'indices of child abuse' (p. 107) to which the social worker failed to pay sufficient attention. In effect social workers should isolate 'high risk' cases from the rest and respond accordingly:

The proportion of 'high risk' cases out of all proved cases of persistent child abuse will be small, and the task of identifying may not be easy. But the attempt to isolate such cases from the majority of child abuse must always be made. (Beckford, p. 288)

Practitioners, these inquiries suggest, should be applying 'predictive techniques of dangerousness' (Beckford, p.289) to their work. It is not the purpose of this chapter to assess whether and how it is possible to predict high risk. Robert Dingwall's chapter shows how difficult a task this is. Our main concern here is to underline that such an assumption may be used to justify particular modes of action and intervention by practitioners and also in the allocation of resources. The Beckford Report concludes that social workers and the personal social services should not waste resources on cases which are likely only marginally to reduce the risk of serious injury if the child stays at home but should remove the children for 'an appropriate time'. Not only would such a policy save lives it would concentrate scarce and costly resources on 'the "grey areas" of cases where something more than supervision and something less than long-term removal, is indicated' (p. 289). The assessment of high risk or 'dangerousness' thus becomes the crucial focus. Such thinking is evident in the DHSS circular (1988a) and is perhaps made most explicit in the circular's recommendations in relation to training. Not only should specialist in-service training be 'directed to those involved in the investigation of abuse and provision of protective services' but the knowledge and skills required should be 'related to child care law, the concept of child protection and the assessment of danger, and alternative forms of intervention' (p.43). The concept of child protection and the assessment of danger thus hang together. The major priority is the identification and assessment of high risk or dangerousness. Once identified, the focus becomes the protection of the child – or child protection – in which comprehensive legal knowledge, which invests social workers with a particular form of authority, is crucial. The Tyra Henry Report suggests that 'preventing danger' and 'firm protective steps' are the two fundamental pillars on which modern practice should be based (p.21–2). The inter-relationship between the law, child protection and the assessment of dangerousness is therefore at the core of the social work task in this area of work.

In the process, the notion of prevention is constructed in a very particular way. For while the conceptualisation of child abuse in the DHSS circular is a broad one and is concerned with providing guidance to agencies in order to prevent abuse, the prevention of child abuse is defined in terms of child protection. We are thus to have Area Child Protection Committees, child-protection reviews, child-protection registers and inter-agency protection plans. Not only has the NSPCC recently reorganised itself into child protection teams but many social services departments have been re-designating case conferences, registers and certain specialist posts in terms of child protection. At one level the term 'child protection' is helpful in underlining for all concerned that the primary focus is the child. It may also be a clearer reflection of professional focus than the more global phrase 'child abuse'. At another level, however, we feel it symbolises much wider changes in thinking, policy and practice which are prescribed by a changing relationship with the law and a more central reliance upon the assessment of dangerousness. For in a period when, on the one hand, the definition of the problem of child abuse has broadened and public awareness has increased, while on the other resources have been curtailed, the concentration on the protection of children from serious harm has provided a rationale of priorities for agencies and practitioners.

High risk and the assessment of dangerousness

Discussions about 'dangerousness' are not new. They have been a part of the language of the law, psychiatry and other clinical professions for many years (Hinton (ed.) 1981; Hamilton and Freeman (eds) 1982; Monahan, 1981). However it is only in more recent years that 'dangerousness' has been taken seriously again as central to policy and practice, particularly in the areas of crime and mental health. There are three essential elements in understanding what is meant by 'dangerousness'. Firstly, it is assumed that there are some individuals in the population who are prone to cause serious and lasting violence, both physical and psychological. Secondly, while these individuals may come to official notice for only minor infractions, their propensity to violence, 'danger-ousness', must become the central focus in any decisions about disposal – which may mean a long period of incarceration. Thirdly, it follows therefore, that we crucially need to improve our predictions of dangerousness in research and practice, so that such individuals, when identified, can be treated or, if untreatable, contained.

Bottoms (1977, 1980) has demonstrated that during the mid to late 1970s the idea of dangerousness became a major topic for discussion by a number of prestigious groups and reports on penal policy, including the Working Party on Dangerous Offenders set up by NACRO (Floud and Young, 1981) and the Howard League for Penal Reform, of which Louis Blom-Cooper, chair of two subsequent child-abuse inquiries, was a member.

Bottoms noted that this increased official interest in the idea of dangerousness coincided with the growing tendency in penal policy to advocate or impose more severe penalties for offenders regarded as 'really serious', while advocating a reduction in penalties for the ordinary or run-of-the-mill offender. The use of long sentences *increased* in a period when there was a general *decrease* in sentence severity, which Bottoms referred to as 'bifurcation'. For bifurcation to become a reality one has to believe in the possibility of separating the dangerous from the rest and have the expertise to carry that through. Assessments of actual and potential dangerousness therefore become the central concern and activity. As Walker commented 'what has made the concept of dangerousness a really live issue is the shortening of the periods of detention which legislators, sentencers, and psychiatrists regard as justified on other grounds' (1978, p.38). Such issues have proved of even greater significance during the 1980s.

It is now widely recognised, however, that there is a major empirical difficulty in attempts to isolate and identify the dangerous in this way for the purposes of imposing a special sentence. Research on the prediction of future violence does not instil confidence in either the reliability or the viability of such assessments. Whatever is done prediction rates rise no higher than two wrong judgements for every right judgement. The empirical support for the prediction of violence is very poor. As a consequence there are inevitable problems of wrongly identifying some (false positive) and failing to identify others (false negative) (Von Hirsch, 1985; Parton, 1985a, pp.139–44; and Dingwall in this volume (Chapter 2)). It is only recently that such issues have been explicitly applied to the area of child abuse. The work of Cyril Greenland is particularly significant in this respect.

Cyril Greenland seems to have proved an influential expert witness to the Beckford Inquiry and his evidence is favourably referred to at various points in the Report. It is probably fair to say that few people in Britain in the child-abuse field had heard of his work prior to then. Interest in his research and recommendations for policy and practice thus probably reflect, in part, the recent reappraisal of what to do about child abuse. He has been trying to develop predictions of dangerousness for many years. While this was previously in relation to the dangerous mentally ill and the violent offender (Greenland 1978, 1980a), in recent years he has been applying it to child abuse or, as he prefers to call it, 'lethal family situations' (Greenland 1980b, 1986a, 1986b, 1987). His most recent book (1987) provides a full, if confusing, account of his approach, research and recommendations. It is notable that in certain passages the book bears a close resemblance to the Beckford Report, particularly when the latter is discussing the importance of the law to practice and 'high risk' situations.

While Greenland makes reference to social factors such as unemployment, poverty, poor housing and 'underfunded, poorly staffed and overworked social services agencies' in contributing to child abuse, they are reduced to contextual issues or items which attach themselves to certain families. His central focus and hence his strategies for intervention, are based upon the practitioner's ability to predict high risk and thus isolate the dangerous. In the process prevention becomes defined as 'the identification and management of high-risk cases' (1987, p. 26). He has been refining a high-risk checklist for some years and has applied it retrospectively to 168 cases of death from child abuse and neglect in North America and Britain. Sexual abuse cases are not included. There are two sets of factors itemised – in relation to the parents and to the child – as shown in Table 3.1. So that, as in the Beckford Report, while 'high risk' is never defined, the checklist is seen to be of particular utility as 'A score of over half of the completed items in either section appears to be associated with high risk'.

While Greenland comments that the checklist has not been rigorously tested *prospectively* and hence does not have any 'demonstrated predictive value' (1987, p. 98) he goes on to argue that it 'may provide a means of reaching consensus among

Table 3.1: Child abuse and neglect high-risk checklist

Parents	Child
1. Previously abused/neglected as a child	1. Was previously abused or neglected
2. Age 20 years or less at birth of first child	2. Under 5 years of age at the time of abuse or neglect
3. Single parent/separated; partner not biological parent	3. Premature or low birthweight
4. History of abuse/neglect or deprivation	4. Now underweight
5. Socially isolated – frequent moves – poor housing	5. Birth defect – chronic illness – developmental lag
6. Poverty – unemployed/unskilled worker; inadequate education	6. Prolonged separation from mother
7. Abuses alcohol and/or drugs	7. Cries frequently – difficult to comfort
8. History of criminal assaultive behaviour and/or suicide attempts	8. Difficulties in feeding and elimination
9. Pregnant – post partum – or chronic illness	9. Adopted, foster- or stepchild

interdisciplinary teams concerned with the assessment of risk' (p.98). In answer to the question 'Can high-risk situations be identified in advance in order to prevent child abuse and neglect deaths?' he asserts: 'A cautious yes, in many cases. Since over 80 per cent of the UK and over 60 per cent of the Ontario victims had been previously injured, it seems prudent to classify all cases of non-accidental injuries to young children as high-risk cases' (1987, pp. 178–9). He comments that, in addition, almost half of these cases were stunted in growth. The immediate problem for practitioners which this raises is – who can be left out, if virtually all cases of non-accidental injury are by definition 'high risk' by the fact of a previous injury? Greenland goes on to argue that there is a pessimistic prognosis for such cases. His review of cases in which children were killed while under the protection of the social services confirms for him the wisdom of Henry Kempe's dictum – 'if a child is not safe at home he cannot be protected by casework' (1987, p. 164). He considers that the existing guidelines, regulations or legislation do enable professionals to intervene 'effectively and selectively in order to protect high-risk children' (1987, p. 179). The problem lies with the practice and attitudes of the professionals.

All recent inquiry reports recognise that a single agency, occupation and area of professional knowledge is rarely capable, on its own, of assessing either whether abuse has taken place or where there may be high risk in the future. For example the Cleveland Report has made it clear that, in the area of sexual abuse, there is no piece of medical information and no form of medical diagnosis which, alone, can fulfil this role. It seems there is now a consensus that the role of the social assessment in the context of the multi-disciplinary framework is crucial for identifying such cases. Professional associations, inquiry reports, the most recent DHSS circular (1988) and the parents' lobby all agree that the social assessment is vital and that social workers should have a particular responsibility and expertise in this area. Such an assessment is the central element in classifying cases in order to select or sift out the actual from the illusory, the high risk from the low risk, and the dangerous from the not-so-dangerous. The assessment of dangerousness thus provides the central focus and rationale for what practitioners should be doing. It should be noted, however, that this emphasis does not simply suggest that certain individuals are inherently dangerous but that it is the situation in which they find themselves which is crucial, perhaps because of added stress or the particular form of family relationships. As Cyril Greenland suggests 'the potential for violence is embedded in a situation rather than implanted within an individual' (1987, pp. 172). For example 'interacting variables such as social isolation, an unwanted pregnancy, and a crying child can precipitate a dangerously explosive situation' (1987, pp. 171–2). If it is the interaction of individual and social situations which leads to dangerousness the *social* assessment becomes all the more important, and all the more difficult. Certainly the Greenland checklist includes an extensive mixture of behavioural, developmental and social factors *associated* with cases where children have suffered at the hands of their parents. Furthermore, one cannot deny that the process of assessment necessitates good professional judgement which draws upon the findings from thoughtful and sophisticated research. The problem with the Greenland-type approach is not only that it is based on a barely controlled retrospective analysis of cases which, by their tragic consequences, have gone dreadfully wrong, but it also comes up with criteria which are likely to lead to the problems (see Dingwall, Chapter 2) of false positives and false negatives. It seems inconsistent, therefore, to lay at the door of professional practice the failures which, at least in part, should be laid at the door of the research itself. There are major problems in developing a form of policy and practice which has at its core the individualised identification of 'high risk' and the assessment of dangerousness.

Dangerous families and therapeutic control

Many of the ideas discussed above have informed the philosophy and practice of the Rochdale Child Protection Team of the NSPCC as reflected in their book, the title of which is in itself instructive, *Dangerous Families: Assessment and Treatment of Child Abuse* (Dale *et al.* 1986). The aim of the book is to outline a model of work in cases of serious abuse where, it is thought, the parents are being offered a final opportunity to demonstrate their abilities to care for their child/ren appropriately. The central goal is to engage the family in an intensive assessment process in which, in addition to making the right decision for the child's future, a therapeutic experience is developed for the parents. The writers have been influenced by the work of Cyril Greenland but are aware of the debates and difficulties in trying to predict danger-ousness in individuals and the use of checklists. However, the authors believe that progress in this direction can be made by considering how the whole family operates as a system. Family therapy and Gestalt are drawn upon to assess the relative danger-ousness of families, so that: 'Violence to children therefore needs to be considered primarily within the context of the family . . . incidents of serious child abuse invariably involve a triangular relationship between the perpetrator,the victim, and the partner, who adopts the role of "failure to protect" the child.' (1986, p.32).

It is felt that the intensive use of such methods over a period of 3–4 months can help to identify the actual or potential 'pathological dynamics within the families' and hence contribute to establishing whether the home is safe.

This book aims to provide a clear model for practice and is at pains to demonstrate how the Rochdale team differs from others in its approach. The team is primarily concerned with the assessment of dangerousness, so that the only reference to treatment in the index is to a critical discussion of how it has been used in the past, with depressing results, particularly by the first NSPCC Special Unit at Denver House (reported in Baher *et al.* 1976). As they point out, the original Denver House team saw their main priority as offering a treatment and therapeutic service to abusing families. The team expressed concern about the disadvantages of removing children from abusing families, including the risk of seriously alienating parents by taking legal action:

> Since our main emphasis was to be on treatment and rehabilitation, we felt that we would prefer that they (the Police) were not involved in our families, as we did not believe they had a therapeutic role to play in battered baby cases. Our intention was to avoid any direct interrogation about the circumstances of the injury, and we were anxious that our parents should avoid this experience from others. (Baher *et al.* 1976, p. 106)

The Rochdale team argue that, while such an approach represented a highly professional application of a therapeutic model, it had serious theoretical and practical flaws. The major feature of such a 'nurturing model' is an emphasis on intrapsychic and social factors, particularly emotional and social deprivations, as determining family relationships. History is seen to dominate, therapy is restitutive and parental maturation is the goal via an encouragement of dependence upon the worker and a 'transference of mothering'. The social workers assumed the parents were essentially powerless to change their situation and hence accepted much of the responsibility on the parents' behalf for bringing about improvement: 'the emphasis was on acceptance and provision, whilst the need for control and the establishment of limits to behaviour was undervalued' (Dale *et al.* 1986, p.9).

By implication the Denver House approach was over-indulgent, encouraged dependency and failed to use authority and recognise the role of law in the work. Perhaps not surprisingly this emphasis on trying to nurture and mother failed to engage the men in the families. The Rochdale team argue that such an approach can never be successful in reality: 'the worker can never be an effective parent to the child'. The results reported by the Denver House team were disappointing, for: 'despite the relatively high rates of rehabilitation, they had to conclude that the children's quality of life had hardly improved *despite* the extended periods of intensive therapeutic intervention' (Dale *et al.* 1986, p. 156).

As a result the Rochdale team have shifted their approach to one which is much more in sympathy with 'modern psychotherapies', where the major element for change stems from the importance of individuals and families themselves taking responsibility for their actions and there is an emphasis on encouraging independence rather than dependence. As the book notes, such a shift was reinforced by the decline in available resources, hence reducing the possibility of developing the re-parenting model in practice.

The Rochdale team are also, however, very critical of what they see as typical practice in social services departments. As a result of the increased publicity surrounding child abuse in the 1970s and the criticisms levelled at departments and workers following very public public inquiries, departments and workers, they suggest, became uncertain and anxious and were more concerned to protect themselves than to influence families and protect children. There was a failure to develop any proper knowledge base with the result that practice was dominated by an anxious surveillance of families. There was a lack of clarity and hard decisions were avoided. The Rochdale team argue that, far from being neutral, such an approach in itself can make situations worse and increase the risk of abuse to children – what they call 'professional dangerousness'. Hence, their model of practice is designed to overcome the problems arising from dangerous families and dangerous professionals.

In order to do this it is seen as vital that social workers use the power vested in their work by statute. Not only does the law provide the mandate for assessment, it provides the therapeutic potential for change. Rather than therapy and the law, or care and control, being seen as separate and mutually exclusive they are interrelated. The one provides the basis for the other. Not only should 'protection' come before therapy, but the potential for change lies in the firm therapeutic opportunities provided by a firm statutory mandate – what is referred to as 'therapeutic control'. The model is influenced by some of the American literature on sexual abuse (see Sgroi 1982) but is applied to all child abuse. Power is seen as both inescapable and central: 'The usefulness – indeed the largely unrecognised therapeutic potential – of powerful statutory mandates to engage highly resistant families in assessment and therapy is demonstrated in this book' (Dale *et al.* 1986, p. 81).

Once established, the focus is upon intensive engagement with the families, the primary focus being upon assessment in order to differentiate the dangerous family from the not-so-dangerous. From the former the children should be removed and placed with long-term foster or preferably adoptive parents. In the latter cases, it should be possible for the children to be quickly returned and the social worker to withdraw. Either way, anxious surveillance, drift and professional dangerousness are kept to a minimum. The primary role for the social worker and the therapeutic team is therefore to make clear, hard decisions based on the assessment of dangerousness. The model attempts to provide clarity and certainty where previously, it is suggested, there was uncertainty and vagueness.

In the process, notions of treatment, support and working with parents in a more equal way become very marginal. The model is based on encouraging, or forcing, parents to be independent and to take responsibility for their actions and situations. The messy material and financial aspects of family life are primarily the responsibility of parents to resolve.

It is not surprising that the Rochdale team are sympathetic to the growth of child-care policies based on permanancy planning, whereby children are seen to require a permanent family placement either with natural parents or a permanent alternative – preferably adoption – and that such decisions should be taken in a relatively short time. Local authority care thus becomes residual and essentially a channel towards securing a permanent home (Parton 1985b). It is assumed that privatised child care within the family, and hence by women, is the best way to bring up children and the state should only intervene when things are seen to go wrong. As a consequence, day care, for example, is seen as a therapeutic service designed to train and support those mothers with parenting problems, rather than a service in its own right. The aim is to return families, and thus mothers, to independent functioning. The underlying assumption seems to be that normal mothers and families cope without state services. We are thus presented with a model of practice in which assessment of dangerousness is central and in which parental independence and responsibility is explicit. Social workers therefore need to be clear, decisive and have no quibbles about using the power which statute gives them. In doing so they take on the guise of becoming a somewhat distant, powerful expert to whom parents have to prove themselves and whose main priority is the protection of children. Such an approach is presented as qualitatively different from that of the earlier NSPCC Denver House team and typical social services departments. In many ways it seems to encapsulate the main elements of what some see as good child-protection work in Britain in the late 1980s.

Childhood innocence

We have argued that the current emphasis on identifying dangerousness and child protection, while attempting to provide a clear rationale for what should be done about child abuse particularly in professional practice is based on a narrow conception of prevention and a restricted view of underlying causes. It is seen as a particular, local problem that occurs only in certain families and requires an exceptional response. We are provided with a narrow concept of child protection, a restricted view of underlying causes and, as a consequence, an over-confidence about individualised assessment/predictive methods. However, we have tried to outline how this concentration on dangerousness and child protection in the mid to late 1980s is qualitatively different from the response developed in the early 1970s.

Underlying this discussion are deeper issues concerning the social construction of child protection. This extends beyond official inquiries, research reports and practice books to its construction in the media and popular discourse – much of which has recently been focused on the issue of sexual abuse. Those, both professionals and feminists, who have been trying to bring the issue out into the open in recent years, have been determined to change the common assumption that most victims, usually girls, have been active and willing participants. Partly as a result children have been presented as being both innocent and weak. Not only do children not lie but 'childhood is presented as a time of play, an asexual and peaceful existence within the protective bosom of the family' (Kitzinger 1988, p. 79). Such romantic notions are not only based on idealised visions of the normal nuclear family but are seen to contrast markedly with the experience of children reared in abusive and/or dangerous families. Such 'innocence', by definition, means that children are not able to look after themselves alone and they do not really know what is in their best interests. Because they are weak, both physically and in what they 'know', they need protecting. Such paternalism fails to locate the problem in the structural power inequalities between adults, particularly men, and children. The notion of child protection confirms stereotypes of the innocent weak child, defends the nuclear family, avoids identifying male power and denies children's access to both knowledge and power (Parton, C. 1989; Parton, N. 1989).

The restructuring of state welfare

Why have the identification of dangerousness and the idea of child protection, concerns of policy and practice for many years, now become of such significance? As we have noted earlier such changes do not apply only to the area of child abuse but are reflected in similar changes in the areas of crime, mental health and social regulation more generally.

Bottoms (1977) and others have suggested the major reason for the 'renaissance of dangerousness' is a decline in the belief in the rehabilitative ideal and social reform more generally. Over the past 15 to 20 years a growing scepticism about the social democratic consensus and the success of wide-ranging state welfare programmes has developed. The confident belief that even the most recalcitrant individuals can be made to improve their characters, values and habits via state-sponsored treatment efforts has been replaced by a far more pessimistic and 'realistic' approach. Such pessimism results in part from a recognition of the poor results of benevolence, as shown by a series of research findings in the 1970s, particularly in relation to crime and delinquency (Fischer 1978; Croft 1978; Gaylin *et al.* 1978) and also that such interventions, in the form of casework and treatment, have less chance of success in a deteriorating economy. In this context it seems to make sense to retrench and emphasise 'less harm rather than more good'. Thus there has been an emphasis on reducing the role of the state and on concentrating its resources and efforts where it is thought they will be most effective.

As Cohen suggests: 'Liberal crime-control solutions were attacked as tried, found wanting and hopelessly optimistic. The message here is again "realistic" and again in favour of a selective state retreat: concentrate on the hard cases and let the soft take care of themselves' (1985, p. 130). Prevention is thus defined in far narrower terms. Rather than trying to bring about general changes and improvements in families, communities and the wider society, prevention should concentrate on identifying the high-risk or dangerous individual or family and thereby stop 'it' before 'it' happens.

However it is not simply that the role of the state, and hence its relationship with civil society and the family, is being reduced. It is being restructured into a new form and with new priorities. Our analysis of changes in thinking about child abuse should not be divorced from those, for example, in the areas of taxation and social security where the values of individual and family independence and responsibility are similarly legitimated. In the shift from a democratic welfare state to one based on a social market economy, the law becomes crucial in at least two ways. Firstly, it must provide a general framework to underwrite contracts between individuals and between individuals and the state with the aim of giving a certain predictability and certainty to the rules governing social behaviour in general. Secondly (paradoxically it may seem), the extension of the law, in theory, can reduce intrusion by state bureaucrats into other sections of society, whether it be the market, civil society or the family. Freedom and liberty is to be defended by the law which in turn encourages independence and responsibility and prescribes the areas of activity of both the state and state officials. When the state does intervene it does so with the full weight of the law informing it.

The renaissance of 'dangerousness' and the decline of the

rehabilitative ideal seems therefore to discredit the more traditional forms of treatment associated with the growth of social work
in the late 1960s and early 1970s. At the same time the problems in
the clinical prediction of future dangerousness are recognised. It
seems that such efforts are being abandoned in favour of procedures based on more apparently observable behaviour such as the
social situation or the family system. It is argued by some (Dale *et
al.* 1986) that this method offers better opportunities for assessment and prediction. Such a move is similarly quite antagonistic to
post-war liberal reforms where the emphasis was upon *indirect*
attempts to improve the functioning of individuals, families and
communities through universal improvements in social security,
health, education, housing and the personal social services. The
emphasis now is much more upon the *direct* observation and
regulation of behaviour rather than the indirect and voluntaristic
provision of state services in a more mutually-negotiated form.

Conclusions

Certainly it may be argued that the emphasis on the statutory
mandate of child-protection work should not only ensure children
are removed from dangerous individuals and families but also
ensure that the rights and interests of parents are not unwarrant-
ably undermined. It may also be argued that the authoritative
model of child-abuse work developed by Cyril Greenland and the
Rochdale team in trying to concentrate efforts on serious cases
may, for some parents, offer a last chance for them to keep their
children where previously they might not have done. There may
well be parallels here with attempts to develop intensive community alternatives for offenders who previously may have been
incarcerated. In the same way as incarceration may be kept for the
dangerous offender, so the permanent removal of children will be
reserved for the dangerous family. The problem still remains
however as to how the idea of serious, dangerous or high-risk is
defined and put into practice. Certainly our discussion of the work
of Cyril Greenland above suggests that this is particularly difficult.
It may also be that the whole approach is itself misplaced. As
Anne Cohn has concluded from her comprehensive review of what

is known about our attempts to predict and hence prevent abuse:

'Because child abuse is a vastly complex human problem, we have not been able to develop a perfect enough understanding of it to allow for successful prediction. At the moment we are unable to predict with accuracy who will or will not abuse. In developing a strategy for prevention, we clearly are concerned with certain characteristics or circumstances that increase the likelihood of abuse. We cannot, however, offer services or supports only to high-risk parents, for we simply do not know for sure who they are.' (1983. p. 171)

Further, she argues that child abuse is a complex problem because families have many needs and these vary through the life cycle. As a consequence it is doubtful that any preventive programme will have much success unless it is integrated into the values and norms of any community. Therefore, for most children to benefit from preventive activities they need to be made available to all families on a voluntary basis, and 'they probably need to be relatively non-obtrusive and in essence, common'. Prevention, far from being based on residual, individualistic interventions which rely on assessing dangerousness and the use of statutory authority, should be based on universal services which work to support those rearing children and rely on voluntary realtionships. This is not to say there will not be the need for the former but it starts from a very different framework. Certainly children's needs for protection, both by adults and from adults, would be substantially reduced if they had more access to practical, economic and political resources. If we are to tackle the roots of child abuse, we have to consider the whole position of children in society. This is a much deeper issue than current concerns with child protection and the identification of 'high risk' may suggest.

CHAPTER 4

EUROPEAN CHILD-ABUSE
MANAGEMENT SYSTEMS

JAMES CHRISTOPHERSON
Lecturer in Social Work, University of Nottingham

This chapter considers similarities and differences between perceptions of and responses to child abuse and the way it should be
handled in 8 different European countries: England, the Netherlands, France, Germany, Sweden, Norway, Italy and Turkey. It
arises out of research into this field which I have been undertaking
over the past decade. In England and the Netherlands I have
analysed samples of case-conference minutes and other filed
material on samples of 126 and 56 cases of actual or suspected
child abuse, and in order to determine public attitudes a questionnaire was sent to volunteer samples of members of the general
public in the UK and the Netherlands. Data from this research has
been published in papers presented to International Congresses on
Child Abuse and Neglect in Amsterdam (1981), Paris (1983) and
Rio de Janiero (1988). It is hoped to publish the full results
shortly.

Introduction

Continental European countries have been aware of child abuse
for as long or longer than have the UK and the USA. The original
version of the *Code Napoléon* included sections prescribing
penalties for the abuse of children, but the rapid rise in awareness
of the problem began with the Mary Ellen case in New York. In

that 1872 case a young girl who was being abused by her adoptive father was wrapped in a horse-blanket and taken before a judge under the terms of the law against cruelty to animals, and successfully removed from home. Legislation in most countries was enacted during the following 30 years and professional interest in the subject has developed rapidly since Henry Kempe's identification of the 'battered baby syndrome' (Kempe and Helfer 1962).

However, it would be wrong to suppose that these countries have necessarily followed the American lead in deciding how to deal with child-abuse cases. Each country's method of intervention has been affected by its legal and social structures, and by its general attitudes to the nature of deviance. Child abuse is a phenomenon which is dependent for its existence on the perceptions of those involved in the interaction and those external audiences who must first identify and then intervene according to law in the lives of those involved in the behaviour. Systems will be affected by the different weight given to the codes of ethical conduct of the various professionals involved. Furthermore, there are marked differences in the degrees of priority which it is felt should be given to the right of the child to be protected, the right of the alleged perpetrator not to be falsely accused, and the duty of the state to punish those who commit crimes against its most vulnerable members. The recent report into the events in Cleveland show how complex can be the task of responding to these often conflicting priorities.

In addition, it is taken as axiomatic in English-speaking countries that legal intervention to protect the child or punish the perpetrator is an essential part of intervention in child-abuse cases. Professionals may reflect the social situation of which they are a part and hold an essentially pessimistic view of human nature, which suggests that people do not change, and in particular do not abandon deviant behaviour which they may enjoy unless they are forced to do so by the power of the state. Even a highly therapeutic project such as the Child Sexual Abuse Treatment Programme in San Jose, California, regards it as essential that perpetrators are prosecuted, although such is the speed of the programme's intervention strategy, and the slowness of the legal process, that by the time a case comes to trial the therapeutic programme may be complete, and successful completion of the programme may serve as a mitigating factor in selecting a penalty (Giarretto 1982). Similarly, in the UK, Dale *et al.* (1986, p.61) recommend the obtaining of Care Orders in abusing-family situations, even where the family are willing participants in a therapeutic programme and there is no intention to remove the child from home.

By contrast, many European countries take a more libertarian and optimistic view of human nature in which people are seen to be able to change if they have the will to do so. Furthermore, it is felt that statutory intervention will be resented by the family involved and may indeed serve as an obstacle to effective change. In the Netherlands, where the system revolves around a paediatrician or general practitioner who acts as a 'confidential doctor', cases of child abuse are only referred to the Child Protection Board for compulsory intervention when parents are unwilling to cooperate in an intervention process, and prosecution in child-abuse cases is so rare that statistics are no longer kept. In Sweden the Care of Young Persons Act 1980 expressly provides that compulsory care proceedings shall only be taken where there is a lack of cooperation on the part of the parents. That should not be taken to mean that children are less likely to spend time away from home following an abusive incident, and indeed European countries tend to have higher rates of children in substitute care than is the case in this country, which in turn has more children in care than has the USA (Christopherson 1986; Mech 1983). Whether the stress on voluntary admissions is in the interests of parents and children is a question that can only be answered from one's own cultural perspective. In the UK we take it for granted that voluntary admission to psychiatric hospital is preferable to admission under a section of the Mental Health Act. Dutch professionals, coordinated as they are by doctors, would see the problem of child abuse in exactly the same way.

It would be tempting to analyse these differences in terms of the theoretical grounding of the workers concerned, and to suggest that American and English workers tend to take either more Freudian or more structuralist standpoints than their European colleagues, and consequently take an essentially deterministic view of their clients' capacity for change. Indeed, structuralist writers such as Gil (1979b, p.45) and more lately feminists, in relation particularly to sexual abuse, have argued for severe

penalties against perpetrators, and consider that to seek to maintain the family is to collude with the perpetrator against the
interests of the other members of the family (Nelson 1982, p.73).
However, structuralists such as Wolff (1975, p.36) in Germany
describe child abuse as a result of punitive social structures, and
argue for therapeutic intervention.

What seems more relevant is the history and ethos of the
professions concerned, and the societal and legal context in which
they operate. In the USA, intervention from the case of Mary
Ellen onwards has always been based on the centrality of law. The
Child Sexual Abuse Treatment Programme grew out of concerns
in the probation service about the inadequacy in the management
of sex offenders. In the UK, child abuse has been seen as a matter
for legal intervention and policing. Indeed, NSPCC inspectors
wore uniforms similar to those of policemen until 1962. In some
European countries, present-day systems arose out of medical
concerns, and child abuse came to be seen as an 'illness'; furthermore, both in the Netherlands (Baneke 1983) and in Sweden,
emphasis on voluntary methods of intervention arose at least in
part from concerns about the numbers of children in compulsory
care and the quality of care they received. In the Netherlands, for
example, children in statutory care are housed in establishments
operated under the auspices of the Ministry of Justice while those
in voluntary care are the responsibility of the Ministry of Welfare,
Public Health and Culture. Children in voluntary care are thus less
stigmatised (Doek and Slagter 1979, p.37). In Sweden the number
of children in compulsory care before the introduction of the Care
of Children Act in 1982 was attracting adverse international
publicity (*The Observer* 1984).

Southern European perceptions of child abuse

However, in Southern Europe, the central issues change. Caffo
describes how in Italy, unlike other countries, the number of cases
of child abuse brought before the court fell over the years from
1965 to 1976 from 6,005 to 3,305 (Caffo 1983). Caffo argues that
this is not the result of a fall in the amount of abuse but a reduction
in interest in the topic on the part of the authorities. Reported

cases of abuse of the kind described above, physical abuse, neglect and incest, all fell during the period. However, Caffo describes quite different areas of concern not encountered in present-day north-west Europe, including the black market sale of babies, emigration and the problem of child labour. Caffo also includes institutional abuse on his list of the most important issues, and while some north-west European countries are aware of it, it is often glossed over because of the institutions' centrality in the very process of rescuing children from abuse. Caffo points out that illegitimacy is still a stigma in Italy and very high numbers of illegitimate children are placed in institutions. Over 103,000 children were in institutions in 1976, as compared with 35,000 in England and Wales, and in 1978 30,000 Italian children were taken abroad for adoption, particularly from Southern Italy. By contrast, in the UK, there is growing awareness of the damage that was done by a similar policy of emigration which ended over 20 years ago (Child Migrants' Trust, 1988). There is little or no framework in Italy, other than the criminal law, for confronting child abuse. Abandonment of the child, unless in physically dangerous places, or even selling the child, is quite legal.

The same phenomenon is seen even more clearly in considering the issue of child abuse in Turkey. There, too, intolerance of illegitimacy leads to a large number of children being abandoned – over 1,000 per year according to Günçe, and Konanç-Onur (1983, p.137). A few of these were abandoned in remote places, in the same way as were children in classical times. Even if legitimate, female children may be abandoned because of pressure to have male children.

Sexual abuse of children in Turkey also appears widespread. In a country with a population of some 51 million, over the 5 years from 1975 to 1980 almost 32,000 people were charged with raping children under 15, more than 10 times the figure for all rapes in the UK in the same period. Günçe and Konanç-Onur point out that the child victims of rape are often killed. In the same period 3,283 people were charged with prostituting children and a further 2,333 with the more serious offence of prostituting children for whom they are responsible. Turkish law also considers from its own national point of view the issue of the kidnapping of children. In north-west Europe this is an extremely rare and extremely serious offence. In Turkey there are two forms of the offence: 'kidnapping with sexual desire and intent to marry' and 'kidnapping without sexual desire or intent to marry'. Over the same 5 years 1,353 children were subjected to this second kind of kidnapping, but 76,928 children between the ages of 12 and 18 were subjected to the former, as were 267 children under the age of 12. This massive number is explained by the fact that girls are kidnapped for marriage to avoid paying a large bride price. Prosecution is suspended if the perpetrator marries the victim.

Legal comparisons

All the countries studied have criminal sanctions against child abuse, and all have legal processes for protecting the child from the parent. Sometimes the criminal and civil legal processes may be linked. For example, section 474 of the Turkish Criminal Code empowers the court to take away a person's legal rights to parenthood, while Article 312 of the French *Code Pénal* provides that if an abused child has to be hospitalised for more than 20 days, the perpetrator will be sent to prison for at least 2 years and will lose 'his or her civil rights'. These may include some rights in relation to parenthood. Conversely, in the Netherlands, on the extremely rare occasions when the drastic *ontsetting* procedure is used by the civil court, the perpetrator loses not only his or her right to care for the child, but also the right to vote. This procedure was only used in 5 cases out of 1,729 reported to the confidential doctors in 1979, and in Turkey there were only 700 cases from 1975–80 where parental rights were removed.

Legal traditions differ from country to country. Only England has a non-codified system based on common law; all the others have systems based on Roman law. As such they are essentially inquisitorial. It is the task of an official of the court to ascertain what happened, and then present that information to the judge, who will then decide what should happen. In the Netherlands the Public Prosecutor may even negotiate with an offender what the penalty should be (Hulsmann 1978).

However, far more frequently the civil and criminal procedures for processing child abuse are managed separately, and may indeed often be in conflict. In England care proceedings which may be the start of a rehabilitation programme for the child may have to wait until the prosecution of the perpetrator has been completed, although the Court of Appeal has recently decided that this need not be the case (Court of Appeal 1988). Indeed there may be resistance to the idea of providing any support for the victim in case his or her evidence is contaminated. Conversely, the events in Cleveland show clearly the dangers of attempting to pursue the interests of the child at the expense of the legal rights of the perpetrator and the family as a whole (Cleveland 1988).

Legal approaches to the issue of confidentiality vary from country to country. In France the right of the social worker to keep information secret is guaranteed by Article 378 of the *Code Pénal*. This was confirmed in February 1978 by the Court of Appeal at Rennes, which overturned a fine on a social worker who refused to give an examining magistrate information on how a child, whom she had taken into care voluntarily, had been injured. In the Netherlands confidentiality is so central to the child-abuse intervention structure, and indeed the structure of social work generally, that the issue of criminal prosecution becomes marginal. Indeed, in case conferences I have observed when a family's lack of cooperation has reached the point where the professionals feel that statutory intervention is inevitable, there was often a debate as to who at the case conference was going to compromise their duty of confidentiality and inform the Child Protection Board which has the responsibility for instigating legal proceedings.

Strict rules of confidentiality can of course obstruct effective cooperation. This can be the case in Germany, for example, where responsibility for managing child abuse is shared between the Youth Office, a local statutory agency which combines the functions of the British youth service with those of the former English children's departments, and a national voluntary organisation, the *Kinderschützbund*. Neither agency can report cases to the other, and indeed hospitals are not allowed to report cases of injured children who are brought to them (Schenker 1978). The law clearly regards the price that would be paid in discouraging clients to seek help if agencies were not to guarantee confidentiality as outweighing the value of inter-professional cooperation. The experience of children's helplines, both in the Netherlands and in the UK, suggest that this view is valid (Childline 1987).

Countries may also vary in the way they view the gathering of information. For example, in the UK the protection of people reporting child-abuse cases is seen as crucial. This was backed by the House of Lords decision in *D. v. NSPCC* (House of Lords 1978) which ensures that identities of referrers are kept secret. The same applies in the Netherlands. In Norway, by contrast, it is believed that information given anonymously is inherently unreliable, although Kjönstad (1981) argues that this belief, coupled with social pressure not to be seen as an informer, are considerable bars to effective reporting of child abuse.

It has been shown above that different forms of abuse and neglect, whether physical, sexual, emotional, or institutional, may be included or excluded from a country's legal or professional definition of child abuse. Countries also vary in their criteria for registering concern. Sometimes it will be necessary for abuse to have taken place; elsewhere, concern that there is a danger that it might take place in the future is sufficient. A country, such as the UK, where all decisions must potentially be justified to a court, will have a definition of abuse which will be couched in terms which can be justified to a court, and which may indeed have a moral element. Hence the Children and Young Persons Act 1969, Section 1.2(a) uses the phrase that the child's: 'proper development is being *avoidably* prevented or neglected'. The use of the word 'avoidably' suggests that a local authority would not be entitled to take care proceedings if the problem were unavoidable, or if the parents had done all they could reasonably be expected to do in order to safeguard the child's proper development, even if their efforts were unsuccessful. The equivalent section in Germany states precisely the opposite: the 1979 amendment to the German Civil Code reads:

If the physical, mental or psychological interests of the child are endangered because of an abuse of parental care or neglect *or guiltless failure of the parents* or because of the acts of a third party, then the Court of Chancery must take steps to alleviate that danger if the parents are not willing to, or capable of, doing so. The court may also take measures affecting third parties. [author's italics]

The extent to which these approaches are different in practice can be seen from responses to emotional abuse. The 1980 DHSS Circular LASSL (1980a) expressly includes emotional abuse in its terms but then defines it very narrowly. In order to bring proceedings, the local authority must show *both* that the child's behaviour or emotional development *have* been severely affected *and* that medical and social assessments find evidence of persistent or severe neglect or rejection. This can be compared with a German case quoted by Deutsch, where the court granted a 14-year-old boy permission to undergo psychotherapy when his parents were unwilling to consent to it, on the grounds of the likely damage to his emotional health in the future if he did not receive such treatment (Deutsch 1984, pp.61–2). It could be that the increasing use of wardship in the English courts and the more flexible terms of the Guardianship of Infants Act 1971, despite its far greater cost, is a reflection among *English* professionals of a desire for a similar degree of flexibility.

In the Netherlands court action is unlikely to follow identification of a situation as abusive, and this leads to a much wider definition of abuse. Increasing numbers of cases which relate solely to emotional abuse are being processed by the confidential doctors, although these include some which might not even be considered appropriate for social-work intervention. One example in the author's study of cases handled in one confidential doctor's area involved a child who was being used as a pawn in the parent's matrimonial battles. That case resulted in the child being placed voluntarily in a 'therapeutic institute'. Other extensions of the concept of child abuse have been possible allowing, for example, the identification of 'sexual neglect', which Koers regards as including 'denial of bodily pleasure, no physical affection, denial of the body's potential for being physically attractive, forbidding contact with age-mates, not allowing physical adornment' (Koers 1981, p.133 [*my translation*]). Such extensions of the concept would be seen as highly contentious in Britain, and indeed might be seen by some cultural groups as defining good care as abuse.

Extending the concept of abuse

Koers envisages the extension of the notion of abuse to include notions such as 'cognitive abuse', Eiskovits and Sagi go further and argue that professionals should break away from the concept of abuse as 'damage' or 'harm' which is located in 'traditional parent-child interaction', and consider the issue ecologically, based on the following propositions about children's normal development:

1. All children have development potential.
2. Actualisation of this potential is largely a function of environmental opportunities.
3. The opportunities are controlled by incumbents of powerful social roles, in this case adults.
4. The quality and direction of the environmental opportunities must be congruent with the development potential (Eisikovits and Sagi 1984, p.22)

To achieve this potential, they argue, children need to be able to participate as equal members in the social systems they encounter in their daily lives, to have responsibility for making decisions, to learn the meaning of interdependence at both peer and adult level as adult protection is gradually withdrawn, to have opportunities to discuss contrary value systems in order to derive their own, and to experiment with identity without irreversible consequences. Koers's extension of the operating definition of child abuse could be seen as part of the same conceptualisation, and a move away from the process by which inappropriate power assertion on the part of the parents towards the child is met by power assertion, sometimes equally inappropriate, on the part of the state over the parents.

This power is exercised by the state ostensibly in order to protect the child but in no case is it exercised automatically. Even among children who have been found to be abused, some are removed from home and some are not. There is no necessary link between seriousness of abuse, and likelihood of removal. In my own study of 126 case conferences in one NSPCC Special Unit area in 1979 and 1980, no specific type of injury led to automatic admission to care although significantly more children who had suffered bruising to the buttocks were removed than children who had suffered bruising to the head ($\chi^2 = 5.37$, p <0.02). Children with bruises to both head and buttocks were excluded, and there were no other differences in the samples to suggest an alternative explanation. This suggests that the moral blame attached by social workers to the ritual infliction of corporal punishment severe enough to cause bruising carries greater weight than does the loss of temper implied by bruises to the head, notwithstanding the potentially far greater physical danger to the child of the latter form of attack. Minutes of Dutch case conferences so rarely describe injuries in any great detail that it is impossible to make statistically significant comparisons.

Perceptions of the causes of abuse

Opinions vary from one country to another on the causes of child abuse, and on the factors likely to facilitate or impede a successful outcome for intervention. The supposed link between child abuse and the excessive use of alcohol provides an interesting example of this. In France, Leulliette states that 70 per cent of children brought to the *Hôpital Bretonneau* in Paris following abuse had alcoholic parents. In more serious cases the figures rise to 75 per cent or even 90 per cent (Leulliette 1978, p.62). Furthermore, Leulliette argues that 'the children's judge who returns these little ones to their drunken father condemns them absolutely, for the alcoholic is never cured.' By contrast, in the Netherlands in 1983, alcohol consumption was only seen as a factor in 20 per cent of cases. In my own English study 29 per cent of the cases had a father or father substitute with a drink problem, and 5 per cent a mother with such a problem. There was no significant difference in the number of English children taken into care between those where a parent had an alcohol problem and those where they did not.

In relation to the problem of parental drug abuse, my study of 56 cases dealt with by one confidential doctor during the 1970s found 14 parents who were seen as having drug problems compared with only 3 out of 126 in the English sample. A Dutch child was also significantly more likely to be taken into care if the mother had a drug problem than was the case in this country ($\chi^2 = 6.29$, p < 0.02). Whether in the light of the decision of the House of Lords in *D. (a minor) v. Berkshire County Council and others* (House of Lords 1988) this would still be the case in a debatable point. Interestingly, chronic drug abuse is one of the grounds put forward by Rädda Barnen in Sweden as justifying permanent removal of a child from its parents (Barn 1985, p.71).

Thus there is a process by which parents are labelled as deviant, for example by abusing their children or by being identified as having a drink or drugs problem. This labelling process does not necessarily imply moral or still less criminal blame, but does involve the loss of civil liberties by the parent being expected to submit to intervention and to the assessment process which that involves. Stress factors are perceived as impairing the capacity of these parents to develop adequate parenting skills. *D. (a minor) v. Berkshire County Council and others* has shown that given a sufficiently powerful deviant label, in that case 'drug user', then parenting capacity may be seen as inevitably impaired even before the child is born. Where moral blame is imputed, it may be reduced if the reason for the abuse can be located in the child, as evidenced by my finding that the police are less likely to take action, in the form of a formal caution or prosecution, when the child itself is seen to have problems, such as being 'difficult', 'whingy', or even handicapped. The deviant label will of course still remain by virtue of having a child who is 'difficult' or handicapped.

Discussion

This chapter has sought to show that although most European countries recognise to a greater or lesser extent the existence of a phenomenon called 'child abuse', and north-west European countries would share a general perception of the kinds of behaviour in which it is appropriate to intervene, they have some very different assumptions, arising from different philosophies, about the nature of the intervention. Southern European countries may feel that there are higher priorities in terms of structural change than the provision of individual casework to abused children.

There are implications for a system based on voluntary intervention such as that in the Netherlands. Where what is essentially moral pressure to cooperate is applied to alleged abusing parents it becomes difficult for parents to resist the loss of privacy involved in receiving help, even if they believe themselves to be innocent of what is alleged. So many forms of help are offered to Dutch parents to divert them into cooperating with professionals that it must seem much easier for the family to admit the abuse, especially as they know that it is extremely unlikely that any criminal consequences will follow. In the Dutch casenotes which I studied, details of the abuse were often, to say the least, sketchy, because, as we have seen, the abusive incident is of secondary importance to the family's overall functioning and needs. No doubt this is an example of criticising a system from one's own national perspective, but when one is brought up in a tradition steeped in the tenets of the common law, the removal of the opportunity to have oneself acquitted of what one has not done has profound civil liberties implications. On the other hand, the organisation Parents Against Injustice has encountered many examples of situations where pressure to confess in the interests of therapy has been applied even where criminal or civil legal sanctions may still follow. The Dutch system has eliminated the conflict between the needs of justice and the needs of the child and the family but it has done so by excluding justice from the equation.

European initiatives are beginning to be taken up in this country. One example of this is Childline, the children's helpline, which is modelled, at least in principle, on the Dutch *Kindertelefon* system and the Swedish organisation *BRIS* (Swedish equivalent of Childline). We in the United Kingdom may have to learn that those professions at present involved cannot hope to meet all the needs for intervention in child abuse. If 10 per cent or even 1 per cent of children are abused, whether sexually, physically or in other ways, and all decided to seek help, then processing of cases by professionals, already creaking under the strain, would become totally impossible. It seems important, therefore, that the UK learns from the Netherlands about the use of other professionals such as teachers or youth workers, and from Italy to develop the use of volunteers to provide support for children and families. In one project in the Netherlands, called Children Help Children, even children are being enlisted to provide support for their abused contemporaries (Korf 1987).

In the longer term we may be forced to accept intervention on the basis of providing assistance to abusing families on a voluntary basis, simply because of the resource implications of processing every case through a case conference, let alone through one or two courts, with the many adjournments that each is likely to entail. American experience with diversionary systems in sexual abuse cases suggest that such a change would be in the interests of all those involved (Topper and Aldridge 1981). Necessity may force us to make progress.

CHAPTER 5

DECISION-MAKING AT THE GATEWAY TO CARE

JEAN PACKMAN
Senior Lecturer in Social Work, University of Exeter

JOHN RANDALL
Assistant County Adviser (Child Care), Devon Social Services Department

In the glare of today's spotlight it is difficult to remember that victims of abuse form only a small proportion of children who are admitted to local authority care. Of the 28,500 who entered the care system in the 12 months ending 31 March 1985 less than 1,500, or 5 per cent, had been placed on Care Orders because of ill-treatment or neglect under section 1(2) (a), (b) and (bb) of the Children and Young Persons Act, 1969. Other children at risk are almost certainly admitted under different headings: committed to care for being 'in moral danger' for example, or received voluntarily from 'unsatisfactory home conditions', or for 'other reasons'. Even so they represent a minority of all admissions to care.

Nevertheless, the vulnerability of such children is evident and their tendency to remain within the care system for long periods is well-established. A quarter of the children *in* care in March 1985 had come into care on court orders related to neglect and ill-treatment, compared with the tiny number admitted in the course of a year. The contentious nature of such decisions, vividly demonstrated by the Cleveland Inquiry (Cleveland 1988), also means that the processes and outcomes of such decision-making are important and require close scrutiny. In order to contribute to such scrutiny we shall draw on material from our study of decision-making about children considered for local authority care

(Packman *et al.* 1986). As one of a number of DHSS-financed research projects that have been widely disseminated (DHSS 1985b), it has the advantage of setting the dilemmas and deliberations about children at risk within a broader child-care framework. This is potentially valuable, both in the search for connections between abuse and other child-care problems, and as a means of achieving a sense of proportion at a time when the shadow of child abuse threatens to eclipse the entire child-care system.

The limitations of our material must nevertheless be borne in mind. The inquiry was conducted in the early 1980s and, as such, it shows its age. Concern about child abuse had been great and growing since at least the early 1970s and, as in other authorities, social workers in our sample counties were working within a framework of detailed departmental guidelines and an elaborate pattern of collaborative, multi-disciplinary machinery. All the same, looking back it is now evident that new peaks of anxiety and new facets of the problem were yet to come. For example, numbers of children on the child-abuse register in one of our study authorities had been declining since 1979 and continued on the downward path until 1985, when a huge upward surge began. By 1987 there had been a 33 per cent increase in the numbers registered at the time of our main study period in 1980–1. This simply mirrors the national scene where, as the ADSS reported, there was a 22 per cent increase in numbers on child-abuse registers between 1986 and 1987 (ADSS 1987). So we were researching at a time when public and professional anxieties may have been somewhat less intense than they are today, with probable but unverifiable consequences for decision-making processes and outcomes.

Sexual abuse was also rare in our study cases – again an indication of how rapidly the picture changes. Only 7 per cent of children on the register in one study authority were categorised as being sexually abused at the time – a proportion which had trebled by 1987. So we have little to add to the important debates on a subject which has dominated the latter part of the decade. The study was also small-scale, being an examination of decision-making in only 2 local authorities in the south of England. There is plenty of evidence that departments vary in their policy and practice – indeed, our 2 authorities were chosen to demonstrate this – so they cannot be regarded as representative of the country as a whole. On the other hand, many of the issues they raise are universal and are not limited to a particular time or place.

It has been possible to look afresh and in more depth at the circumstances surrounding 62 children within our original sample who were on child-abuse registers and at the nature of the processes leading up to the decisions that were made about them. They represent 17 per cent of all the children considered for care by a dozen teams in the 2 authorities in 1 year. Roughly half had been identified as being abused, or at risk of abuse, and were already on the register at the time of consideration. The rest were placed on the register as a result of the decision-making processes we were studying. We have drawn on our records of interviews with all the social workers and with a majority of the parents who were involved. These were interviews conducted first at the time admission to care was being actively considered, and again approximately 6 months after a decision had been reached. We have also studied the minutes of the many inter-agency case conferences which were held on behalf of this group of children, as well as our contemporary accounts of the conferences we were able to attend.

A striking feature of the decisions made about the child 'victims' in our study was the tendency to keep them out of the care system, rather than taking them in. Comparisons between all the children who were admitted during the year in question, and those who were considered for care but were kept out, showed that there was little to choose between them. Their family backgrounds, their own characteristics and the complex web of relationships and behaviour that social workers were attempting to evaluate were apparently very similar. Only a few factors differentiated the 2 groups to any significant degree and a small cluster of these concerned 'risk'. Perceived low standards of parental care, concern about the child's health and development, a history of neglect or abuse and the presence of the child's name on a child-abuse register were all significantly more likely to be associated with a decision *not* to admit the child than otherwise. This unexpected paradox forms a backcloth to the discussion which follows, although its meaning has been explored more fully elsewhere (Packman and Randall (1989).

Family circumstances

First, what of the family circumstances of the 62 children who were identified as being abused, or at risk of abuse? How did they compare with other children who hovered at the gateway to the care system? The short answer is that they were very similar, sharing the same overriding characteristics of poverty and its associated deprivations, alongside family disruption and turbulence. But within this characteristic picture certain features were rather more prominent. Very young children were heavily represented, well over half being below school age, compared with a little over a third in the sample as a whole. A modest, yet significantly higher proportion were living in two-parent families (2 out of 5, compared with just over a quarter in the whole sample), but many of these lived in reconstructed family groups, where stepfathers were present (28 per cent compared with 22 per cent in the whole sample). Families were, on average, larger than those of other candidates for care – half had 3 or more children, compared with 41 per cent in the whole group. The picture was not dissimilar to that found by Brian Corby in a northern town, also in the early 1980s (Corby 1987). Another striking feature was the extent to which the families were already known to the social services departments when admission to care was receiving serious consideration. Only 5 per cent were, in fact, new referrals with no previous history of contact and more than 1 in 3 had been known for at least 5 years. This was an exaggerated version of patterns across the whole sample.

One vivid and poignant form of departmental 'knowing' came from the fact that some parents had themselves been children 'in care'. In fact the proportion of mothers and fathers who were old girls and boys of the child-care system was no greater for the child 'victims' than for others being considered for care (approximately 1 in 5) but the way this could influence the perceptions of parents and social workers is well-illustrated within this small group. As an example, one infant's young and volatile mother had first been admitted to care, aged 10, for 'entertaining sailors', and her 'beyond control' behaviour later led to assault on a policeman, expulsion from an Approved School, and excessive drinking and drug-taking. In the words of the social worker, 'she's never had a home, and always wanted a home and a baby'. Her motivation and capacities for parenting were therefore understandably suspect. From the mother's viewpoint, she acknowledged that she 'was a little swine', but reckoned that this didn't excuse the fact that 'social services treat you always as a child and want to control you'. In contrast, she saw the probation officer as treating her 'like an adult'. Her wish to save her child from admission to care was fiercely expressed, in consequence.

Another depressed and ill and much more apathetic young mother, caught up in a sequence of fraught but transitory relationships, had been in care for most of her childhood. In her own words 'I've had social workers all my life. I was in care. A lot of people said it was because of my Dad but I found out it was because Mum beat me as a little baby. Then my Dad went to prison.' A failed fostering and poor relationships with her natural family left her bitter and equally sure that she didn't want her own children to go into care because 'I know what it's like'.

Thus, the families of children in our sample who were placed on the register displayed many of the well-documented 'risk' factors, in terms of family structure, environmental pressures, and the childhood experiences of parents, which are offered and used as predictors of abuse. But they also shared these characteristics (albeit sometimes in a more emphatic way) with most of the larger group of children (361 in all) who were being considered for care over the same time period. So the problem for professionals of identifying risk with any certainty, from within this wider child-care population – a problem which has been discussed at length by other writers (Parton 1985a; Dale *et al.* 1986) – is highlighted once again.

Reasons for considering admission

What, then, was the nature of the 'risk' that led the 2 departments to place the 62 children's names on their abuse registers; and what were their reasons for considering (but not necessarily effecting) an admission to care of these same children? The two issues were separable because, as we have indicated, approximately half of the children were already *on* the register when admission was being discussed and reasons for care were not necessarily directly connected with the reasons for registration. Indeed, it emerged that one of the effects of being a 'registered' child was to lower professional resistance to the idea of admission. Rather than being seen as a 'last resort', as it appeared to be for most other cases, quite trivial incidents – a mother failing to collect her child from relatives on an agreed day, for example – could trigger a serious consideration. This was one among several factors which seemed to account for the paradox of the significantly *lower* rate of *actual* admissions of children 'at risk'. Once the circumstances had been more fully explored, the option of admission was sometimes reassessed as an unnecessary over-reaction.

In 90 per cent of cases, however, reasons for considering the child's admission to care were directly related to concerns which had already led – or were about to lead – to placing the child's name on the child-abuse register. The largest group (42 per cent) consisted of actual physical injury, with a further 19 per cent who were thought to be at risk of physical harm. (The departments were identifying 'at-risk' children, in advance of DHSS guidelines defining such a category.) Neglected children and children who were emotionally abused each represented 12 per cent of the total, and the 4 sexually abused children formed the smallest group of all. The pattern today would look very different, with 'at risk' and 'sexual abuse' categories dominating the register.

Behind the shorthand of categorisation, however, lies a much greyer, less distinct and less dramatic picture. Physical injuries were often of a relatively minor kind – bruises, scratches and severe nappy rash – all taken as warning signs of rough and inadequate handling which might lead to more severe conditions if they were not checked or monitored. Only 2 out of the 62 children had broken bones and, mercifully, the extreme cruelties of the newspaper headlines were not in evidence. One teenager in the sexual-abuse category had been beaten by her stepfather with a hairbrush, and his reaction to her perceived waywardness was regarded as having 'sexual overtones', but there appeared to be no other supporting evidence.

This is not to diminish or overlook the very real harms and deficits in their upbringing that these children were suffering.

What was apparent was that signs of physical injury were much easier to detect and demonstrate than the more subtle but no less damaging forms of neglect and emotional deprivation or abuse, from which many were perceived to suffer. The visibility of physical harm was sometimes used, therefore, as a convenient peg on which to hang registration, when concern for the child's well-being was much wider and more complex – a point to which we will return.

Consultation and coordination

Deciding whether or not these children should be admitted to care was usually a complicated process, involving not only the social worker, but departmental managers and/or specialist advisers and, in most cases, personnel from other services as well. The degree of consultation which took place in advance of a decision was, in fact, considerably greater for these children than for others who were being considered for care, where 'risk' was not an explicit concern. In the vast majority of cases an inter-disciplinary case conference was convened. Where this was not so, three main reasons were apparent. In a few cases urgent action was taken by means of a Place of Safety Order and a conference followed after the event – an appropriate procedure for emergencies, recognised by the DHSS (DHSS 1986). In other instances families were already on the register and were being regularly reviewed, and key workers and their managers felt confident in making a decision without immediately involving the coordinating machinery. A third more dubious reason concerned social workers' perceptions of departmental policy in certain circumstances. An example was an 'at-risk' family, threatened with eviction, where the social worker asserted that children in her authority must never be admitted to care for homelessness: an interpretation that focused only on the immediate crisis, ignoring serious concerns about standards of parenting.

But even where a conference was not convened, levels of intra- and inter-departmental consultation were high. Two social service department managers, a health visitor and grandparents were all involved, following a complaint of ill-treatment by a neighbour, before it was decided there were no grounds for further action. In another crisis, no less than three managers and the police were party to discussions before a Place of Safety Order was taken. There was little evidence of social workers acting entirely alone, or of taking such decisions lightly.

Such informal deliberations tend, however, to be regarded as of secondary importance to the formal, inter-disciplinary case conferences, whose value has been stressed repeatedly in government circulars and in the conclusions drawn by many child-abuse inquiries. Indeed, such significance was attached to the failure to call a case conference in the Kimberley Carlile Inquiry that it was regarded as a key contributory factor to her death – the missing 'crucible' in which different professionals could have pooled their knowledge, anxieties and expertise with, hopefully, more decisive and protective effect (Carlile 1987). The responsibilities of case conferences are generally recognised as vital, but limited. They are for sharing information and expertise for purposes of identifying abuse or risk; sharing assessments of families and children to inform decisions about intervention; deciding whether the child's name should be placed on (or taken off) the abuse register; identifying a key worker and holding reviews to monitor any change or progress in the child's situation. Decisions about admission to care belong outside the conferences, with the social services departments themselves, but can still be strongly influenced by the multi-disciplinary discussions within. It is therefore to the case conferences in our own study that we will now turn.

We have already indicated that case conferences were held at some point in the process of deciding about entry to care for the majority of children where 'risk' was a recognised factor. But we have confined a closer examination to those held in only one of our two sample authorities, where minutes of 21 conferences concerning 19 children – two-thirds of the at-risk group in that authority – are available. The children came from 12 families. In addition, we have drawn on the researcher's notes, taken virtually verbatim, at half of those conferences. In doing so we rely on our qualitative material and the focus shifts from the landscape of trends and patterns to people and processes in close-up. Hallett and Stevenson's study of conferences held in the mid-1970s, (Hallett and Stevenson 1977) and the DHSS draft guidelines of 1986 for inter-agency cooperation (DHSS 1986), form useful reference points for an examination of practice in 1980–1.

The composition of the conferences was very much as described by Hallett and Stevenson. The Chair was invariably taken by an area manager of social services who was not directly concerned with the case – a practice that the DHSS recommended. An additional manager was present at half the meetings, and at one there was even a third. At least one, and often two, field social workers attended, and occasionally a residential social worker as well. Surprisingly, a specialist child-care adviser was a rarity, but the overall effect was of a heavy social service presence at every conference. Health visitors and their managers were the next most frequent participants, with a range of other health service professionals – psychiatrist, paediatrician, nurse, community physician – all appearing once or twice. The much-lamented absentee general practitioner was a feature of this, as of other studies, and appeared at only one conference. At one time or another, representatives from the police, schools (generally headmasters and only rarely teachers), educational welfare and educational psychology, probation, NSPCC, DHSS and the electricity board made up the rest of the group where a membership of between 8 and 10 people was the norm.

Parents, children and relatives were not invited, so these were traditional meetings of professionals and officials talking about, rather than with the families causing concern – a format confirmed as appropriate by the DHSS in 1986, but regarded less favourably by some of the parents. 'They had a big committee meeting at the hospital. We weren't even allowed to state our case. We would have liked to get it through to them that we don't beat our kids up.' Without direct experience of a family presence at such meetings, we cannot usefully add to the debate on the subject.

As already outlined, case conferences have several purposes, but we will confine our comments to those of direct relevance to decisions about entry to care. In the event, about half of the 19 children were admitted to care during our monitoring year and others were not, but a number of the former did not enter care until after a second, third or even fourth case conference had taken place. This, in itself, puts a different gloss on our finding that only a minority of 'at-risk' children were admitted to care. At 'first consideration' this was, indeed, the case, but active work with their families generally continued, surveillance was close, and recurrent crises and changes of circumstance meant that decisions had frequently to be updated and changed. The degree of volatility and unpredictability in families, and the shifting sequence of decision-making that it entailed was a feature of many of the cases in our wider study, but it was especially marked in the 'at-risk' group.

Family turbulence, at its extreme, also made clear how difficult it often was for professionals to take hold of a case and 'plan' or 'manage' it, however well they communicated and collaborated with one another. Though absent from the conference table, the parents and children were a powerful influence, frequently baffling or wrong-footing the 'experts'. The problem can be exemplified by the case of a family of mother, stepfather and 2 young daughters. The health visitor referred the family because of marital violence, the mother's mental health history and her current symptoms of depression, and a conference of health and social services personnel was called. The shared assessment was that the marital problem was at the root of all difficulties, but as the mother was very likely to leave her husband (about whom she expressed murderous feelings), this would reduce tension and risk to the children. Support and counselling by the social worker and health visitor should see her through the transition to an independent life with her children. A positive bond between mother and children was warmly acknowledged and admission to care was ruled out in consequence.

Three months later, at a second conference, the picture changed. Mother had made no move to leave her husband, but the marital friction had worsened, and she had been offered first day, and then residential care in a psychiatric hospital: the professionals had enabled a separation to take place. Because the stepfather had been reluctant to cope, the children had been received into care. The psychiatrist voiced concern that the mother would harm her children under stress – which was again defined as 'marital' – and all again agreed that the couple's permanent separation was the answer. The housing department was asked to find accommodation for mother and children only, on medical grounds, and reference was again made to the mother's caring relationship with her daughters. Another month on, and a review conference found the basic situation unchanged, though there had been a worrying incident when the mother had carried a knife when visiting the marital home. The social worker was also expressing concern that she was not visiting her children regularly, and voiced doubts about her ability to 'get things together well enough to have the children back'.

At a further conference, only weeks later, all plans had collapsed. Mother was refusing the new accommodation that had been offered, but was still expressing extreme anger about her relationship with her husband. The psychiatrist was proposing to discharge her, because her bed was needed and she was not considered 'mentally ill'. The health visitor was now expressing *her* doubts that the mother 'really wanted the children back', and the psychiatrist agreed, perceiving her as 'too dependent' with 'no responsibility'. The housing officer said he would be unable to rehouse her as a single person, but social services were reluctant to discharge the children under the present ominous circumstances. Since the children's foster home was only temporary, they were to set about finding a new placement for the girls. The children were not, for the moment, at direct risk from parental instability, but they were about to experience the turbulence of the care system itself.

Such a pattern of rapidly changing circumstances, which cannot be either controlled or accurately predicted was fairly common. It can be argued that part of the problem lies with failures of professional expertise. Perhaps, in the example given, rather than looking towards separation as the solution, one of the workers – health visitor, social worker, or psychiatrist – should have 'grasped the nettle' in Mattinson's terms (Mattinson and Sinclair 1979) and worked with the couple, together, on their fraught relationship. The outcome might then have been different. Perhaps, too, there was too much planning *for* the family and not enough planning *with* them, to engage their cooperation. But the fact remains that inter-professional goodwill and cooperation, which was evident in this case and in several others that we witnessed, was not enough to enable the frontline workers to do more than run to keep pace, and to behave in a reactive and even defensive manner. Criticism of social workers' passivity and their failures to plan to be decisive, have been widespread in recent child-care research – our own included (Packman *et al.* 1986). But such criticism must, in our view, be tempered by recognition of the complex and fluid family situations with which they are often faced and which, quite evidently, bemuse and confound workers from other disciplines – some much more prestigious and highly trained then their own.

Family turbulence does not always engender either professional togetherness or purposeful response and we observed participants at odds with one another, mirroring the conflicts in the cases they were discussing. A conference on 2 boys from a chaotic and deprived family plunged into lurid and circular discussions about the appalling state of the home – no electricity supply, broken meter, unsafe fire, dog excrement in kitchen and living room, 4 sleeping in 1 bed, an indecent exposist living on the floor above. As the pooling of each dreadful piece of information proceeded, antagonism to each other, as well as to the family, grew. The DHSS and WRVS (Women's Royal Voluntary Service) discovered, to their chagrin, that both had paid for the cost of the same summer holiday. The constable was outraged to be informed – by the man from the electricity board – that the police were going to drop charges against the father. 'I don't know about that! The shoplifting was not just a twopenny-halfpenny thing!' As indignation was whipped up, the conference moved angrily towards a joint decision.

'We either pay the electricity bill, or we take care proceedings' (SSD Manager).

'We could say the parents are not exercising proper control' (Police Constable).

'We *do* have moral danger – the exposist may have been there a year and we should also say we'll take a Place of Safety Order if she's sent to prison' (SSD Manager again).

Finally, it was agreed that payment of the electricity bill should be refused and legal advice sought on care proceedings. The stage was set for admission to care.

In the event, father paid his electricity bill with the unexpected windfall of a tax rebate, and the children stayed at home. The family was in the driving seat again!

At its worst, the chaotic and uncooperative family which is suspected of abuse can, in the absence of good chairmanship, throw a conference into such turmoil that the obvious is missed and no firm direction for the work is ever agreed. One such family, newly arrived in the area after 4 years on the abuse register of another authority, raised such alarm and exasperation in the group that at times all were talking fast and furiously at once. As various members groped for a way out they wondered if their own anxieties were actually exacerbating the family situation.

'She's bombarded agencies and agencies have bombarded her. I can't help feeling we may be causing some of this.' (Wartime analogies are not uncommon in the jargon of beleaguered social workers.)

Later, the NSPCC worker warned, 'If they're pressured much more something dreadful will happen.'

The 'dreadfulness' was perceived as physical harm to the children and the 'grounds' for action were seen in those terms alone. To the research onlooker, massive evidence of emotional damage and deprivation seemed to be overlooked, and the conference ended in mid-air, with no pulling-together conclusions, and no minutes taken. As a footnote, it is perhaps reassuring to know that one bad case conference does not necessarily lead to immediate disaster. After 6 months 1 child had apparently benefited from being admitted to a special school and another was receiving speech therapy. But serious concern about parenting standards rumbled on and all the agencies were gloomy about future prospects.

Family relationships

What emerges from all the case material is, in fact, the complex processes of interaction between family members: between the families and the professionals, and between the professionals themselves. If we take, first, relationships and behaviour within the families, the crucial significance of the marital relationship was evident in almost all the cases we studied. Most were unhappy parents, at loggerheads with one another, frequently expressing their tension and dissatisfaction by rows, separations and marital violence. In several families the father was in the forces and his frequent absences on duty placed further strain on taut and fragile relationships. For some the partnership seemed barely to have got off the ground, as with one depressed young mother who had drifted into cohabitation with the intense and overpowering father of her child – and was now stranded in a disturbing and alien relationship over which she felt she had no control. In a few families there was no constant marital pair, but a succession of partners passing through the home, and in one case a complicated *ménage à trois* lurched from crisis to crisis and from local authority to local authority. The quarrels and violence that erupted between the couples had obvious repercussions on their children. For some it was apparent in the depressed and withdrawn or aggressive and uncontrollable behaviour they exhibited, which in turn fuelled parental discontents. Some children were directly in the firing line, as likely to be struck in anger as their warring parents.

The severity of marital disharmony and the threat this posed to the children was, in fact, strongly reminiscent of Mattinson and Sinclair's *Mate and Stalemate* (Mattinson and Sinclair 1979) where the worst marital problems were to be found amongst the most chronic and risky child-care cases that the social services department carried. Some of the same features of ambivalence, failures in parenting and continual threats of separation were apparent in and less upon the *parents* in families where abuse is suspected. Certainly important lessons have to be learned in this respect and specialist child-abuse workers (Dale *et al.* 1986) and offering help to improve that relationship and developing the professional skills to do so would seem, from our own study, an essential ingredient of protective intervention.

For this reason we feel bound to reject too literal an interpretation of fashionable exhortations to focus more upon the *child* and less upon the *parents* in families where abuse is suspected. Certainly important lessons have to be learned in this respect and failures to observe, assess and communicate with children on a regular basis, when risk is at issue, have been painfully apparent in some well-publicised tragedies (Colwell 1974; Beckford 1985; Carlile 1987). But there are dangers, too, in ignoring the behaviour and well-being of any family members and in neglecting the core relationship between parent and parent which can have such a profound influence on the relationship between parent/s and child. Abuse is, after all, a sad aspect of interaction between adult and child, which can in turn be shaped by the interaction between adult and adult. The most hopeful and helpful form of intervention would seem to be to strive for balance, and to emphasise neither at the expense of the other.

Children's behaviour

The child's own behaviour was another aspect of family dynamics which was clearly of great significance in many of the cases we studied. For instance, over half of the 62 children 'at risk' were said, by social workers, to be 'unmanageable' – an imprecise but useful umbrella term that indicated disruptive and disobedient behaviour that was proving beyond the parents' ability or motivation to control. A third was labelled 'aggressive'. Given the young age of so many of the children, these are large figures. Much smaller proportions were thought to display the classic symptoms of emotional disturbance, like bedwetting, soiling or timid withdrawal, but case conference discussions suggest this may have been an underestimate on the social workers' part. From interview and conference material, there seemed no doubt that here were important factors associated with risk, though it has to be said that proportions of problem behaviour among the children on the register were little different from those in the study population of children as a whole: another indication of the difficulty of accurately identifying 'risk' from within the wider population of troubled families whose children are considered for admission to care.

Problematic child behaviour can be seen from at least two perspectives. Regarded as a response to the way children are being parented and to the aggressive and disruptive relationships and behaviours they see around them, it can act as an alarm signal, indicating the occurrence or the threat of some form of abuse. Unruly or disturbed child behaviour can also be seen as a dangerous trigger, which puts pressure on harassed and often ignorant or immature parents, stretching their parenting capacities beyond their limits. Whether abuse occurs in response to a child's behaviour, or the behaviour occurs as a consequence of the abuse scarcely matters however, as the process is most likely to be circular.

There were plenty of examples of children's behaviour as cause and consequence of abuse in our case material. Thus, one mother spoke of the effect of her colicky baby's insistent distress: 'I threw her on the couch because she wouldn't stop screaming and I thought I was going to kill her!'. Another mother responded to her boisterous 4-year-old, who had bitten a toddler brother, by deliberately scratching her face; a harsh punishment she believed would fit the crime. We have already referred to the teenaged girl beaten for staying out at night – a punishment repeated with more severity when she returned home from care, but resumed her old patterns of behaviour.

In other cases, children's behaviour appeared to be a reaction to grossly neglected and disorganised family life. One family's 8-year-old 'roamed wild', thieving; another's 7-year-old pilfered and was hyperactive, while his sister was described as backward and withdrawn. A teenager from a family where father figures came and went was 'eager, bright and no real trouble' to his school-teacher, but came to the attention of police and courts through his shoplifting, and was removed from home in consequence. Of a family with a 6-year history of suspected abuse – scratches, bruises and cigarette burns – 2 children were smearing the walls with faeces, had speech defects, and were described as hyperactive and out of control. This brought them massive attention from education, social services and the NSPCC, with benefit to their behaviour and general well-being – at least in the short-term. For the parents, improvements were at the cost of constant surveillance, and at follow-up, the mother's despair was palpable. 'I can't see any future at the moment, really.'

Professional roles and relationships

We have already illustrated some of the effects that the children's plight and their families' lifestyles had upon the deliberations of case conferences. But the professionals were not mere reflectors; they had their own agenda, and their roles and relationships with one another, inside and outside the conference room, are also of interest. Not all behaved according to stereotype. When the police were invited to attend they did not always take a tough line, or find themselves at odds with 'soft' social workers. Asked by the social services chairman if he had a role to play in a case where a boy had been severely beaten by his father, the CID detective answered: 'If we go in, would we do more damage? He [the father] is really making an effort. If it happens *again* we must move.' Nor was the social services department always left 'holding the baby' by workers in other agencies. A concerned schoolmaster was anxious that a delinquent boy in his class should not go into care, because 'he'd get into the wrong crowd'. He proposed an alternative plan. 'I'd rather see him in a creative situation. I think it would be far better to get him involved in constructive activities at school. I want to teach him.'

In contrast, behind the scenes a health visitor was apparently busy sabotaging the efforts of the social worker to treat as significant a series of minor injuries to a child. The latter explained, 'My concern was the *pattern* of recent events: three incidents in the last month and four in the last year, of minor injuries. It's not the individual injuries themselves, but the pattern.' At the case conference the child's name was placed on the register, and it was decided to increase day nursery attendance. The social worker was to offer 'ongoing social-work support and marital guidance'. Meanwhile the health visitor who was assigned the task of 'monitoring' the family pursued her own line. 'He fell over a little while ago and blacked his eye,' the mother confided to the researcher. 'The health visitor said, "Don't let the social worker see it! Put a plaster on it if she comes, or hide it!" She's like a Mum to me!'

What, then, can be concluded about the processes by which social workers and other professionals attempt to coordinate their approach to working with 'at-risk' children and their families? The evidence from our study suggests that the approved machinery for collaboration is frequently and faithfully used and, at its best, enables a fruitful sharing of information, anxiety and expertise which can, in turn, lead to clear strategies for action. But equally it can falter and fail, not only through the lack of skill or commitment of the participants – poor chairmanship, absenteeism and the like – but also, we suggest, through the powerful influence of the problems it seeks to address. The sheer complexity and dynamism of these painful problems can, at times, defeat attempts to predict or accurately assess, to plan and manage, or to marshall skills effectively, and can clearly contribute to inter-professional rivalries and even outright warfare. Case conferences are a valuable tool for coordinating work with child abuse, but they provide no panacea or magic answer.

The decisions

We will turn, finally, to the decisions that followed on from these procedures. As already indicated, most of the children at risk (over three-quarters) were kept out of care, at least in the short term. For roughly 3 out of 5, such a decision was positive: the risk was not considered serious enough to warrant removal, or the potential for improvement was viewed optimistically. In 2 out of 5 it was a negative decision: though assessments were pessimistic, evidence was regarded as insufficient, or courts were forcing a preventive strategy on unwilling workers. Not all of these children stayed at home. A few were steered towards sympathetic relatives and a handful were offered boarding places by a cooperative education service. In some cases the parent who had inflicted harm left, and 'risk' evaporated. The care system was not the only available protective environment.

Where children were left at home, social services and other agencies almost invariably continued to be active, 'monitoring', 'supporting', 'counselling' and marshalling resources, with the aim of minimising risk. Social workers were usually designated as 'key workers' and the children and their families were visited with considerably greater frequency than others in our study and were often the recipients of a range of 'preventive' resources. Day care for pre-school children offered relief to overburdened parents, care and stimulus for the children; it acted as a safety measure, keeping the children at risk under watchful supervision. Family aides were few in number but were highly valued as props and models for some disorganised families. It is disturbing that at least one of our sample authorities is now fighting to maintain this precious resource in the face of cash crises and cuts. Material assistance could have benefited most of these needy families, but was thinly spread, given in small amounts from limited budgets. The crucial areas of marital counselling and guidance in handling the children's behaviour problems were, in a few cases, tackled by specialist services. But, for most, it was up to the social workers to try to help: a matter of significance for both their training and supervision.

Those children who entered the care system were usually removed compulsorily: the majority, in the first instance, by means of a Place of Safety Order. Only 4 children were received into care with the consent of their parents. A general suspicion of 'voluntary' admissions under the 1980 Child Care Act was evident across the whole of our study, but it was particularly acute in relation to children at risk. Some crises clearly demanded urgent and peremptory action, but even where concern was not so acute the parents were generally regarded as too dangerous and unpredictable to be trusted to cooperate without legal sanction. This seemed to us unfortunate, when several parents were so openly afraid of their own actions and were seeking help to avoid crises: 'They should be put away from here. I'm frightened of what I might do to them. My mind goes blank when I hit them.' Responding to such cries for help by sharing the responsibility of arranging an admission would surely be a more positive and preventive act than awaiting the next crisis before removing the child on an order. It would certainly be in the spirit of the proposed changes in child-care legislation (DHSS 1987).

We have few means of evaluating these crucial decisions, except in the crudest sense of what happened next. Approximately 6 months on, all cases were followed up and half of the admitted children had been discharged from care, but a quarter of those kept out had subsequently come into care. Movement in and out of care had been continuous and there was a sense in which the whole at-risk group hovered very close to the gateway to the child-care system. Nevertheless, the majority – roughly three-quarters – were still living with their families in the community, though for all but a handful their case was still 'open' and active and social workers anticipated that it would be so for a long time. Not surprisingly, few problems and anxieties were swiftly solved or allayed. For a third of the small group of children who were still in care at follow-up the plan was to rehabilitate them with their families. Stringent time-scales which would have ruled out the chance of return after more than a matter of months were not operating in either authority. For the remaining two-thirds, social workers discussed long-term care, sometimes with adoption in mind.

From the parental perspective there were mixed reactions.

Predictably, parents whose children had been removed compulsorily were frequently angry and critical, especially if they had 'asked for help and got control instead'. Those few who collaborated in a 'voluntary' admission were less dissatisfied. A mother whose social worker had negotiated a careful contract for a short-term admission spoke of feeling 'not angry – upset but relieved really', and saw the future in more hopeful terms. Those whose children stayed at home also had their criticisms. There was little evidence that they felt neglected and abandoned by social services, as many of the families of children who were *not* considered to be at risk had done. But the continuing close surveillance and 'monitoring' were sometimes blamed for contributing to tensions and difficulties, rather than relieving them.

In the longer term, in 1987 we were able to ascertain a few key facts about the 35 children who had been at risk in 1 of our 2 authorities. In the 6 years since the study 5 children had moved from the authority while still on the register, so their status was unknown. None of the remainder were still on the register, though 3 names had only been removed in the previous year; 1 child was on a supervision order and 4 had been adopted. None were by then in care.

Conclusions can hardly be drawn from such a partial and cryptic picture, but it puts the problems that had loomed so large in 1981 in some perspective. First, being placed on a child-abuse register is not a life sentence, and the authority's records confirm this. Removals from their register had outstripped additions in every year until 1986, when the sharp upsurge in referrals changed the pattern. We cannot, of course, be sure that deregistration meant that risk was no longer present – as the Beckford tragedy sadly reminds us (Beckford 1985). But it appears that, despite the difficulties they posed and the anxieties they generated at the time of our study, the majority of these families had soldiered on without major disaster – at least, so far as we can tell. In contrast, for a small minority of children risks had been considered too great to restore them and permanent homes had been found instead. Given the growth in 'permanency planning' since the beginning of the decade we can only speculate that the balance between children restored to their homes and children in permanent substitute homes might look rather different now.

Much else has changed in the wider child-care scene since our research was undertaken, and developments in the sample authorities reflect those in the country as a whole. There has been a steady growth in family centres based on different models, ranging from casual drop-in centres to intensive therapeutic regimes for the most damaged families and run by both statutory and voluntary agencies. In response to the rising tide of abuse referrals, specialist posts and teams have been created – a development viewed with ambivalence by the generic social workers who value their training and advisory expertise but resent their own perceived loss of status and responsibility in consequence. Joint work with abusing families has become more common, promising better assessments of their complex dynamics and a more tolerable sharing of the fear and anxiety they impose. Direct work with children, individually and in groups, to enable the disclosure of abuse and to repair some of the psychological damage done, has become more prevalent.

Less optimistically, cash crises in local government (one of our sample authorities amassed a serious overspend) have threatened an already dwindling amount of residential care, since it is too readily assumed that closing homes saves money. Further, the pressure of abuse referrals, their need for an immediate response and the disproportionate time they demand are at the expense of other, vital aspects of child care, like finding and supporting foster homes and preparing children properly for a return home or for placement elsewhere. In the meantime, the departments' myriad responsibilities for other age groups and other problems are further squeezed. It is as if the monstrous cuckoo of child abuse threatens to push all else out of the nest.

What then is the relevance of a local child-care study, completed several years ago? The answer lies we believe in its contribution to perspective and a sense of proportion about child abuse. Despite the increase in referrals it is still the case that children who have been abused or seem to be at serious risk of abuse form a minority of those who come to the attention of social services departments. Further, they and their family circumstances are not peculiar or unique. In many respects they are indistinguishable from a larger population of deprived and troubled families where poverty and strained or fractured relationships interact to produce behaviours in parents and children that are potentially damaging and dangerous. This, in turn, means that knowledge of warning signs and predisposing factors associated with abuse, though an essential part of the professional helper's expertise is still an imperfect tool with which to identify the 'high risk' cases. Accurate prediction and positive identification of risk is not, and possibly never will be, something that more research or better training for social workers will deliver, and we cannot share the Beckford Inquiry's (Beckford 1985) retrospective confidence about this.

To this basic uncertainty is added the volatility and turbulence of many of the families whose children are believed to be at risk and the powerful emotions their perceived dangerousness evokes. For those who work closest to the maelstrom – and usually this is the social workers, who nowadays are almost invariably cast in the role of key worker – the task is formidable and failures to protect or to protect unnecessarily may be inevitable. Acknowledging the complexity of the task is one step towards a less condemning and more constructive stance towards those who take it on. It argues the need for strong and consistent supervision (or chairmanship, in the context of the case conference) which offers support but also challenges, enabling workers to pull back from the muddles and emotions they encounter and to achieve a clearer perspective.

Finally, there is a sense in which it is all too easy to place too much emphasis on the investigatory aspects of child abuse and too little on what comes after. Coordinating machinery and inquiries into tragedies lean heavily in this direction, and our own focus upon the gateway to care unwittingly contributes to this bias. But deciding whether or not abuse has occurred and whether the child should therefore come into care cannot be viewed in isolation. The quality of assessments and the decisions made in consequence are inextricably bound up with the quality and quantity of services and skills available to help all children and families referred to social services departments. The child will be 'protected' by admission in only the most rudimentary sense if there is no choice of foster or residential placements, or if the placements are of poor quality or fail for lack of preparation and support. Similarly, only a plentiful and flexible array of supportive services for families can enhance (though never guarantee) the protection of children in their own homes. Policy and practice in child abuse both influence and depend upon the wider context of services for children and their families and sophisticated decision-making can never be a substitute for welfare provision.

CHAPTER 6

CHILD-ABUSE INQUIRIES AND PUBLIC POLICY

CHRISTINE HALLETT
Reader in Social Policy, University of Stirling

There is, in British public administration, a long and continuing tradition of the use of committees of inquiry or tribunals to resolve difficult issues of public policy and to investigate scandals, tragedies or other causes of public concern (Wraith and Lamb 1971). A marked feature of the response in Britain in recent years to the emergence of child abuse as a public issue has been the selective use of ad hoc committees of inquiry in circumstances when child deaths have occurred. This chapter explores their procedures, purposes and impact and appraises child-abuse inquiries as instruments of public policy.

Types of inquiry

The list compiled for the Kimberley Carlile Report suggests that there have been some 34 child-abuse inquiries to date. The number is, however, difficult to estimate precisely, given the low publicity accorded to some local inquiries. The 34 inquiries have taken three main forms: internal inquiries (or case reviews) conducted by senior management; locally-commissioned external inquiries with an independent chairperson and sometimes, but not always, external panel members; and inquiries instituted by the Secretary of State for Social Services. Of these the most common is a locally-commissioned panel with an independent chairperson.

The DHSS guidance *Working Together* (DHSS 1988b) suggested that when cases of confirmed or suspected child abuse occur resulting in death or serious harm to a child a case review should be set up. It also suggested that the local Area Child Protection Committee (formerly Area Review Committee) should indicate whether there are aspects of the case which seem to justify further inquiry. This seems sensible advice. Senior management staff in local agencies will want to review their policies, procedures and practices when such events have occurred, both to learn lessons for the future and, in certain circumstances, to establish whether there is a case for disciplinary proceedings (although this is not mentioned specifically as one of the five purposes of such reviews in the DHSS guidance). In the past, these internal reviews have been conducted by and on behalf of individual agencies, often the social services department, as for example, in the case of Jason Caesar (Caesar 1982), Graham Bagnall (Bagnall 1973a) and Claire Haddon (Haddon 1980), or they have been initiated and staffed by members of the Area Review Committee as in the Wayne Brewer Inquiry (Brewer 1977). In several of the inquiries which have come to public knowledge this type of investigation has proved sufficient. In the Jason Caesar case, for example, a specific recommendation was that having fully investigated the case they could find no grounds for holding a formal inquiry. Such case reviews seem, in the past, often to have been successful in allaying such public anxiety as existed and in constituting a workable and effective low-key, low-cost response to the problems. They have not in all cases, however, proved sufficient to satisfy the public, the media, local agencies, or central government.

In such circumstances, where an independent inquiry is required, the DHSS recommends in the guidance issued for consultation in 1985, that it should generally be locally commissioned. This accords with the recommendations made by a working party on *Ad hoc inquiries in local government* appointed in 1977 by the Society of Local Authority Chief Executives (SOLACE) and the Royal Institute of Public Administration (RIPA). They expressed the hope that:

Ministers would agree with our arguments that formal inquiries should be regarded as a last resort, and that when a situation arises in which it seems necessary to appoint one, the Minister would normally deem it appropriate for the local authority to appoint it rather than himself . . . we therefore proceed on the assumption that . . . when a formal inquiry is held to be necessary, local inquiries would be preferred and ministerial inquiries would be exceptional.

This has proved to be the case. In 1980 the Secretary of State finally agreed to appoint an inquiry (the third) into the case of Paul Brown (Brown 1980) in the Wirral after having refused to do so in 1978. The only other statutory inquiry into child abuse to take place in the 1980s is the Cleveland Inquiry (Cleveland 1988). In practice, however, the distinction between inquiries sponsored by local authorities and those sponsored by the Secretary of State may be less clear-cut than this implies. Formal inquiries are usually only instituted when there is considerable public disquiet, and in such circumstances local authorities and central government have usually been in close touch about how the issue should be handled. In Cleveland there is no public record of local agencies themselves having asked the Secretary of State to institute an inquiry. In the Jasmine Beckford case it is reported (Beckford 1985, p.36) that if Brent Borough Council had not set up an independent inquiry the Secretary of State would have ordered a statutory inquiry. Similar events are reported to have occurred in the case of Kimberley Carlile (Carlile 1987) (Social Services Insight 1987). In both cases, the local agencies decided to commission the inquiry. Whether other local agencies would act similarly in the future is uncertain, but perhaps unlikely. There are several drawbacks to their doing so.

One concerns the absence of powers in locally-commissioned and thus non-statutory inquiries to compel the production of documents and the attendance of witnesses. Although the earliest of the inquiries in recent years (Colwell 1974) was set up by the Secretary of State, it too was non-statutory and relied on the voluntary cooperation of witnesses. This was forthcoming and the Committee record that all those from whom it considered necessary to hear evidence agreed to assist. The difficulties which might have occurred were noted, however, and a statutory power to set up an inquiry into local authority social services departments in respect of child-care matters was vested in the Secretary of State by Section 98(2) of the Children Act 1975. A related power, under Section 84 of the National Health Service Act 1977 already existed in respect of health services. Although successive Secretaries of

State have exercised these new powers, in response to requests by local authorities to do so, in the case of the Darryn Clarke Inquiry (Clarke 1979) and in the Paul Brown Inquiry, and also in Cleveland, the majority of child-abuse inquiries have been non-statutory. This has been a source of increasing difficulty. One problem concerns the production of documents and the power of public authorities to disclose confidential information to inquiries. This was an issue which, in different ways, troubled both the Kimberley Carlile and Tyra Henry (Henry 1987) Inquiries. Both panels managed to negotiate a way round it, but without changes in procedural guidance and the law of the kind recommended by the Kimberley Carlile Inquiry the problem could seriously disrupt any future inquiry.

The associated difficulty of the lack of power to compel the attendance of witnesses is better known. This has caused a variety of problems. In some inquiries, for example Lucie Gates (Gates 1982), the panel was apparently pressurised to take certain actions such as seeing witnesses in a particular sequence in order to retain the cooperation of participants. They write (Gates 1982, p.199): 'The panel had to yield to this example of the many pressures we encountered, otherwise some of the key participants threatened not to give oral evidence.' In other circumstances key witnesses have refused to appear altogether. The majority report of the Lucie Gates Inquiry listed 10 or more witnesses whom the panel had wished to see, and stated that they would not have proceeded without an agreement that one of the social workers involved would give evidence.

The locally-commissioned Heald Inquiry into the Paul Brown case (Brown 1978) which preceded the statutory inquiry, faced a 'severe handicap' since staff followed the advice of their trades union, the National Association of Local Government Officers (NALGO), and declined to give oral evidence. In the Reuben Carthy case (Carthy 1985), the general practitioner (who had seen the child with a fractured rib a few days before his death and had not informed the social services department) refused to give oral evidence on the advice of the Medical Defence Union. So did the police surgeon in the Lester Chapman Inquiry (Chapman 1979), and the general practitioner and senior social worker in the Malcolm Page Inquiry (Page 1981). More recently, the social worker with the major responsibility for the case of Tyra Henry and the health visitor and probation officer involved all declined to give oral evidence. So did the social workers from the Wirral Social Services Department who had been involved with the case of Kimberley Carlile. Their absence is fully discussed in the Report where it is suggested firstly, that the Wirral social workers believed that the inquiry should have been set up by the Secretary of State and not by the health and social services authorities in Greenwich; secondly, that they doubted the comprehensiveness of the inquiry since other relevant witnesses from the Wirral had not been invited to attend and thirdly, they wanted an inquisitorial mode of proceeding with questioning undertaken by Counsel for the Inquiry but cross-examination by the legal representatives of other parties restricted. The inquiry panel appeared unpersuaded of the force of these arguments and concluded:

> It is hard to think of a more serious breach of a social worker's obligations to (a) the public he or she serves; (b) the profession of which he or she is a member; and (c) to their colleagues in other authorities . . . whatever objection there may be to these inquiries – and we sympathise with some of the objections – there is no excuse for the non-attendance of the Wirral social workers and their Director. It was not in the public interest – nor in their interests – to remain silent (Carlile 1987, p.25).

The committee's report goes on to note, however, that the effect of their absenteeism was 'that we have thought it unfair to criticise by name, their individual conduct of the Carlile case'. This is of no small importance to the staff concerned, given the notoriety of some social workers following inquiries and the summary dismissal of others without disciplinary proceedings, notably Gunn Wåhlstrom and Diane Dietmann, following the Beckford Inquiry. We have come a long way from the trust and perhaps naïvety with which social workers and others voluntarily gave evidence at the Colwell Inquiry. It seems reasonable to predict that trades unions, professional associations and legal representatives will advise their members and clients not to appear at future inquiries where their presence is voluntary. Unless, as the Kimberley Carlile Report suggests, new powers are granted extending the power of subpoena to non-statutory inquiries, their days may be numbered.

A second factor which might lead local agencies to hesitate before bowing to central or local pressure to commission an inquiry is the cost. This varies depending upon the personnel involved in the panel and the procedure adopted by the inquiries, especially in matters such as the legal representation of parties and production of a daily transcript. The Jasmine Beckford Inquiry in Brent in 1985 was estimated to have cost £250,000. The costs of the Cleveland Inquiry are variously estimated at between £2 million and £4 million, of which a proportion has been borne by central government. The DHSS consultative paper on inquiries (DHSS 1985a) suggested that they would only be required when there was continuing public concern or issues emerging from the case review which could not immediately be resolved. The Beckford Inquiry Report suggests that such inquiries should only be set up if 'the inquiry deals with issues of general public importance and will, by its recommendations and educative function, make a major contribution to the development of the management of the child abuse system, nationally as well as locally' (Beckford 1985, p.36). In such circumstances, local agencies may be increasingly reluctant to establish external inquiries or to address national issues of public policy, which are likely to generate huge local costs.

Finally, local authorities may be increasingly reluctant to sponsor and fund local inquiries if, by so doing, they imply that the problems in the child-protection services are local in origin and can be resolved by local action. As will be discussed later, this local emphasis can obscure the responsibilities which central government carries in these matters.

The consultative paper on inquiries (DHSS 1985a) urged local authorities to consider carefully whether there was a need for further inquiries following internal case reviews. The experience of recent locally-commissioned inquiries without full statutory powers has revealed major weaknesses in their suitability for handling problems of this kind. It would seem that, in future, when and if local case reviews do not suffice, and an inquiry is deemed to be necessary, the choice might be for an independent statutory inquiry sponsored and financed by the Secretary of State. The era of local but independent reviews may be over. The 1988b DHSS guidance, however, offers no direction on this particular issue. Indeed, little is said at all about inquiries in the new guidance compared with the consultative paper solely devoted to the topic in 1985 (DHSS 1985a). The guidance suggests a 'hands-off' approach by central government. It notes simply that, Area Child Protection Committees, having indicated whether matters arising in the recommended internal case review justify further inquiry, 'it will then be for agencies individually or jointly to consider what form an inquiry will take'. The government's intention is clearly to ensure that, in circumstances where inquiries of various kinds have been set up in the recent past, internal case reviews are the customary response in future.

Procedures

Although child-abuse inquiries are ostensibly similar policy instruments for addressing similar problems, they use diverse procedures to accomplish their tasks. Arthur Mildon QC, who chaired the Lucie Gates Inquiry in 1981, noted with surprise that there were then no DHSS guidelines as to procedure, despite 20 inquiries in the space of 10 years. On occasions, those commissioning inquiries at central or local levels have specified the procedures to be adopted, for example whether the inquiry should be held in public or in private. More often, however, these procedural matters are at the discretion of the chairperson and, to varying degrees, members of the inquiry panel. The inquiry reports usually contain an account of the procedures followed and the reasons for selecting them.

The balance of power and influence between the chairperson and panel members in these decisions varies. In some circumstances, for example in the Cleveland Inquiry, the panel members were appointed in the role of assessors to assist in a judicial review. The Report, and presumably final decisions about procedures adopted in the course of the Inquiry, were the 'sole responsibility' of Lord Justice Butler-Sloss. In others, where all members are full members of the committee, the chairperson none the less often acts as *primus inter pares*, and occasionally in a somewhat high-handed manner, treating other members merely as advisers not as full panel members. The precise limits to the authority of the chairperson, the nature of the working relationships between panel members and related procedural matters are rarely, if ever, spelled out on appointment and can cause problems later. Often the pressing political need for action leads to setting up inquiries in haste, leaving the details to be worked out 'on the run'. John Chant, who served as an assessor in the Cleveland

Inquiry is reported as saying that it 'was set up in the most desperate hurry and this showed in the first week when the inquiry team was holding public hearings and was still in back-stage discussion on how to fulfil its remit' (Fry 1988a, p.15).

An insight into difficult working relationships is provided in the Lucie Gates Report which records:

> Preparatory to the hearing, at a conference of members of the panel, representatives of the convening authorities and an observer from the DHSS, the Chairman [*sic*] had outlined the procedure he had provisionally agreed with the convening authorities . . . No one dissented at the conference. Within a few days of the commencement of the inquiry, however, some members of the panel raised strong objections. . . . (Gates 1982, Vol.2, p.5)

In the Maria Colwell Inquiry a number of difficulties arose. One followed from the Chairperson's view that the public hearings should avoid causing further pain to the foster-parents who had cared for Maria. A panel member, Olive Stevenson, while sharing this aim, none the less pressed, unsuccessfully, for full evidence to be heard on the social worker's assessment of the foster placement in order to appraise the professional decision-making concerning the 'tug-of-love'.

In both the above cases the tensions in working as a committee during the inquiry and the difference of perspective on key issues between the chairperson and some or all panel members led to the production of minority reports. Such problems can be exacerbated by the small size of most inquiry panels and the intensity of the experience of a child-abuse inquiry for the panel members. It is unlikely that such matters are much considered when appointments are made from the ranks of the British establishment. The names of suitable lawyers as chairpersons 'emerge' from the Lord Chancellor's office and members from the list of the 'great and the good' held by the Public Appointments Unit in the Cabinet Office. A director of the Unit is reported by Hennessy (1986) to have described his task recently as 'to find chaps of both sexes for posts'.

Inquisitorial or adversarial inquiries

The decisions reached by inquiry panel members in procedural matters are of considerable importance. These decisions affect matters such as the extent of legal representation – and thus the length of time taken by the inquiry and the costs – who will be called as witnesses and the nature of the experience faced by those participating. One of the most significant is the form of the inquiry itself.

The basic distinction between the forms of inquiry is commonly termed inquisitorial or adversarial. In some ways, however, expressing the distinction in this way is misleading. All inquiries are set up to inquire and their task is therefore inquisitorial. The essence is how they proceed to accomplish it and in particular whether they adopt an approach which 'mimics' litigation, as the Tyra Henry report puts it, in which there were contending parties, full legal representation and 'the truth' is established through examination and cross-examination. The characteristics of this, the so-called adversarial approach, are described in the Kimberley Carlile Report (p.8):

Few words are more misleading as a description of a legal procedure than 'adversarial' with its overtones of hostility, antagonism and confrontation. In reality the word simply connotes one of two main ways, familiar in civilised legal systems, of conducting the legal process. Under the adversarial system the tribunal sits to hear and determine the issues raised by the parties who bring their dispute forward for adjudication, or examination on behalf of society at large. It has distinct advantages. It is based in part on the traditional dialectical approach that the truth will most likely emerge if each interested party is allowed to put his or her own case, from their own perspective (Carlile 1987, p.8).

Of the child-abuse inquiries to date only 10 have adopted an adversarial or quasi-litigious approach. The list, comprising the reports on Maria Colwell, John George Auckland, Richard Clark, Darryn Clarke, Paul Brown, Jasmine Beckford, Tyra Henry, Kimberley Carlile and Cleveland, none the less includes the inquiries which have generated most publicity and public interest.

In the inquisitorial approach, the tribunal or inquiry panel defines the issues, calls such evidence as it thinks is necessary to establish the truth and directs the areas of questioning of witnesses. Most child-abuse inquiries to date have used a form of inquisitorial procedure. Some have relied largely on the study of documentary material, such as case records alone in the case of Claire Haddon (Haddon 1980), and supplemented by written, but not oral, statements in Graham Bagnall (Bagnall 1973a). In many other cases, the committees of inquiry have sought a degree of informality in conducting the proceedings, exemplified by referring to 'participants' rather than 'witnesses' and to holding 'interviews' or 'discussions round the table' (Page 1981) rather than hearing oral evidence. The precise arrangements have varied. In some (e.g. Fraser 1982), participants were allowed to be accompanied by a friend but not a lawyer, in others (e.g. Mehmedagi 1981) participants could be accompanied by a friend, union official or lawyer. In the Steven Meurs Inquiry the panel 'determined to see each witness entirely alone and to take our own notes so that we could dispense even with the presence of a secretary in the hope that in this close and informal setting those who came to talk to us would be ready to speak freely and openly' (Meurs 1975).

The advantages claimed for the 'adversarial approach' centre on its alleged superiority as a means of reaching the truth and its fairness. The Salmon Royal Commission on Tribunals of Inquiry (often referred to as the Salmon Committee) which reported in 1966 (Cmnd 3121) rejected the suggestion that informal methods of discussion around the table might more likely lead to the truth than the usual methods of examination and cross-examination and argued that there was a 'real danger in departing from well tried and proved methods of arriving at the truth' (Tribunals of Inquiry 1966, p.36). The adversarial approach is designed to ensure that the evidence is tried and tested openly before legal representatives of all parties, and that those whose interests are affected by it can challenge it, thus limiting the possibilities of loose talk or falsehood. It is argued that interviews conducted in private by inquiry panels do not carry such safeguards. The Chair of the Lucie Gates Inquiry expressed this as follows:

If parties directly involved do not hear and have opportunity to challenge what is being said, although it may affect them, they may feel aggrieved, the panel may be misled, and weaknesses in a system may be perpetuated to the disadvantage of those it is intended to serve. (Gates 1982, Vol.1, p.xxiii).

Such arguments held sway in the Kimberley Carlile Inquiry which adopted an adversarial style 'both to assist in examining every facet of the matters under inquiry and to ensure fairness to those who may come in for criticism' (Carlile 1987, p.8). Other panels have, however, reached different conclusions. The Maria Mehmedagi

Inquiry defended its adoption of the inquisitorial mode in the following terms:

We believe that our method of working whereby witnesses were questioned only by the Chairman [*sic*] and members of the panel and by their own friends enables us to establish the truth about this case at least as well as the method whereby witnesses have to face cross-examination by a series of people representing other witnesses or organisations. Our witnesses spoke very frankly and fully to us about their involvement in the case (Mehmedagi 1981, p.4).

The effect on witnesses of cross-examination mentioned above is of some significance, especially in inquiries without powers of subpoena relying upon the voluntary attendance of participants. While cross-examination may be conducted in child-abuse inquiries in a temperate, courteous and restrained way, the impact on witnesses and indeed panel members of adversarial proceedings should not be underestimated. It is difficult to avoid a court-like atmosphere in which workers feel they are on trial. This proved to be a problem in the Maria Colwell case in which counsel and the chair were heard to use the words 'defence and defendants' (Society of Local Authority Chief Executives, 1977, p.28). One of the participants in the Maria Colwell Inquiry, Jeanne Wall, recalled the experience:

It was so beyond one's experience to be a sort of pawn or puppet, pushed and pulled. It felt so totally unreasonable, so totally unjust, so totally untrue. The whole thing was unreal. One was quite unable to talk freely about what had happened. Because of the quasi-judicial set up, like a trial, the cross-examination, one had to answer only what was asked, with no opportunity to talk (Shearer 1979).

Fifteen years later, the participants in the Cleveland Inquiry experienced similar feelings, as Mike Bishop, the Director of Social Services in Cleveland made clear in his graphic account of giving evidence at the inquiry:

For me, used to facing committees and the media, it was hard. But for those unused to facing public criticism, it must have been ten times as hard. Lord Justice Butler-Sloss and the three assessors sat above the witnesses. On the same level as the witness was a horseshoe of eleven legal teams fronted by a QC, backed up by a junior barrister and two solicitors. It was daunting facing all these lawyers.

The QC examined each witness and the back-up team sent notes about the answers. Each witness had to go through this 11 times . . . It was terrifying . . . We were told it wasn't a trial but it certainly felt as though we were in the dock – and where else in the judicial system does the defendant wait for months for sentence? (Fry 1988b, p.12).

The Royal Commission on Tribunals of Inquiry had recommended that in such situations 'every effort should be made by the Tribunal and counsel appearing on its behalf to put witnesses at their ease' (Tribunals of Inquiry 1966, p.36). They had 'no doubt this can be done' but, in practice, it is far from easy. It caused major difficulties in the Lucie Gates Inquiry where a full-blown adversarial model with counsel for the inquiry leading followed by cross-examination of both other parties was abandoned after 4 days in favour of a procedure whereby the panel initially asked questions of witnesses. The adversarial procedure had been outlined by the chair of the panel, a QC accustomed to such ways of working, at a preliminary meeting with panel members, but, in practice, they found:

that the agreed procedure meant that individual witnesses, initially neighbours of Miss Gates, were being cross-examined by legal advocate after legal advocate in sequence. The hostility between the neighbours and the official parties, together with the adversarial approach resulted in a distressing situation for witnesses and for members of the panel. By the time this process had been completed the panel members were reluctant to ask the questions which we considered relevant to the terms of reference and in an inquiry into professional practice by fellow professionals. We found this unsatisfactory and said so (Gates 1982, Vol.2, p.198).

If they had known the trial-like appearance which resulted they would not have agreed to serve. This provides a clear example of panel members resisting a role described by Dingwall as 'spectators to an adversarial drama' (Dingwall 1986a, p.505).

Adopting an adversarial mode does not, however, only affect the ambience of the inquiry. It carries important implications for the cost of inquiries (the cost of appointing counsel for the inquiry and granting full rights of legal representation are very considerable) and for their length. Once representation is granted, lawyers must be allowed to represent their clients and protect their interests, but this may not be central to the panel's interests. In the Kimberley Carlile Inquiry, legal representatives were invited to question every witness called before the Inquiry but they were restricted to asking questions on issues which directly affected their clients' involvement, or when they identified any relevant issue which had not been covered elsewhere in the inquiry. With this procedure, the panel concluded: 'By and large, our experience has been that the advocates adhered to the principle of self-restraint. We are not conscious that the time taken in eliciting all the evidence we needed to hear was appreciably lengthened by unnecessary questioning' (Carlile 1987, p.9).

However, the Tyra Henry panel reached a different view. They drew attention to the conflicting duties of legal representatives in inquiries in assisting the panel and in protecting their clients' interests, but argued 'there is no comfortable seat on this fence'. The panel concluded that much of the questioning of the witnesses was not particularly helpful to them, although almost all of it was legitimate once legal representation had been granted. They suggested that in future inquiries a central consideration should be 'whether a forum composed of contending parties is an appropriate or economic format' (Henry 1987, p.161).

While there are disadvantages inherent in both ways of proceeding, the case for inquisitorial methods seems persuasive. They are generally cheaper and quieter, less stressful for participants and, perhaps, better suited to situations where complex issues of policy, practice and professional judgement are for determination, rather than establishing the proof or otherwise of concrete and specific allegations. Appropriate safeguards are necessary to ensure both that informality does not lull witnesses into a false sense of security and that if individuals are likely to face criticism, the substance of the evidence against them is conveyed in writing (in so-called 'Salmon' letters) and they are given an opportunity to answer it. However, if these measures are taken, a procedure whereby the panel sees witnesses, accompanied by a friend or lawyer if desired, and asks the questions it wishes to address, seems preferable to an adversarial mode. As the Tyra Henry Report suggested:

Witnesses may be more open and candid in a setting where they are not testifying from a proof of evidence prepared by lawyers and then defending themselves from multiple criticism, but are simply doing what they can to tell the panel things it needs to know. And correspondingly the personal stress on witnesses will be much lower – a factor of importance first in attracting reluctant witnesses and secondly in lifting the shadow which an impending inquiry must cast over the lives of those centrally involved (Henry 1987, p.162).

Public or private

Many of the considerations relevant to choosing between inquisitorial or adversarial inquiries, such as which is more conducive to establishing the truth, safeguarding fairness and encouraging cooperation, also affect the choice of whether to hold inquiries in public or in private. Of the 34 inquiries held to date the majority have been conducted in private, with only 7 (Maria Colwell, John George Auckland, Darryn Clarke, Paul Brown, Jasmine Beckford, Tyra Henry and Cleveland) held wholly, or mainly in public. In some inquiries the commissioning authorities directed that the panel should be held in public (for example in the case of Tyra Henry) or in private, as in the cases of Lucie Gates, Carly Taylor, Richard Fraser, Heidi Koseda, Steven Meurs, Richard Clark. In others, the panel exercised its discretion in the circumstances of the case.

The statutory power to institute inquiries under Section 98 (2) of the Children Act 1975 incorporates a presumption of public inquiries in specifying that the Secretary of State may direct that it shall be held in private or the person holding the inquiry may hold it or parts of it in private. The Tyra Henry Report (p.162) suggested that sitting in public is a check on arbitrary or capricious conduct, presumably by the panel or by witnesses. Others, notably the Beckford Report, have argued the importance of public inquiries for demonstrating public accountability and restoring public confidence. This was the argument of the Royal Commission on Tribunals of Inquiry. They said:

. . . it is, in our view of the greatest importance that hearings before a Tribunal of Inquiry should be held in public. It is only when the public is present that the public will have complete confidence that everything possible has been done for the purpose of arriving at the truth (Tribunals of Inquiry 1966, p.38).

However, this was written about tribunals of inquiry which the

Royal Commission recommended should be set up only rarely on issues of national importance when there is a major crisis of public confidence. The Cleveland Inquiry may be viewed as constituting a serious crisis of public confidence but this has less often been the case with the succession of inquiries into individual child deaths. The recommendation for public hearings was made at a time in the mid-1960s, when the Royal Commission was 'confident that the Press in general can safely be relied upon to be fair to all persons involved in an inquiry.' A questionable assumption in the 1980s.

Some 20 years later, the DHSS recommended in the consultative paper (DHSS 1985a) that inquiries should normally be held in private. This was also the view of the majority of a sample of 35 panel members and witnesses who participated in a survey organised by the British Association of Social Workers (BASW 1982). This appears to be more likely to secure the voluntary cooperation of witnesses and to encourage participants to speak freely and openly, and is less likely either to lead to injustice through media reporting of evidence before those affected have had opportunities to rebut it or to cause undue stress to participants and damage morale.

The circumstances in which committees are appointed

The essence of child-abuse inquiries is that they are discretionary. There is no legal requirement upon local or central government agencies to hold inquiries in specified circumstances, as there is, for example, with planning inquiries. Thus, in tracing the origins of inquiries an understanding of how discretion was exercised in particular cases is critical, but as with so much in public policy it is often veiled in official secrecy. Rhodes (1975, p.51) suggests that, in considering the purposes which committees of inquiry serve in public policy, the basic question is why governments choose to use this device which 'involves looking both at the circumstances in which committees are used and at the motives of governments in appointing them'.

The specific origins of child-abuse inquiries are usually local. Local interest sparks off campaigns in the local media and in those cases when it escalates beyond the local scene there can be uncontrollable pressure for an independent inquiry. This is not always the case however. In the Tyra Henry case, the national tabloid press took an early interest. The press had apparently obtained very quickly what the panel describe as 'an unusual amount of detail about Tyra's injuries . . . and the police inquiries' (Henry 1987, p.75). Parton (1985a) traces the process by which initially local pressure built up for the Secretary of State to institute a public inquiry to supersede the locally commissioned one in East Sussex in the Colwell case. There are, however, few other systematic accounts of these processes in other cases.

The criminal trials of those charged with inflicting injuries and their reporting in the media clearly play an important part. The origins of the Darryn Clarke Inquiry held in Liverpool in 1978–9 are typical in this respect. The report records that the disclosure at the trial of the terrible injuries inflicted upon the child led to a public outcry. This was intensified by local press stories that reports of his ill-treatment had reached certain agencies but nothing appeared to have been done. The outcry was increased by further published allegations that anonymous telephone calls to the social services department appeared to have been ignored. The Liverpool City Council then requested the Secretary of State to appoint a statutory inquiry. Several of the inquiry reports record their origins as lying specifically in the remarks made by judges in court during the trial of those responsible for killing or injuring the children. In the Simon Peacock case, the judge is recorded as having expressed the view that an inquiry should be set up because of an apparent breakdown in services. In the Carly Taylor case, the judge said that he had planned to express his grave disquiet at the apparent absence of any effective action by the responsible authorities to protect the child and to invite the Secretary of State to consider holding an inquiry. On learning that an independent inquiry would be set up locally, he refrained from doing so.

Not all judges are restrained, however, and their comments are particularly criticised in recent reports. In the criminal trial of Morris Beckford and Beverley Lorrington, Judge Pigot remarked that it appeared that Jasmine Beckford's social worker 'was fobbed off time and time again by excuses which would not then have deceived a child' and that she displayed 'a naïvety almost beyond belief'. He did not discuss the work of the health visitor but expressed the view that 'it is quite clear that no blame can be attached to the school authorities' – a conclusion with which the inquiry panel, after reviewing the case, disagreed. The panel comment: 'the personnel of the social services department found the public display of judicial criticism, with little or no opportunity of defending themselves, very distasteful' (Beckford 1985, p.38). The panel recorded that they, too, were much troubled by the 'extra-judicial utterances'. They expressed the hope that their comments would lead any judge in similar circumstances simply to note the setting up of an inquiry as a satisfactory response to a socially disturbing event.

The remarks of judges made in the course of criminal proceedings and their subsequent reporting by the media are therefore important precursors to child-abuse inquiries. But there is an element of chance about this and it is likely that comparable cases across the country which escape this form of attention are dealt with as effectively by internal review. The key to whether or not an independent external inquiry is held seems to be the degree of public concern and consequent political pressure refracted and amplified through the media. Arthur Mildon QC, who chaired the Lucie Gates Inquiry wrote: 'I suspect the inquiry procedure is too often resorted to as a means of taking the heat out of an awkward political situation and casting on others responsibility for deciding what, if anything, went wrong and what should be done' (Gates 1982, Vol. 1, p.xxvi).

The purposes served by child-abuse inquiries

Not surprisingly, those appointing committees of inquiry rarely specify clearly the purposes they are intended to serve, but analysis of the inquiry reports themselves identifies the following four often-stated purposes: establishing the facts of the case; learning the lessons for the future to prevent further tragedies; meeting or allaying public concern and restoring public confidence and, less often, establishing who was responsible for actions and inactions and where responsibility should lie. They form convenient headings under which committees of inquiry may be appraised.

Finding the facts

The essence of child-abuse inquiries is to inquire into the facts of the case, to find out what happened. While some go well beyond this task, all inquiries attempt with varying degrees of thoroughness to establish what happened and to reconstruct the story. This focus on what happened in the specific case (or, in Cleveland, series of cases) is at the heart of the working of these committees. It is both a cause and, perhaps, a reflection of the practice of appointing lawyers to chair the inquiries. The Royal Commission on Tribunals of Inquiry noted that it was the usual practice to appoint members of the judiciary and eminent leading counsel to Tribunals and recommended that the law be amended so that those chairing Tribunals in future should hold high judicial office. They argued that having a judge in the chair would assure the public that the inquiry was being conducted impartially and efficiently and would ensure the judicial exercise of the Tribunal's powers in matters such as compelling the attendance of witnesses and the production of documents.

Several of the inquiries have adopted an adversarial procedure akin to that recommended by the Royal Commission and they have all been chaired by QCs or judges. In so far as inquiries handled this way involve determination of issues of fairness, in matters such as the issuing of 'Salmon' letters, and specifying the permissible style and extent of cross-examination, it seems appropriate that lawyers should chair them or at least be influential panel members in such matters. However, the majority of inquiries have not adopted this form of procedure, yet it is the customary practice to appoint a lawyer to chair the committee. When not a QC, these have often been serving or retired chief executives (or former county clerks) from local government as, for example, in the cases of Carly Taylor, Richard Fraser, Wayne Brewer, Steven Meurs and Max Piazzani, or an academic lawyer as in the Karen Spencer Inquiry. Exceptions to the practice of appointing lawyers to chair inquiries include the Stephen Menheniott Inquiry chaired by a member of the (then) social work services of the DHSS, the Simon Peacock and Graham Bagnall Inquiries chaired by local councillors, Malcolm Page chaired by a GP, Heidi Koseda chaired by a social work academic and those (e.g. Jason Caesar, Claire Haddon) undertaken by senior officers or committees in local government. Only 2 (Cleveland and Heidi Koseda) of the 34 inquiries have been chaired by women.

The usual practice, then, has been to appoint lawyers who possess skills in the sifting and assessing of evidence and the determination of specific issues (customarily guilt or innocence). In inquiry after inquiry, the story is constructed or reconstructed in terms of individual actions, of what happened or failed to happen when, who said what to whom. In general, as Dingwall has argued persuasively in relation to the Jasmine Beckford Inquiry, there has been little attempt to consider the individual cases in the wider context of the child-protection system generally and of the daily realities of practice in health and welfare agencies, or to use the knowledge and insights derived from academic study in the social sciences. In a similar vein, the British Association of Social Workers has criticised 'the tendency of inquiries to focus upon the performance of individuals in isolation from the agencies which employ them, authorise them to act, provide them with the wherewithal to undertake their task and which ultimately carry responsibility for their performance' (BASW 1982, p.21). Usually there is a detailed forensic examination of the minutiae of the specific case on the basis of which so-called 'common sense' recommendations for change in policy and practice may be made. Some of these lessons, as will be discussed below, are no doubt useful but whether such elaborate and in-depth processes are required, and so often, in order to reach them is less clear. There is a balance to be struck between establishing the facts with rigour and accuracy (a skill which many lawyers demonstrate) and excessive concentration on matters of detail which do not materially affect the final judgements made in child-abuse inquiries, vital though they may be in criminal trials in matters such as fraud and murder.

Rhodes (1975) in his analysis of independent committees appointed by government distinguishes between the purposes of three different kinds of committee. The first group comprises committees whose sole or main purpose is the investigation of particular events, such as the Aberfan disaster. The third group consists of committees, often standing committees, whose sole or main purpose is to give advice based on the knowledge and experience of its members (a contemporary example would be the Social Security Advisory Committee, the so-called 'independent watchdog' on social security matters). In between is the second group, which combines inquiry into general issues with the formulation of advice (such as the Seebohm Committee (Cmnd 3703 1968) or the Wagner Committee (National Institute for Social Work 1988)). Rhodes suggests that these distinctions do not indicate the relative importance of different kinds of committee; in particular he argues that fact-finding committees of inquiry into individual incidents can attract considerable public attention and have important implications for public policy, as for example in the Aberfan disaster. However, he suggests that there is

a significant difference both in purpose and practical operation between investigating an individual event and investigating a general problem . . . In the former case general questions of policy or procedure emerge only by implication, whereas in the latter they are the raison d'être of the investigation (Rhodes 1975, p.35).

This is important since it is somewhat haphazard which general questions emerge in the examination of a particular case. Furthermore, the salience of these issues for public policy depends, in part, upon whether the case under review is typical or highly unusual.

Examination of the child-abuse inquiry reports suggests that, in some inquiries, the neat distinctions in Rhodes's classifications have been blurred and a fourth hybrid category has emerged which combines the investigation of particular events with some analysis of selected general issues, drawing upon the knowledge and experience of panel members supplemented by some expert witnesses. This has occurred because not all inquiries have restricted themselves to establishing and examining the facts of the case and making limited recommendations. The terms of reference of some inquiries make clear that the sponsors were not seeking wide-ranging recommendations based on the examination of a single case. The Maria Colwell Inquiry is a case in point. The terms of reference simply asked the committee to 'inquire into and report upon the care and supervision provided by local authorities and other agencies in relation to Maria Colwell and the coordination between them'. While recommendations emerge in the course of the text, for example in the section on inter-professional communication, the committee broadly observed their terms of reference, and the report does not end with a specific list of recommendations. Other inquiries have interpreted their terms of reference more widely and trampled more freely through the fields of child protection. Although criticised by some (e.g. Dingwall 1986a and Family Rights Group 1986) for doing so, the Jasmine Beckford Report made wide-ranging recommendations arising from the particular case. The issue is specifically addressed in the Kimberley Carlile Inquiry, which reports:

> Inquiries such as ours are, of course, designed to focus primarily upon the detailed examination of the activities of specific individuals in the particular case . . . like earlier inquiries – and we have particularly in mind the Beckford Report – we felt impelled to go further and, in making our recommendations for future legislation, governmental guidelines and professional action, to examine a number of general issues thrown up by the particular case (Carlile 1987, p.28).

It was put to the committee that such recommendations would more properly be made by a committee specifically appointed, resourced and staffed to review child protection generally and, in particular, to take evidence concerning cases which had not ended in tragedy. Perhaps not surprisingly, since the inquiry was well under way, this view was rejected. The point may none the less have been taken for the future, since the Report notes:

> Behind issues relating to a protection service lie the chronic resource implications that go a way beyond the remit of any child-abuse inquiry. Such a task is appropriate only for a Royal Commission and not for the partial investigation of a single child abuse, however amply its terms of reference are interpreted (p.30).

When the requisite legislative provisions are on the statute book, the panel recommends 'it should be possible thereafter to deal with the occasional tragic death of a child through parental abuse by much less costly inquiries that do no more than elicit the facts of the particular case and expose the particular weaknesses and deficiencies' (p.31).

Meanwhile, the focus on the detailed specific actions of individual staff has affected the performance of the three other purposes cited earlier, namely learning the lessons, establishing account-ability and meeting the public interest.

Accountability

One of the most powerful outcomes of the child-abuse inquiries has been to establish in the public and professional consciousness who is to blame. The word 'who' rather than 'what' is used advisedly, for a consequence of the approach adopted in generally appointing lawyers to chair inquiries and the centrality of finding the facts is the attribution of individual responsibility, usually, and almost exclusively, to front-line workers and, occasionally, to their senior managers. The issue was first addressed in the context of recent child-abuse inquiries in the Maria Colwell Report. The majority report commented as follows:

The overall impression created by Maria's sad history is that while individuals made mistakes it was the 'system', using the word in the widest sense, which failed her. Because that system is the product of society it is upon society as a whole that the ultimate blame must rest: indeed the highly emotional and angry reaction of the public in this case may indicate society's troubled conscience. . . (Colwell 1975, p.86).

The Report continues, however, 'certain local authorities and agencies can not escape censure and must accept responsibility for the errors and omission of their workers.' It is interesting to note that although workers had been identified by name throughout the public hearings and in the Report, the blame was attributed to agencies and not to individuals in the Report's conclusions. The effect of the associated publicity during the inquiry and subse-quently was very different. Perhaps for this reason, Stevenson, in her Minority Report, wrote:

Although, as is apparent from the report, I agree with some of my colleagues' final list of criticisms, I do not think a hierarchy of censure is appropriate and therefore disassociate myself from it. For one thing, it leaves a predominant impression of weakness rather than strength in the East Sussex social workers which is misleading. There was much that was excellent in their work . . . As to others involved, all played a part in the tragedy, including the schools. But the narrative will speak for itself and I do not wish to apportion degrees of blame (minority report in Colwell 1974).

Subsequent inquiries have grappled with this discomfiting issue. The Malcolm Page Report, for example, stressed that although the inquiry had to look at the actions of individuals and agencies, 'the object is to help others in the future not to answer the question who is to blame?' (Page 1981, p.7). In similar terms, the Lisa Godfrey Report noted that while its detailed examination of the case had led to a critical appraisal of the actions of the people and services concerned, their brief was 'not to assess culpability but to consider what might be done to reduce the risk of a recurrence in the future'. The Karen Spencer Report noted that while the terms of reference did not focus on questions of responsibility or of blame, 'an inquiry of this sort must examine the way in which agencies and individuals acted and it is inevitable that many of those who read this report will have in the back of their minds the questions "What went wrong?" and "Who was to blame?".'

The description earlier in this chapter of the origins of inquiries suggests that the question may be at the forefront rather than the back of people's minds. Inevitably, when an investigation of *what* has happened takes place, implicit or explicit conclusions are drawn about who was responsible and *why* it happened. When the account of what happened is forensic, detailed and individualised, conclusions as to why tend to follow a similar path. This is evident both in many of the inquiry reports themselves and in their reporting in sections of the media. Yet child-abuse inquiries have major deficiencies as instruments for establishing accountability in cases of this kind. The first, noted above, stems from their essential mode of inquiry and their focus upon individual actions and explanations. This locates responsibility at the front-line and is an outcome inherent in handling issues of public policy by appointing one, or a succession of, ad hoc committees. It is not restricted to cases of child abuse.

This apportioning of responsibility was demonstrated clearly in the succession of inquiries into scandals concerning standards of care in long-stay hospitals in the 1970s. But it can also be seen in other spheres, such as the Crichel Down Inquiry in 1954 in which civil servants were singled out for criticism in circumstances in which, some argue, Ministers bore at least a partial responsibility.

A more topical example is the inquiry into the Zeebrugge ferry disaster (Department of Transport 1987) which apportioned blame not principally to the management of the ferry company for failing to instal warning lights on the bridge of all its ships, nor to successive governments for not having legislated to prevent such occurrences, but to those who failed to close the bow doors and check that they were closed on this particular ship on this occasion. One effect of inquiries, therefore, is to individualise blame. The basic issues of accountability for resources and the frameworks of law and policy remain largely untouched.

Clearly, public servants should expect to be held accountable for their actions. There are existing mechanisms for securing accountability in our health and welfare systems. They are particularly complex in respect of social work, with its multiple accountability to users of services, to senior management, to local councillors and to its own professional ethics. Despite their importance in determining accountability, the yardsticks or standards used in the child-abuse inquiries have been varied and far from clear. Some inquiry reports do not specify the standards by which performance was assessed. Others give some clues. The Malcolm Page Report used the following standards: 'We have assessed this case on what we judge from our collective experience to represent standards of good practice which it would be reasonable to expect' and also 'the only proper criterion is to look at decisions and actions within the context in which they were made or taken and this context must necessarily encompass the knowledge and experience of the individuals involved and the pressures on the agencies for which they worked' (Page 1981, p.8).

In the Lester Chapman Inquiry, the test was that provided people perform conscientiously and to the best of their ability, they should have nothing to fear and should be given the confidence and full support of their superiors. In the Kimberley Carlile Report the standard – adapted from that used by Mr Justice Hodgson in the case of *Dietmann v. Brent London Borough* (an action for wrongful dismissal following the Jasmine Beckford case) – was whether workers had applied the 'standards of skill, judgement and care that could objectively be expected from a worker of their respective grade and experience '. It is, however, hard to see how this can be a matter of *objective* rather than subjective assessment.

In the Lucie Gates Inquiry Majority Report, the panel ask how it is possible to evaluate performance in one case 'without comparisons with the handling of other similar cases by the agencies involved and more generally'. They suggest that 'considerable difficulties arose when it became obvious that mechanisms to evaluate professional competence in child abuse do not exist. The terms of reference involve judgements about the quality of professional practice.' They do indeed. However, the problem is not that mechanisms for evaluating competence do not exist. Rather, there are several standards in operation and they are essentially matters of judgement. The child-abuse inquiries represent an important departure from the principle that standards of professional practice are normally judged by disciplinary committees composed of professional peers. In some circumstances matters will arise which can be judged by those who do not hold the professional qualification of the individual concerned. One example arose in the Heidi Koseda case where it transpired that the NSPCC officer had falsified his casenotes, fabricating an account of a visit to the family which he had not in fact made. However, in other circumstances, particularly where the quality of decision-making on the basis of specified available information is at issue, it may be argued that professional peers are required to reach such judgements. An interesting facet of the inquiries to date, including Cleveland, is that while many professions have been criticised, the activities of the legal profession and the working of the courts have generally gone unremarked, although there are exceptions, notably the Beckford Report which criticises the remarks of the trial judge and also the magistrates in the juvenile court.

The risk of unfairness in child-abuse inquiries is that the standards appear to comprise the common-sense views of the panel members, sometimes helped by expert witnesses on particular issues. In consequence, the principle of fairness, that a person whose conduct is under review should know the substance of the criticisms, the nature of the evidence to be called and the basis on which judgements will be reached, is often breached in child-abuse inquiries. The delivery of 'Salmon' letters takes care of the first two, but they rarely specify the test which will be applied in passing judgement on individual performance. In the inquiry reports to date it has been social workers and health visitors to whom this issue has applied in particular, although major shortcomings have been revealed also in the work, for example, of the NSPCC and of doctors. In the Cleveland Inquiry the question of the test of medical competence has been central.

The issue of which standards of professional practice are being applied is especially important given the close links between the inquiry findings and disciplinary matters. The consultative document on inquiries (DHSS 1985a) made clear that inquiries are not disciplinary proceedings. The 1988 guidance in *Working Together* lists 2 (of 5) main objectives of case reviews as 'to assess whether decisions and actions taken in the case were reasonable and responsible' and 'to check whether established procedures were followed'. The actions to be taken in consequence are not specified. It is, in any event, hard to separate 'findings' from disciplinary matters, especially since the attempt by Hammersmith councillors to use the Shirley Woodcock Report to discipline staff (Community Care 1982) and the summary dismissal, without a disciplinary hearing, of the key social work staff involved in the Beckford Inquiry following the publication of the Report. The Tyra Henry Report notes that 'although as we have repeatedly stressed, ours is not a disciplinary tribunal, we have had constantly in mind that what we say nevertheless affects the careers of staff who are involved in Tyra's history' (Henry 1987, p.158).

The issue has been poignantly highlighted recently by the question marks raised (but now resolved) over the future employment in a voluntary social-work agency of the social worker principally involved in the Kimberley Carlile case. Despite the disclaimer that 'our considered opinion, now that they [the social worker and the health visitor] are to be criticised should not be taken as meaning anything other than criticism of their respective conduct in this case' (Carlile 1987, p.216), there was a firm recommendation that the social worker should not in the future perform any of the statutory functions in relation to child protection. Such judgements are more properly the province of a disciplinary hearing than a child-abuse inquiry.

It may be that if a General Social Work Council were established, it could promulgate standards of practice in social work in child protection. However, to be useful in this context, it would need to identify achievable good practice in the straitened circumstances of many social services departments. A General Social Work Council might also and usefully hear disciplinary charges arising against social workers. Given the multi-disciplinary nature of child abuse, however, such a Council does not seem an appropriate body to undertake the broader review of cases of child abuse which have ended in tragedy. To do so would risk endorsing the view that child protection is the sole prerogative, rather than a principal responsibility, of social workers. To date, however, the issues of accountability in cases of child abuse have been incompletely, unfairly, variously and somewhat haphazardly addressed by the succession of inquiries.

The public interest

The public interest which, as the Tyra Henry Report notes, is difficult to differentiate from media concern, is important both in the circumstances surrounding the setting up of inquiries and in decisions about whether their proceedings should be held in public or in private. Those inquiries – a minority – which have been held in public have cited legitimate public interest and the restoration of public confidence as important reasons for so doing. Inquiries held in private have also considered their role in public education. For example, the Malcolm Page Inquiry expressed the hope that their Report would 'contribute something to the process of informed and constructive criticism', pointing out, as it does, that 'the burden of dealing with cases of child abuse does not rest solely with social workers but that there are other professions and agencies who have to be involved' (Page 1981, p.66). In a similar vein, the Simon Peacock Inquiry hoped that their Report would 'bring to the notice of the general public the very real difficulties facing those responsible for the prevention of non-accidental injury to children' (Peacock 1978, p.1).

The Jasmine Beckford Report suggested that the public hearings were themselves a learning process for professionals and for the public. 'We think this aspect of a public inquiry cannot be underrated. It provides an insight into social welfare services that will have a lasting impact that can only be for the good of public understanding of what is being done in the name of the public' (Beckford 1985, p.27). It is hard to dissent from the view that there has been a lasting impact, but whether it has only been for the good of public understanding is much more questionable. There may be a potential for the direct education of the public through witnessing public hearings. However, the numbers are likely to be very small. Many more will receive their education as the inquiries are refracted through the media.

An analysis of the social construction of news, and of media representation of social work in particular, is beyond the scope of this chapter. The role of the press in publicising and amplifying concern before inquiries are set up has, however, been the subject of critical comment in several inquiries. Similarly, despite the carefully-worded reports of many committees, the burden of reporting, especially in the tabloid press, has been to emphasise only the failings of individual workers. Until recently, the harshest treatment has been reserved for social workers, but doctors have become the focus of attention in reporting of child sexual abuse in Cleveland and elsewhere.

There is an important task of public education to be performed. In particular, the mobilisation of neighbourhood community concern for the protection of children and the support of vulnerable families is to be welcomed, as would be wider community awareness of what action to take when anxieties and suspicions are aroused. The outcome of the inquiries and the selective reporting of them are likely to have shaped popular consciousness in particular ways. Firstly, since the subjects of inquiries are by definition serious and tragic cases in which often horrendous and repeated injuries have been inflicted upon children, the public image of child abuse and of child abusers is atypical. Child abuse covers a broader range of conditions and, in many cases, much less disturbed behaviour by parents or caretakers than the reporting of these inquiries would suggest. Secondly, the popular image of the child-protection agencies, social services departments in particular, resulting from the inquiries is likely to be one of, at best, incompetence and, at worst, callous indifference and neglect: an image hardly likely to encourage confidence and the prompt and appropriate referral of neighbourhood concern.

The inquiries are, of course, a legitimate source of public interest, and news reporting. They have undoubtedly heightened public awareness of child physical and sexual abuse. But, in the absence of counter-information about child abuse, child abusers and the routine working of child-protection agencies, their effect upon popular consciousness is a decidedly mixed blessing.

Learning the lessons for the future

The inquiries have undoubtedly played an important part in shaping policy, procedures and practice in child protection in the UK. In many instances, resources are increased locally and procedures changed while an inquiry is still pending. The response of local health and welfare agencies in Greenwich to the death of Kimberley Carlile before the inquiry provides a good example of this. The reports, when published, do contain some learnable lessons for inter-disciplinary work and social-work practice in matters such as the recording and transmission of information, assessment, supervision and professional education and training programmes. It is difficult to know how effectively such 'lessons' have been learned. One characteristic of the reports, as the Carly Taylor Report itself noted, is the repetitive nature of many of the findings. The DHSS (1982) Report on child-abuse inquiries which summarised the inquiry reports published between 1973 and 1981, was also rooted in an acknowledgement that similar and repeated failings were being revealed in successive inquiries. By definition, however, these cases form a very biased sample. As Hutchinson (1986) notes:

Child-abuse inquiries by their very nature highlight, for the most part, mistakes, omissions, errors of judgement and the shortcomings of systems and individuals. A great deal of good social-work practice goes on unnoticed, unacknowledged and unpraised because it has never been brought to the attention of the public, clearly there is no mileage in it for the media (p.181).

Comparable in-depth examinations of successful cases are rarely found in the public domain. There are some exceptions, such as the study by Dingwall and his colleagues of routine work in child protection (Dingwall *et al.* 1983), but such studies are comparatively rare. In general, they do not counterbalance the firm hold on professional, and certainly on popular, consciousness, of the failings repeatedly and vividly depicted in the inquiry reports. Social services departments generally are not renowned for their skill and effectiveness in public relations and image promotion and there is little testimony to the quiet but apparently effective work in much child-protection work taking place across the country. Much of this work is likely to be drawing on the lessons revealed in the inquiry reports.

Appraisal

A broader appraisal of the varied impacts of the child-abuse inquiries needs, however, to move beyond an assessment of their effectiveness in meeting the four purposes outlined above, which were set for them by the commissioning authorities and the panel members. The effects of the inquiries have been varied. Some have been low-key and local and have made little or no impact beyond professional consciousness in the immediate locality in which the events occurred. Others have been of huge public and national significance and instrumental in consolidating child mal-treatment as a social problem in the UK, a process well-documented by Parton (1985a). They have been of critical impor-tance in effecting a shift of resources and of the focus of work within social services departments. This is remarkable for having been accomplished without major legislative change and without significant additional resources from central government. The whole machinery of child-abuse procedures, area child-protection committees, case conferences, and at-risk registers, is based not on law but on circulars of guidance. The exposure to public and media scrutiny provided by the inquiries and the associated fear among professionals has been a powerful catalyst for action. Some of the consequences for social-work practice and the nature and direction of child-welfare services as they shift from child care to child protection are explored by Packman, Parton and Parton and Stevenson elsewhere in this book. The focus of the inquiries has largely been on the individual pathology of the abusive families and the individual actions and inactions of practitioners. This concentration and mode of proceeding has left other issues off the agenda. It is a predictable outcome of responding to child-abuse tragedies by a succession of public inquiries, set up in traditional ways, and so presumably is not an unintended consequence for those in central and local government who sponsor them. Among the most important issues left largely unaddressed by this process are the paradigms surrounding the social construction of child abuse as a social problem, the dominant modes of response to child protection in a liberal democracy, and the issue of resources.

The first is discussed elsewhere by Parton (1985a) and the second by Dingwall *et al* (1983) and Dingwall (1986a). The third issue of resources is considered below. The 'common-sense quasi-judicial' approach has by definition drawn little on social science theory and done little to challenge the 'taken for granted' assumptions about child abuse. The actions of individuals are criticised but in general the fabric of the basic social order is unchallenged. For example, there has been little, if any, questioning in the inquiries of the processes of socialisation which lead adults to harm children, and especially which sanction male violence in the domestic arena. The Cleveland Inquiry Report (1988) is a good demonstration of this point. The inquiry concluded that 'sexual abuse occurs in children of all ages, including the very young, to boys as well as girls, in all classes of society and frequently within the privacy of the family' (Cleveland 1988, p.243) and reported that in the case of only one child considered by the inquiry was the perpetrator alleged to be a woman. Despite this the societal context in which abuse occurs, particularly the power imbalance within families between men and women and adults and children, especially that involving male violence and male sexuality, goes unremarked. Nor have the social structures and conditions in which families, black and white, struggle to bring up their children in harsh and depriving conditions in Britain's cities generally been addressed. Many of the inquiry reports (e.g. Charlene Salt, Lucie Gates, Kimberley Carlile) describe the housing and social circumstances inimical to the welfare and well-being of children in which the families lived. The Tyra Henry Report does so with feeling and some anger. But, in general, the wider implications for public policy are not considered.

A key issue camouflaged by the focus on individual action is the resourcing of the child-protection system. Some of the 'lessons' from the inquiries are learnable, given adequate resources for matters such as qualifying and in-service training, clerical staff and record-keeping systems and adequate numbers of basic grade and supervisory staff. But similar recommendations are repeated in inquiry after inquiry without significant additional resources being made available to address the problems. Despite devoting some attention in recent inquiry reports to the resource issue, the messages about resources are often muted and drowned by the concentration on the part played by individuals. The Kimberley Carlile Report is a good example. It argues: 'It is beyond our terms of reference and beyond what can reasonably be considered relevant to what happened to Kimberley to go into these complex calculations in detail' (Carlile 1987, p.67).

The 'complex calculations' refer to the method of calculating the grant-related expenditure component of the block grant from central to local government. The problem is that such calculations are critical in determining spending levels on local services in rate-capped authorities. The borough, regarded by government as an inner London borough for rate support grant purposes, was rate-capped at the material time and had the lowest levels of fieldwork and administrative staff per 1,000 population of all the Inner London boroughs. If the resource context is considered to be beyond the terms of reference of a committee of inquiry of this kind, the instrument is seriously inadequate for examining public policy. The Kimberley Carlile Report notes (p.65) that 'resources were available in this case. Kimberley had a health visitor and a social worker . . . .' But Kimberley did not 'have a social worker' in the usual meaning of that phrase. The case was unallocated and held by a newly-appointed and overworked team leader since it was not possible to allocate it to a social worker because of staff shortages and pressure of work. Since that time, the staffing position in the Inner London boroughs appears to have got worse, with very high turnover rates reported in some authorities. Particular difficulties in recruitment have been reported in those authorities such as Lambeth (Tonkin 1988) and Greenwich, Brent and Cleveland (Eaton 1988) which have suffered low morale and damaging publicity in the course of inquiries.

The following letter, published in the professional social work press under the heading 'The very harsh realities of tackling child abuse' bears eloquent testimony to the continuing problems:

Sir – I am an area manager working in a busy London SSD, and am writing to you after reading *A Child in Mind* – the report of the commission of inquiry into the circumstances surrounding the death of Kimberley Carlile.

The report is strong on analysis but fails hopelessly to deal with the realities of our current services. It is not helpful to scapegoat individuals rather than addressing the present 'overload' of the child-abuse system. There are very important lessons for health authorities and SSDs.

My own SSD improved its child-abuse policies and resources over recent years – but we still have a long way to go. I believe that we are fairly typical of London SSDs – possibly better than many. Nevertheless, colleagues acknowledge that many of the faults pointed out by recent inquiries are being continued by us. Of course one must acknowledge that individual skills, knowledge and wisdom are vital; but the overload of a poorly-resourced system means we are forced to cut corners.

Here are some illustrations of the realities of responding to child abuse in my authority in 1988:

> line managers (team managers and area managers) routinely chair child-abuse conferences – we have no independent chairperson;

> emergency consultation with staff is often by telephone;

> I do not record on the case file all consultation, supervision and discussions following discussions with colleagues and other professionals;

> I regularly work overtime (unpaid) as do all my team managers. I recognise my decision-making and judgements may not be as good by the end of the week when I am tired;

> my area has unallocated cases of children on the child-abuse register which are not allocated to team managers. We have insufficient experienced and trained social work staff to take on all these cases;

> we have had no commensurate increase in social work resources to match the large increase in reported child-abuse cases over the past three years;

> my staff have often not been able to attend vital training courses, including child-abuse training;

> more often than not we do not have proper legal advice at child-abuse conferences;

> there are no family centres in my borough which cater for abused children and their families;

> child-abuse conferences are not usually called within 24 to 48 hours.

The responsibility for improvement in the resourcing of child-abuse services does not rest with those of us who operate them. Surely directors, social service committees, and indeed central government must accept responsibility to improve resourcing. I would be interested to hear from other managers and social workers of their experiences of child protection services.

Do we not have a professional responsibility to speak out?

JEREMY AMBACHE
Putney, London SW15 (*Community Care* 31 March 1988)

The failure to respond centrally to these issues is, perhaps, exemplified most clearly in respect of social-work training. Successive inquiry reports have pointed to major deficiencies in the basic professional training of social-work staff on 2-year qualifying programmes. In two Reports (Jasmine Beckford and Kimberley Carlile) powerful calls were made for an extension of social-work training to incorporate additional periods of specialist learning. Despite widespread support for such a change, the government has refused to implement and fund these changes. The unwillingness of central government to address the implications of the inquiries for developing a well-resourced child-protection system was reflected in the draft circular of guidance – *Child Abuse – Working Together* (DHSS 1986) which suggested that the recommended changes could be effected without substantial increased resources: a view challenged by many.

The procedural difficulties outlined earlier in this chapter and the examination of the varied impacts, suggests that the modern era of child-abuse inquiries, stretching from Colwell to Cleveland, may be at an end. The voluntary participation of professional staff in such procedural devices in the future looks increasingly unlikely, and even foolhardy, and the government may now be reluctant to institute statutory inquiries which could compel people to attend.

There is likely in the future to be a greater concentration on routinised, low-key internal review within agencies and review committees when child deaths occur, comparable to the investigations into perinatal mortality and surgical accidents in the health service. These regularise the acceptance of a degree of error in complex service-delivery systems and attempt to improve practice without seeking scapegoats. Other reviews of administrative action, possibly involving the ombudsman, may also be used to examine child-abuse deaths without attracting the glare of publicity associated with some of the formal inquiries. The inquiries to date have had a significant and varied impact on policy and practice and on public perceptions of child abuse. As this chapter has demonstrated, they have been contradictory in their effects – beneficial in some respects and harmful in others.

In 1869 Gladstone wrote 'A committee keeps a Cabinet quiet' (Morley 1905(i), p.691). Increasingly in recent years inquiries seem to have been used as a political expedient to allay public disquiet. Those sponsoring inquiries in this form could be relatively confident that attention and blame would be laid at the feet of individuals, and political responsibility for the child-protection system, its modes of operation, its legislative framework and its resources would largely escape public scrutiny. For some time now committees have served these purposes. But the frequency with which they have been used and the repetitive nature of their findings suggests that different instruments of public policy will be required in future when, as sadly they will be, children are killed or seriously harmed by those who care for them.

CHAPTER 7

REFLECTIONS ON SOCIAL WORK PRACTICE

OLIVE STEVENSON
Professor of Social Work Studies, University of Nottingham

The issues explored in this chapter are concerned with social work practice. The aim is to reveal some fundamental problems which lie behind much of the commentary upon child abuse. These are highlighted in the reports of the numerous inquiries which have been reported since 1974 and extensive use is made of these in what follows. However, these detailed commentaries are located here in the wider context of present and past child welfare practice in the UK and seek to draw out the relevance of some of the earlier chapters to this theme.

It is understandable that the inquiries have been combed for evidence which might lead to better prediction of risk, 'warnings which should have been heeded' and, if heeded in subsequent cases, might prevent tragedies. As Dingwall (in Chapter 2) shows so clearly, the search for predictive factors is full of definitional, statistical and methodological pitfalls. The predictive value to be derived from inquiries is very limited. Furthermore, the fact that, in certain of these cases, social work practice fell below commonly accepted standards of good practice, does not tell us anything about the general state of the art.

However, readers will look for guidance and help in this complex and stressful work, and will not be content with academic analyses which discredit attempts to understand or to characterise the problem of child abuse, but offer no indications of where progress may be made. The inquiries raise certain general matters which through practice, experience and knowledge of child wel-

fare are instantly recognisable as of central and critical importance. It is upon these that we have to concentrate.

There are two issues which run through child-welfare literature
and are vividly highlighted in the inquiries. These may be summarised best by presenting a stereotypical view of the extreme versions
of the argument. The first concerns 'the child versus the family'.
At one extreme it is asserted that the protection of the child from
abusing families is of primary and overriding importance and that
the needs of feelings of adults must at all times be subservient to
that. Associated, but distinct, is the concept of children's rights.
At the other extreme, the needs and rights of the families are
asserted: their need for support and confirmation of their status as
parents: their rights, including social justice and in particular a
right to procedures and mechanisms which protect them from
unjustified allegations.

The second issue concerns the theoretical frameworks within
which child abuse may be treated. Some see theories of individual
and familial psychopathology as of paramount significance; others
stress structural factors, social and economic disadvantage which
lead to familial stress. A third contrasting analysis emphasises
social and cultural forces. For example, some feminists stress male
patriarchy, by which gender roles and parental behaviour are
defined; the abuse of male power in the wider society is exemplified and sustained within the family.

It is on these two issues that the discussion pivots.

'The child versus the family'

This is central to all the inquiries, Cleveland (1988) included. As
Parton and Parton have shown (in Chapter 3), the increasing use
of the term 'child protection' has wide social and political significance. In recent inquiries, (Beckford 1985; Henry 1987; Carlile
1987) its use seemed designed to stress that part of the social
worker's duty which, it was suggested, had been inadequately
emphasised. How far the emphasis on 'child protection' has led to
more controlling and 'policing' activities on the part of social
workers, in particular to a greater readiness to remove children
from their homes, is a contentious and complex matter on which
clear empirical evidence is lacking.

In this book, Parton and Parton (Chapter 3) discuss the implications for policy and practice of the increasing use of the term 'child protection'. Earlier, Parton (1985a) argued that 'social work practice . . . has become more authoritative and decisive and has increasingly come to intervene in ways which can be experienced by families as threats or punishments' (p.127).

Packman and Randall's findings (reported in Chapter 5), however, do not appear to confirm that assertion, insofar as one might expect such trends to result in a greater readiness to remove children from home. In the sample of children and families studied in the mid-1980s, they found that 'a striking feature of the decisions made about the child "victims" [i.e. abused children] . . . was the tendency to keep them out of the care system' (p.90).

Packman and Randall explore this issue in more depth elsewhere (forthcoming 1989). They found that, in their sample, there were few significant factors to distinguish the characteristics of the 'victims', 'volunteers' and 'villains' from each other. Their 'perplexing and paradoxical' finding was that 'past and present anxieties about abuse, about standards of parental care and development, and even the presence of the child's name on the child-abuse register, were all more likely to be associated with a decision *not* to admit the child' (to care). (This was in contrast to the 'villains'!). To explain this simply in terms of a preoccupation with the needs of parents, is, they suggest 'too narrow and inadequate'. Their analysis shows that 'admission to care is *considered* more readily and more frequently' (for children at risk). Indeed, a quarter of the at-risk children initially kept out of care were in care 6 months later. Some others left home but were not in care (for example, by using a boarding hostel); some perpetrators left home.

Thus, the picture drawn is emphatically not one of indifference or insensitivity to child protection but neither is it one of readiness to resort to admission to care. What Packman and Randall do show, however, (and this is excellently illustrated in their chapter in this book), is that, on occasion, 'work seemed trapped into anxious monitoring and waiting for the worst to happen', or that reluctance to admit was extreme. In such circumstances, prevention was conceived in a narrow, negative way – in contrast to its use in a fuller sense 'achieved by a well-planned admission with parental involvement'.

Dingwall and Eekelaar (1984) analysed child-care statistics for the period 1970–81 and concluded 'there is no . . . solid evidence of dramatic expansion in the scope and aggressiveness of welfare intervention since the second world war' (p.103).The authors do not specifically examine intervention in relation to child abuse. Furthermore, it is possible that analysis of later figures would show different trends.

Solidly-based large-scale research is urgently needed. Without it, we do not know what general foundation there is for the suggestion that, on the one hand, social workers are over-ready to remove children or, on the other, that they are too reluctant. We are swept to and fro by the winds of rhetoric, by topical examples of the 'shock horror' variety, exemplified in inquiries, and by the prejudices of influential people in key positions. That social workers are affected in their decision-making by public concern is not surprising, nor, one might argue, undesirable, if it indicates a proper degree of humility and uncertainty. However, two examples indicate a degree of vulnerability which is of concern.

Table 7.1 shows the rise in Place of Safety Orders around the time of the Maria Colwell Inquiry in 1974, the first major inquiry of the kind which was to become commonplace in the next decade.

A second example is from *The Sunday Times* (9 October 1988):

Doctors last week expressed concern that Cleveland may no longer be adequately protecting victims of child sexual abuse. In the last 6 months there have been 154 suspected cases referred to social workers, most of them by the police. Only two have been removed from their homes and only 10 have been made the subject of legal supervision.

A complex web of attitudes, beliefs and feelings underlie this debate, which constantly recurs in the literature. One concerns the notion of 'child abuse' or 'child saving' as Platt (1969) described it. Once the idea of parental ownership of children had been breached, this was a dominant theme in the early work of the voluntary children's societies, illustrated for many years in the publicity of the NSPCC but also, strikingly, in the policy of Dr Barnardo's to settle children 'in the colonies' – Australia, New Zealand and Canada. (It is not widely known that children were thus 'exported' up to the late 1960s.) The idea of a fresh start, free from harmful influences of parents, was fundamental to much of this work.

Table 7.1: Place of safety orders 1972–7

Date	No. of place of safety orders*
March 1972	204
March 1973	214
Maria Colwell inquiry sitting: March 1974	353
Publication of Maria Colwell Report: March 1975 March 1976	596 739

* In force to local authorities at 31 March 1972–6.
Source: Hallett, C.T. and Stevenson, O. *Child Abuse Aspects of Interprofessional Cooperation* (Allen and Unwin 1980).

Countervailing forces in more recent years were, however, powerful. There were two main elements in these. One concerns parental rights. The Children Act 1948, which laid the foundation for contemporary child welfare, contained various provisions designed to ensure that parental contact was not arbitrarily severed or curtailed. Yet the adequacy of these provisions has been increasingly challenged, for example in relation to the procedures for assumption of parental rights by the local authority. The Family Rights Group, the organisation of 'Parents against Injustice (PAIN) are contemporary symbols of a continuing inevitable tension, which erupted with sensational force in the Cleveland episode.

A second element, paradoxically, relates to what is perceived to be best for children. This is derived in part from the painful experience of those who, operating in child welfare from the 1950s with considerable initial optimism, saw how badly the 'care system' treated many children. They saw the damage done by discontinuities of experience, that children cut off from parents were damaged by this and that the career of a child in care was often troubled and further deprived. In short, they became more and more averse to breaking the tie if that could be avoided. This point of view was expressed quite forcefully in my Minority Report in the Maria Colwell Inquiry:

. . . there is much confusion, some of which was apparent in this inquiry, regarding social workers' attitudes to the so-called 'blood tie'. The phrase is one which may trip off the tongues of lawyers much more readily than those of social workers. If that phrase means that emotional relationships, which in some way take precedence over others, exists simply because of consanguinity, then this is not generally accepted by social workers and was explicitly rejected by the East Sussex social workers at the hearing. For those who work with children separated from their parents, the issue is seen much more in terms of the development in a child of a good self image and sound sense of identity (Colwell 1974, p.109).

There are two elements, I argued, in this: that children should know who their parents are and that their perception of them, coloured as it is by the adults who care for them, should not be such as to make them feel they come of 'bad stock'.

It is as pertinent today, 15 years later. Indeed, Blom-Cooper went over some of this ground in the Jasmine Beckford Report and concluded:

There is a body of evidence in the literature of criminology and psychiatry to lead social workers to a recognition that council provided care can be as damaging in its long-term effects as in the experience of incompetent parenting at home. We are confident that the majority of social workers work hard at holding the balance between effectively preventing child abuse and striving not to deprive natural parents unnecessarily of the privilege, if not right, of bringing up their children in the normal way. The situation still involves criticial decision-making and involves, therefore, a degree of risk, a risk which is particularly present at an early stage in any referral before overt evidence of cruelty has emerged. We trust that our report and its recommendations will not in any way disturb the balance that social workers must endeavour constantly to strike between parental rights, limited as they are when those rights have been abused, and child protection (p.15).

There are, of course, two elements in that debate. One concerns keeping children within their families, one with keeping children in touch with their families. Yet underlying both is a powerful assertion of a fundamental position on what is best for children. Writings over the years such as those of Holman demonstrate this commitment. Holman's seminal article on inclusive and exclusive fostering, in which he produced evidence that fostered children benefit from parental contact is entirely consistent with his more recent publications on prevention (Holman 1975). It is also significant that even in adoption – that most abrupt and complete severence – the law now permits adopted persons, when they are adult, to attempt to make contact with their natural parents. The powerful drive to do so is well illustrated by Toynbee (1985) in her accounts of the searches undertaken by various individuals.

The importance of these links is taken a stage further in the current debate about the placement of black children for fostering and adoption. Some argue strongly that the self-esteem derived from a secure sense of racial identity is crucial to children's well-being. Hence transracial placement would be frowned upon, even where there is no contact with natural parents.

More recently, in keeping with an increased emphasis upon the concept of 'rights' as distinct from that of 'welfare', children's rights have been the subject of a growing literature (Franklin *et al.* 1987), and are epitomised by some of the work of the Children's Rights Centre. The activities of the National Association of Young People in Care (NAYPIC) has presented a view of life in care which is predominantly negative. This is understandable and justifiable in drawing attention to the deficiencies of the care systems. It has resulted in the articulation of statements of basic rights for such children and young people. Interestingly, some of those who espouse this cause also emphasise the child's right to contact with parents. Lavery (1987) points out that:

A growing body of opinion has begun to question the tendency towards permanency as it has been developed by SSDs. Greg Kelly, for instance, in a discussion of relevant theories and research, has argued that continued parental contact may well be beneficial to the emotional adjustment of children in care and in accordance with many of their wishes, even though rehabilitation may not be immediately possible (p.84).

Dingwall and Eekelaar (1984) draw attention to the fact that children's rights may be formulated in two different ways. The libertarian position encompasses two rather different claims, both of which are often formulated in the language of children's rights. The first, and weaker, claim proposed that 'children should be afforded the same civil status, with associated rights and duties, as adults'. This overestimates 'the physical, moral and psychological capacities of children' (p.104). The extreme assertion of this view leads to absurdity and is not one which concerns us here, although it should be noted that it has stimulated healthy questioning as to the extent to which children and young people can and should be accorded the same rights as adults.

The second formulation relates to 'a family autonomy ideology which appears in both left . . . and right . . .'. It attempts to evade the problem which arises because 'any attempt to accord children specified rights necessarily involves setting up enforcement agencies to supervise the care provided for them'. It does this by 'reformulating children's rights in terms of adult freedoms'. 'Children's rights are identified with a parental right to freedom from state supervision', 'children have a right to develop and maintain unconstrained psychological ties with their parents' (p.104).

The authors show clearly the flaws in this argument; it is 'not a theory of children's rights so much as a political theory about the proper relationship between families and the state' (p.104). It seeks to restrict intervention to the grossest forms of abuse, a position which it is clear our society will not accept. They conclude: 'There can be no escape from the fact that the recognition of children's interests necessarily entails the abridgement of family autonomy. The trade off between these objectives is a political decision' (p.106).

The tension in this debate has been further increased by the position of foster parents. In two of the most highly publicised inquiries, Maria Colwell and Jasmine Beckford, media concentration on the 'tug of love' element between natural and foster parents heightened public concern, although with much less force in the second case, in part because of the differing tone and emphasis of the two reports. As Hallett points out (in Chapter 6), the early decision of the first inquiry to exclude an appraisal of Maria's foster parents, led to an incomplete picture of the situations in which Maria found herself and hence of the social workers' exercise of professional judgement. (That was an important factor in my decision as a member of the panel to write a minority report.) The feeling generated by the case played its part in the passage of the 1975 Children Act which, *inter alia*, defined for foster parents a role as custodians of certain foster children. Of course, this and other legislative moves were presented as primarily protecting the security of children but it would be naïve to disregard the undertone of sympathy for foster parents which played a part in the debate. Their 'rights' were also on the agenda.

During this period, we saw also the rise of a powerful professional group whose primary concern was to improve the quality of placement in adoption and fostering. Spurred on by the sophisticated and energetic voluntary organisation, now British Agencies for Adoption and Fostering, many local authorities appointed specialist officers. While the great value of this work is not in dispute, specialisation of this kind may have the indirect consequence of splitting concern for the child (and his or her prospective parents) from that for the natural family. When, as not infrequently happened, the adoption and fostering specialists were more skilled, more experienced workers and better resourced than the so-called generic worker, concentration on the child and his or her placement needs on occasion was not matched by purposeful concern for the family. Some of the difficulties which can arise were illustrated in the Beckford Report, in which communication between the senior social worker on the case and the principal social worker in the Adoption and Foster Care Section became badly strained.

Associated with this problem was the rise of the 'permanency planning' movement. This emerged as a consequence of major research studies in the USA, confirmed by subsequent Australian and British work (Wedge 1973; McCotter 1981), and showed the tendency of children in care to 'drift'. The movement was reinforced by such influential authors as Goldstein, Freud and Solnit who in their first book (1980) argued powerfully and dogmatically for speedy and final separation and the adoption of children whose parents were judged incapable. A number of local authorities espoused this policy with some enthusiasm. In a research study directed by the author (Stevenson 1986), it was found that some practitioners felt such policies were being imposed on them by management and that they ran counter to their views concerning the needs and rights of both parents and children. This brief and incomplete account seeks to unravel some of the tangled threads in a debate. It is one in which many take part, judges, lawyers, doctors, as well as social workers, while the general public offers spasmodic waves of confirmation for one party or the other and sometimes bays for professional blood.

Some, but by no means all, social workers have become very clearly identified with one party rather than the other. However, the rhetoric often obscures the need for individualised judgements in specific cases. In child welfare, articulation of principle tends to be at a level of generality which is not particularly helpful to field-level workers who often play a crucial part in making decisions –

focused upon what is believed to be best for *this* child and *this* family at *this* time – and acting upon them. There is an air of unreality to some of the arguments and counter-arguments; so many factors, planned and unplanned, legitimate and illegitimate, affect the decisions made about children of families at risk. Behind the use of research findings to demonstrate the needs of children and families, behind the intellectual discussion of 'rights', one has a strong sense that the available evidence and the theorising is being used on both sides to justify what is essentially an emotional position, the roots of which run deep. It is as if each camp is determined to prove a general case rather than grasp and accept the reality of differing circumstances and situations involving complex professional judgements.

This situation manifests itself in different ways at different times but is illustrated most recently with particular force in the events in Cleveland. Here, feelings and views about child sexual abuse apparently led some to believe, or to accept uncritically, that the damage of leaving children at home when there was strong suspicion, outweighed the damage which might be done by immediate removal and subsequent experiences in hospital or elsewhere. Some children, of course, are placed at risk of further, dangerous abuse once allegations have been made. There have been tragic instances of this. Also, disclosure may be more difficult if a child remains at home with the alleged perpetrators. None the less, I am left with an impression – it can be no more – that some of the decisions to remove were not the outcome of measured professional assessment of the risks to a particular child of being left at home. Rather, the certain views of some in positions of responsibility, who believed powerfully, and no doubt sincerely, that sexual abuse necessitated separation, created a climate in which others did not feel free or confident enough to challenge those views. This is understandable, given the normal and valid feelings of revulsion which much sexual abuse engenders and the fact that social workers, as other professionals, were ill-equipped to deal with the anxiety, anger and distress which abuse arouses. However, it does remind us, yet again, how dangerously open social workers are both to immediate organisational pressures and to the influence of leaders with strong opinions. Field workers, however, have had little help with the management of these situations. In the run-up to the Cleveland Inquiry, government guidelines were

not available. Societal attitudes were (and are) profoundly confused and ambivalent. It is interesting to read in the new guidelines, issued at the same time as the Cleveland Report (DHSS
1988a): 'It is recognised that sexual abuse does not necessarily call
for an immediate emergency response as removal of a child from
home' (p.34). Practioners may be forgiven for saying '*now* they tell
us'!

The issues and circumstances surrounding child sexual abuse
have some special features of difficulty. It is, however, useful to
remind ourselves that this most recent preoccupation can be
located in the wider context of 'rescuing children': its opponents
hold similarly powerful views, which often seem to spring from an
identification with the parents of children on the frontiers of care.
Such parents frequently endure multiple deprivation; they are
often financially and materially in poverty; their difficulties are
overwhelming and they seem unable without help to fight or
manipulate the system to their benefit. Anger at such people's
plight may be a driving force behind the efforts to keep the family
together. Indeed, explanations of physical child abuse as an
outcome of economic deprivation and associated stress are common. However, it is more difficult to make the link between the
former and sexual abuse.

A different but important strand in this identification with
parents is illustrated in a number of child-abuse inquiries in which
social workers appear to have been over-involved with the child-
like qualities in the parent, especially the mother. This is seen
most vividly in the Lucie Gates Inquiry (1982) but is also evident in
others such as the Tyra Henry case. Indeed, in the latter, the
report specifically asks whether the social worker 'was parenting
Claudette (the mother) rather than acting as key social worker'
(Henry 1987, p.110). That these feelings of protectiveness should
sometimes exist is neither surprising nor undesirable. What it
points to is the need of workers for advice and support in gaining
insight into the effect which the families, or particular members of
families, have upon them and the way this may twist their
judgement. Few, if any, social workers would dispute intellectually that their first duty is to protect a child at physical risk. The
question which is vital to answer is why that duty, on occasion,
becomes blurred. One reason may be that dismay and anger about
parents' suffering takes over. The hard lesson here is that,

however unjust and traumatic past events may have been, the child's present needs and rights take precedence. In a sense, this is simpler to tackle than the complex emotions and rationalisations which may be at work when child-like parents tug at the heart-strings of workers, with promises of 'doing better next time'. Such difficulties may be reinforced by the unease which many social workers have felt about direct work with children. To get in touch with a child's feelings and needs may on occasion have seemed harder than to relate to these in adults. This is well illustrated in many inquiries and is a matter to which we return later.

Identification with parents has led to accusations of gullibility and naïvity, most recently in the Beckford, Henry and Carlile Inquiries, sometimes harshly expressed, as by Blom-Cooper in the Beckford Report. Of this Inquiry Report I commented elsewhere: 'it is too easy to paint a picture of the disingenuous social worker constantly and persistently deceived by cunning parents . . . Yet it is not implausible that deliberate deception in this case, as at many others, arose at points of crises and stress.' While we need shrewd observation, 'that is not at all the same as systematically approaching clients with distrust. That is a hopeless road to travel . . .' (Stevenson, 1986).

However, we are still left with the unanswered question, why have qualified and experienced social workers been deceived in situations where a general level of suspicion is already present? One reason may be the difficulty which social workers may have in retaining positive feelings about parents who lie to them. A moralising element enters into the relationship, a kind of conditional protectiveness, which is inappropriate and does less than justice to the stresses under which parents may be operating. The inquiries show how important it is to understand the context in which lies are told. For example, in the Kimberley Carlile and Tyra Henry cases the reports show patterns of deceit and deviousness in the mothers over a number of years in relation to different matters. However, this is not always the case. One wonders whether there should be a question in every case conference or supervision session – 'do you think the parents are truthful? If not, why not?'. These questions should be asked in the same tone as 'is the mother in good health?' and should not be used as a form of moral judgement associated with moral positions.

The swing of the pendulum towards parents' rights which we have seen in the wake of the Cleveland affair seems to have strengthened the movement towards parental participation in case conferences. This is epitomised in the changes between the draft guide (1986) and the final version (1988) of the DHSS circulars. The earlier version is unequivocal in its rejection of this.

It may be helpful for the key worker and one or two more members of the core group to meet with the parents from time to time . . . Such meetings, however, should be clearly distinguished from interagency case conferences. *It is not appropriate for parents to attend the latter.* (DHSS 1986, p.19. Author's italics)

In 1988, DHSS advice is as follows:

Parents' views should be sought prior to a case conference to afford them the opportunity to seek advice and prepare their representations. They should be invited wherever practicable to attend part, or, if appropriate, the whole of the case conference unless in the view of the chairman [sic] of the conference their presence will preclude a full and proper consideration of the child's interests (DHSS 1988a, p.30).

Thus, the chair should now show good reason why parents should not attend – a major shift of emphasis.

Well before the Cleveland affair, there was a vocal minority who regarded this as a necessary development of good practice. It is indeed in line with more general trends towards openness and participation between professionals and their clients and an assertion of parents' rights. Such research as has been done (Rousiaux 1984; McGloin and Turnbull 1986) seems to confirm that involvement in conferences does not lead to insurmountable difficulties, although these studies may offer valuable advice on the handling of these situations. However, it is a matter which raises considerable anxiety among some professional participants and chairpersons and which could easily be discredited if sensitive management and chairing of such meetings is lacking. In particular, the DHSS circular does not relate their advice specifically to sexual abuse. It remains to be seen if case conferences concerning sexual abuse can be managed in the same way.

Whatever the complexities of practice, it is beyond doubt that our society will not accept a situation in which the balance to children's rights tips beyond a certain point, whatever 'first duty' the law lays upon social workers. The Cleveland situation has exposed this yet again, after a run of inquiries in which social workers were often criticised for too much concern for parents. Discussion of parents' rights, even when they stand accused, features in the recommendations and merits full quotation.

We recommend:

a. The parents should be given the same courtesy as the family of any other referred child. This applies to all aspects of the investigation into the suspicion of child sexual abuse, and should be recognised by all professionals concerned with the family.

b. Parents should be informed and where appropriate consulted at each stage of the investigation by the professional dealing with the child, whether medical, police or social worker. Parents are entitled to know what is going on, and to be helped to understand the steps that are being taken.

c. We discuss below the position of parents in case conferences.

d. Social Services should confirm all important decisions to parents in writing. Parents may not understand the implications of decisions made and they should have the opportunity to give the written decision to their lawyers.

e. Parents should always be advised of their rights of appeal or complaint in relation to any decisions made about them or their children.

f. Social Services should always seek to provide support to the family during the investigation. Parents should not be left isolated and bewildered at this difficult time.

g. The service of the place of safety order on parents should include a written explanation of the meaning of the order, the position of the parents, their continuing responsibilities and rights and advice to seek legal advice (Cleveland 1988, p.246).

Additionally, with regard to access, the recommendation is:

Whenever and however children are received into care social workers should agree with parents the arrangements for access unless there are exceptional reasons related to the child's interest not to do so. In either event the parent should be notified in writing as soon as possible of the access arrangements and the avenues of complaint or appeal open to them if they are aggrieved (Cleveland 1988, p.246).

Theoretical frameworks for understanding child abuse

We turn now to the second of the two 'great debates' – how to understand abuse (and indeed, many other family problems with which social workers have to deal). There is a sense in which the futility of polarised argument seems evident as soon as it is raised. Surely it is obvious that individual, familial, social and material factors play a part, albeit in differing proportions, in the problems which social work clients experience? Yet one observes, over the years, the pendulum swinging to and fro, the difficulty which proponents of different views have in paying serious attention each to the other. Ever since the late Barbara Wootton's blistering attack (1959) on social workers' use of psychodynamic theory, which coincided with increased awareness of post welfare state poverty and increased sociological influences on social work, social workers have been extremely nervous of utilising such theory. The extent to which such theoretical frameworks ever in fact shaped or underpinned their actions is highly questionable, as Webb (1981) has convincingly shown. But the argument rumbles on, opened up anew by each generation of social-work students. It is bound up with ideological and political positions of great significance, yet the way in which the debate has often been conducted is unhelpful to practitioners and may have adversely affected child-welfare practice in the past 20 years.

Oversimplified, the argument goes like this. Those who seek to explain behaviour in individual and familial terms will seek modes of intervention which may change 'maladapted behaviour'. They are accused of ignoring the powerful impact of social and material deprivation and disadvantage on such families. Most important, they are accused of implicitly, even explicitly, upholding a social status quo which may in itself be oppressive, unjust and in need of radical change. Hence their association with a political right wing. Indeed, it is argued that a right-wing government and its supporters may actively encourage modes of intervention which place responsibility back 'into the family' and are thus relieved of responsibility for amelioration of social conditions.

This is a powerful critique and is commonly heard in social-work circles. To other professionals engaged in child-protection or child-welfare work, psychologists or psychiatrists, for example, this may be an unfamiliar analysis, especially since they may have addressed few of these issues in training. They may be powerfully committed to the belief that problems in parent/child relations are located in the individual or family and that it is pointless to seek to reorganise the outside world round this family or 'simply' to alleviate external difficulties, without strengthening the family. They may see in those who present opposing views a reluctance to face and engage with the complex forces in family interaction. They may even fear that an element of political 'activism' will bring suffering to families who are being 'used' in the interests of wider reform rather than cared for.

The enthusiasm with which some social-worker teachers grasped hold of 'systems theory', in the work, for example, of Pincus and Minahan (1973) and Goldstein (1973), is in part explained because it appeared to offer a way of bridging the divide. Yet it has never been sufficiently convincing and some, notably Langan (1985) have been sharply critical of its underlying assumptions which appear to support a view of social work as upholding the status quo, in particular in relation to gender roles. This criticism cannot be explored here but it highlights a problem for feminists who appreciate the impact of social structure and family life and the complex forces for understanding and intervention which enable social workers to move between these worlds, a point to which we return.

The 9 years of Thatcherite Britain have inevitably strengthened the sense of outrage within the social work profession, as the extent and nature of material and financial deprivation among their clientele becomes ever more apparent. Unfortunately, however, this does not facilitate any resolution of the conflict here described. Rejecting or doubtful of the 'intra-familial' theories of causation and of intervention, many are left in theoretical confusion, or even sometimes in a vacuum, as they seek to understand and grapple with problems of child abuse. Theories which locate social and material deprivation and disadvantage in a framework of class or gender, power and oppression, do not offer an adequate explanatory framework for the wide variety of cases and problems encountered. Only a minority of deprived and disadvantaged people abuse their children. Such theories do not explain 'for example' why some parents live in filthy conditions, 'fouling their nest' in a way unheard of in ordinary families. The Malcolm Page (Page 1981) case is a grim example of this. Malcolm died from hypothermia and malnutrition. The police report at that time is not substantially different from earlier reports by social workers and health visitors.

Walking from the hall up to the bedrooms the smell of urine which was noticeable in the hall became stronger. On the landing at the top of the stairs there was evidence of excrement just lying on the landing. In the main bedroom there was a double bed; the mattress was stained with urine and was damp in parts. There were three dirty pillows on the bed and a very dirty sheet that was also stained heavily with urine and marks of excrement. On the floor there was a plastic mat and lying on top of this were several lumps of excrement and excrement had been trodden into the mat itself. On the bare boards there was excrement some of which had mould on it. There were several lumps of excrement around a small carpet area which was in the corner of the room. The bedroom was in a very poor state of repair. The wardrobe contained clothing which was just piled up to a height of about two feet and consisted mainly of children's clothes.

In the rear bedroom there was one double bed and a cot, the bed had a double mattress on it which was very heavily stained and sopping wet with urine. There was a soiled sheet sodden with urine and mixed with excrement lying on the floor under the bed. There were several lumps of excrement all over the floor and at least twelve empty milk bottles lying in different positions on the floor. There was a cupboard in the room which, when opened, displayed excrement which had been wiped in an area of about six inches square on the back of the cupboard door, apparently in a child's hand. The cot in the room had a small mattress and there was no other bedding on the cot. (Page 1981, pp.46–7)

In this case, conditions similar to those described above at the end of Malcolm Page's life led to the children being taken into care at an earlier stage, while the parents were encouraged to clean up. After the children returned home, there was an inexorable slide downwards. The intervention was ineffective because those involved had apparently no idea of the dynamics which led both parents to tolerate, even to need, these living conditions. Mr Page was, it seems, of normal intelligence and in regular employment as a stock controller. Comments in the report concerning his view that domestic and child care was 'women's work', and therefore left to an inadequate wife, do not explain how he, moving in 'normal' society, presenting himself for 'clean' work, could tolerate such filth at home.

The cases of Tyra Henry, Kimberley Carlile and Darryn Clarke among others raise questions critical both to physical and sexual abuse of children. This concerns the seeming inability of some women to separate from 'dangerous' men. An analysis which explains this solely in terms of economic and social pressures on women with children is not adequate to explain it. Claudette Henry, for example, knew all too well of her partner's propensity. Her first born, Tyrone, was gravely and permanently injured by her partner, Andrew Neil. Her mother and family's support was available to her, as was alternative housing. Andrew Neil was away in prison for various periods of time. Yet contact was resumed, with tragic consequences for Tyra. It is of pressing importance to understand more of the nature of the attraction and interaction in such situations. With hindsight, plans made in good faith to protect Tyra seem extremely naïve. A feminist analysis which stresses the widespread abuse of male power may be an essential starting point but needs to go far enough to understand those women who cannot escape even when they are offered opportunities to do so. Understandably, feminists resent any analysis which lends weight to the offensive 'she asked for it/enjoys it' school of thought. Yet, if we are to help women like Claudette Henry, we have to examine the processes of interaction which lead to such tragic outcomes for mothers as well as children.

In short, the diversity of human behaviour requires, as it were, theoretical subplots which can reside within more generalised social theories of family functioning. Without such theory being available, the social worker, or indeed any other professional, is left floundering. The particular issues and cases discussed above illustrate a more general point – the inadequacy of the theoretical frameworks which the average social worker has at his or her disposal when behaviour cannot be simply explained as a reaction to environmental, material or financial stress. We cannot afford (and neither can the children and families) to sustain theoretical dichotomies which have been so marked in the past 20 years. It is arrogant to assert that this partial understanding is adequate.

Of course, reality is more complex and confusing than the above discussion might seem to imply. For example, there are many different theoretical frameworks, often conflicting, which offer explanations of individual and family behaviour which, in turn, lead to different models of intervention. Some of their exponents hold strong, even messianic, views as is evidenced in the different schools of family therapy. Some of these differences seem esoteric to practitioners, and the general indifference of British social workers to psychodynamic or behavioural theories means that there has been little debate among them, comparable to that sparked off by sociological and political theorists concerning poverty or by feminists. There is a pressing need for these issues to be re-addressed in education and training. Specifically, social workers need first to consider the utility in child-protection work of frameworks for understanding the micro-dynamics of family life and, secondly, the extent to which these can be integrated or reconciled with the analysis of wider forces in society which affect their clients. It sometimes seems that almost any framework for assessment and intervention would be better than the vacuum in which many social workers seem to operate (Parsloe and Stevenson 1978). Indeed, it may be that one of the attractions of the work described by Dale *et al*. (1986) and discussed by Parton and Parton (in Chapter 3) is that it offers an apparently clear framework for assessment and intervention, rarely available in the British literature. The danger is that it will be seized upon too readily, and then distorted or rejected as inadequate because of the lack of readily-available alternative formulations.

Assessment

It is of particular concern that so much emphasis is currently being placed upon 'comprehensive assessment' without apparent acknowledgement of the need for a framework of understanding to underpin such assessment. This is illustrated in the BASW evidence to the Cleveland inquiry when the general secretary of BASW said:

it is absolutely essential that those involved in the family . . . conduct the fullest assessment of the family background. A full family history is being shown repeatedly to be of vital importance. He went on to suggest that the broad principles outlined by Henry Kempe in making an assessment of the family should still apply. It was necessary to assess the family by looking at the parents individually, the parents' relationship, the vulnerability of the child, the child's situation in the family, the family's social situation, their contacts with the extended family etc. as well as considering and recording the family's perspective of events which set the referral in motion (Cleveland 1988 p.214).

The DHSS (1988a) guidelines state: 'Any action to provide for protection, treatment and other services for the child must be based on an assessment of the child's and family's needs, including an assessment of levels of risk to the child' (p. 23).

Indeed, but such activity is only of limited utility if it does not address the meaning of behaviour which perplexes, and which seems to have within itself the seeds of destruction of the family. 'Assessment' is self-evidently a necessary precursor to action. It is currently (post-Cleveland) being used as a kind of 'cooling' device; the lack of it, it is implied, tends to precipitate ill-conceived interventions. It is, of course, an activity which any sensible person – plumber, television engineer, physiotherapist, gardener – routinely undertakes. Indeed, it is as relevant to the domestic domain as to that of work. A mother assesses her child's state of health before she calls the doctor. To make an appropriate assessment she has to have enough information but also to be able to organise it into a framework in which it makes sense. A mother who does not understand that vomiting and diarrhoea lead to dehydration and hence, in an infant, is life-threatening, may fail to take appropriately urgent action.

Discussion of assessment in child abuse is bound up with similar issues of *risk*. This gives it added point and urgency but it should be remembered that it has a much wider application in social work or related practice. Most such assessment has at its root the examination of individual and family functioning with a view to ascertaining the need for particular forms of help. There may, however, be a dysfunction between need and service available which affects the process. Workers may define need in terms of service available. However, they are conceptually distinct and when they are blurred the creative response to another's situation is limited.

In child-protection work, risk to the child is, of course, a part of the assessment of family functioning. However, it is unhelpful to stress risk alone because the work of assessment is not complete once that issue has been dealt with. For example, the decision, following initial assessment, to leave a child at home is an essential part of an overall strategy which must be grounded in an appraisal of the family strengths as well as problems. That appraisal should lead to particular discussions about forms of intervention – or towards non-intervention.

In Chapter 2, Dingwall has shown that prediction of risk in classes or categories of family situations is fraught with difficulty. Parton and Parton also stress this in their discussion of 'dangerousness' (Chapter 3). However, this use of the term 'prediction' should be distinguished from the assessment of risk in relation to particular families. To deny the role which professional judgement may play in that is to deny that there is any consistency in human behaviour. It flies in the face of common sense, for example, to suggest that a man with a long-standing history of violence to children is no more likely to do it in future than a man with no such history. The case of Susan Auckland whose father had previously killed a child illustrates this as poignantly as the case of Tyra Henry. However, this serves to highlight the complexity of such assessments.

First, as Dingwall points out, the more specific the behaviour, the more reliable are such judgements. A man with a history of some kind of violence is not necessarily prone to injure children. That connection would have to be demonstrated. In the Maria Colwell Inquiry, my colleagues wished to criticise the social workers for not giving weight to her stepfather's (one) conviction for violence in a pub brawl when deciding to return Maria to the care of her mother. I dissented from this.

Secondly, as Parton and Parton point out, once one accepts situational factors as relevant, the business of prediction becomes less and less tenable. If a man's history of violence appears to be bound up with situations in which he was under particular stress at a given time, who is to know how he may react in a similar situation? And do we know enough about the precise 'triggering' factors?

A third problem, to which Packman and Randall (in Chapter 5) draw attention, is what they describe as 'family turbulence'. It is a truism that assessment is an ongoing process, which must seek to take account of the dynamics of family interaction and changing circumstances. However, perhaps too little attention has been paid, especially in the inquiry reports, to the 'turbulence' of some of those families with whom social workers seek to engage. As Packman and Randall describe, assessment and intervention plans may be thrown into disarray when relationships and events take a different turn. As Mattinson and Sinclair (1979) have so vividly shown, there are a few families, by no means a majority but well-known and 'long-running' in social services departments, who are characterised by frequent crises of functioning in which care of children is likely to loom large. A crucial part of the assessment may therefore concern fluctuations and unreliability in parenting behaviour – assessment of a moving target, one might say. Discussions of risk in these cases may well be more difficult than those where the behaviour, even when gross, is more systematic and organised. Typically, as in the Lucie Gates case, there are a large number of minor incidents and complaints from neighbours in which carelessness or heavy-handedness predominates. With the Gates children, there were no less than 108 such incidents reported in a 5-year period. It is most instructive to see these gathered together in the report (Gates 1982, p.17ff of Other Members Report). Thus it may be through the aggregation of different incidents that the critical judgements are made. The implications of good and speedy communications between agencies and between workers is obvious. However, unless a decision is taken at the outset that the game is not worth the candle, and the children removed (which has other problems discussed earlier), there will be times when assessment of periods of turbulence will not be sufficiently acute to prevent tragedy. This has to be faced.

A fourth example, which concerns the difficulties for social workers in using theory in assessment, lies in the weight ascribed to past events and experiences in the assessment of present and future behaviour. What is to be made of information that a person suspected of abuse has himself or herself been abused? Certainly, the knowledge that in other cases abused parents have abused their children is not safe information from which to draw inferences. Social workers are not called upon to assess abused persons who are *not* suspected of abusing their children. The evidence from present behaviour and interaction is, certainly, a valuable check on the way evidence from the past is used.

The fallibility of past–present connections was admirably illustrated by Rutter (in Fuller and Stevenson 1983). A study of the

histories of mothers and children in care showed that a significant
number had themselves been in care. Yet a comparable study of
women who had been in care did *not* show that their children were
more likely to be in care or that the children (on Rutter's
measures) were less adequately mothered (Fuller and Stevenson
1983). There is no substitute for professional assessment of the
current situation.

Direct work with children

In no sphere of work is assessment more important and neglected
than in communication and therapeutic intervention with children.
Some 18 years ago, Vann (1971) took the rose tint out of the
spectacles of those who peered back at the days of Children's
Departments and lamented their passing. She showed that in
general, work with children was not highly skilled in those days.
However, there were powerful influences on some of us who
trained in that period, notably Clare and Donald Winnicott, whose
interest in direct work with children was of great significance.
Partly because of the trends discussed earlier, during which
psychodynamic theory became unfashionable and unacceptable to
a majority of social workers, the impetus which they gave to
raising awareness of children's feelings and needs was, if not lost,
at least obscured.

In a much-quoted statement, the Cleveland Report is by implication critical of some of those working in the area: 'There is a
danger that in looking to the welfare of the children believed to be
the victims of sexual abuse, children themselves may be overlooked. The child is a person and not an object of concern'
(p.245). This important observation highlights a problem which
has come to the fore in child sexual abuse, in which much time can
be spent with children in 'disclosure' work. (The word is rightly
criticised by Lord Justice Butler-Sloss.) It is unfortunate that
interest in direct communication with children has escalated in
relation to one particular problem and in the context of legal/
criminal proceedings, when it has been so woefully lacking in
child-abuse work generally (although not in some specialised
aspects of child welfare, as in fostering and adoption).

The inquiries reveal a number of situations in which the feelings of the children appear not to have been 'read' adequately. The first of these, Maria Colwell, offered a particularly vivid example. Maria was 6 at the time when she was 'toing and froing' between her mother (with a new stepfather) and her foster parents. There were episodes of running away from the former; outbursts of sobbing on leaving foster parents and occasional remarks to the social worker such as wishing 'she lived on a farm, where no one could find her'. It was not easy to know what to make of all this. I did not share my colleagues' certainty that it pointed simply to rejection of her mother and stepfather. Yet it was clear that even when the opportunity presented itself, there was little consistent attempt to engage directly with Maria about her feelings. This was in no way unusual in the child-welfare practice of that time – and since. The inquiries reveal little evidence of direct work with children, even when children were of an age and in situations in which it would have been possible. Indeed, there is something rather frightening about the repeated finding that even children's physical development has not been monitored and that such tell-tale signs as weight loss after leaving hospital and foster homes were not picked up (Beckford, for example).

The DHSS account of inquiry findings (1982) is useful on the general point of observation and assessment. For example, a child's demeanour may or may not provide a clue. Not all children show the frozen awareness frequently referred to in textbooks.

Wayne Brewer suffered 'a pretty long history of violence and intimidation' (WB 3.1). Yet when a vigilant social worker visited the family, half expecting the see 'a cowering, frightened child' she was instead impressed by the relaxed relationship apparent between Wayne and his stepfather. Wayne 'showed no signs of apprehension'. The consultant paediatrician and health visitor were also deceived by the child's natural resilience. Similarly, Lester Chapman after being beaten and running away 'was not cowed or frightened', but 'cheerful' and 'revelling in being the centre of attention'. (DHSS 1982, p.31)

(It must be added that Lester's behaviour, as described by the police surgeon who examined him at the station, showed all too familiar signs of over-readiness to respond to attention shown by some deprived children.) The DHSS report also discusses 'children's messages' – what they said about their parents and their lives and the importance of seeking to understand these.

Why have so many social workers been so unskilled in their work with children? Earlier comments concerning the need for frameworks to explain behaviour take on particular importance in relation to children. First, the significance of the age and stage of development is vitally important in understanding children's intellectual and emotional processes. The usefulness of asking children where or with whom they want to live, for example, is related to their conceptual development as well as their emotional state. A second important difficulty is in using children's play to understand their feelings, needs and wishes. Social workers have been nervous and inept in the use of play materials, with little help in training. This has been in part because the use of play has been associated with psychodynamic interpretation, and thus has either been regarded as of doubtful legitimacy or beyond the competence of social work. Yet we now see useful experimental work being undertaken with sexually-abused children. It is to be welcomed but immediately raises questions as to the way certain forms of communication are to be understood and used, such as in the use of 'anatomically correct' dolls. For example, one school of psychodynamic thought (Klein) asserts that children have unconscious innate knowledge of the sexual act. Such a view would challenge the interpretation of sexually-explicit play as evidence of abuse or even of events witnessed!

However, work with children in child abuse raises other difficulties as well. In particular, surroundings often pose major problems. To relate meaningfully to a child at home, whose parents are suspected of abuse, is extremely difficult. This was painfully illustrated in the case of Jasmine Beckford, with whom the social worker was unable to establish communication to get any idea of what was happening. Social workers may be rightly afraid that direct communication with the child will raise parental anxiety and antagonism which will adversely affect the child. This is a long-standing difficulty which can also arise with fostered children. While nothing will make it easy, there is a strong case in these situations for a formal requirement, laid down at the outset (for example when a child is returned home or fostered), that the social worker will want to see a child alone, preferably out of the house. 'Outings' are an obvious way of achieving this. Such a requirement may reduce a little of the tension surrounding these events, although, obviously, the more an adult has to hide the less welcome such action by the social worker will be.

However, the inquiries also reveal missed or inadequately exploited opportunities for other adults to engage with the children and convey their impressions to the social workers. This may indeed be the most effective way of finding out the child's view of the situation. These adults may be teachers, from nursery school upwards. Maria Colwell's primary school teacher saw and heard a great deal and was ignored. Jasmine Beckford's nursery school attendance was erratic and, latterly, waning; it offered a resource which was not utilised. Neither, it seems from the report, was the family aide's opportunity to relate to the children used as part of the formal assessment of the situation. While many of the children who had died were very young and therefore this issue did not arise, it is highly probable that many older children who have been injured but have not died would have benefited from a more sensitive and direct involvement by adults in touch with them. The importance of this is, of course, reinforced by the large numbers of sexually-abused children and young people now coming forward. The creation of 'Childline' by a television news presenter and the large numbers of telephone calls which it receives, tells its own story. It also illustrates the difficulty for social workers who operate in the statutory setting, with which some children and young people may be reluctant to communicate.

Acknowledging the problems and difficulties, one is left with a strong sense that good practice should begin with good observation of children which has often been lacking. This lays a foundation on which various strategies can be built. The implications of this for education and training, including better resourcing, are clear.

Those of us who have been a long time in social-work education, know that our own experience as students and that of the students whom we trained, while that experience was fresh, was profoundly influenced by periods of observation, well-supervised, of children talking and playing. Recently, we have introduced within the Nottingham University course, a 'nursery' placement for all students intending to work in social services departments. Initial reluctance by some students has been overcome and there is universal acknowledgement of its value. As one young male student put it: 'it was the first time I had spoken with a person under five'. Thus, social unease, even embarrassment, may have played its part in the failure to relate adequately. However, such experience should be underpinned by systematic teaching on child development, in particular that which offers a framework for the understanding of behaviour.

Conclusion

The preceding discussion leads to a number of conclusions which, it is argued, are of central importance to social-work practitioners and managers.

The first concerns the inescapable importance of the exercise of professional judgement in individual cases. Birchall, Dingwall and Parton and Parton discuss in more or less detail the difficulties of utilising research, whether it be about prevalence, incidence or prediction. This is not to argue that research should not be undertaken or is of no value to practitioners. It is to suggest that those undertaking it should exercise proper methodological caution in its execution, and in what they claim for it, and that those utilising it are clear as to its status. This, in turn, strongly suggests the need for properly structured national and local resources for advice on research which practitioners should be able to call upon. It is unacceptable that practitioners should alone carry responsibility for relating their work to available research.

What then are the ingredients of good professional judgement in child-protection work? Earlier discussion suggests that it involves the capacity to manage within oneself the inherent and essential ambivalence engendered by the (at times) conflicting needs and rights of parents and children. There is no place for dogma; the unending challenge (and, let it be said, fascination) of the work lies in the attempt to balance these sets of needs and rights in a way that does least harm to all parties, while accepting a first duty to protect children. It may well be, as the new DHSS guidelines suggest, that on occasion, this balance can only be achieved by the allocation of different workers to the parties; in this way conflict is externalised – but it will still have to be managed. However, realistically, human resources are often not available to do this, and the tension has to be held within. In order to help in this most stressful aspect of child-welfare work, supervision, which examines the feelings engendered and professional dilemmas it poses, is critical. Such interaction should help to identify the dangerous times and cases, as when workers identify unhelpfully with an immature mother to the exclusion of the child.

The second element is good professional judgement, which, as this discussion emphasises involves use of theory. It is argued, first, that models which locate the source of the problem *either* 'outside' *or* 'inside' the family are unhelpful to practitioners. Secondly, it is suggested that the negative attitudes towards 'micro' theories of family functioning, have resulted, for a majority of social workers, in a paucity of appropriate theoretical explanations for family functioning and child behaviour.

The implications of both points are far-reaching. We urgently need models of interaction betwen internal and external systems which will be meaningful to contemporary social workers in British society and which, in particular, relate constructively to feminist perspectives, and to the experiences of black families in Britain. Secondly, we need to examine the relevance to child-protection work of a range of theories about family functioning, including their application to families in ethnic minorities. Such work would permit more precise experimentation in intervention, and improved measurements of outcome. There is at present a danger that over-confident, even dogmatic, assertions by an exponent of one theoretical position will be seized upon uncritically by social workers, who, understandably, crave certainty in an uncertain and stressful area of work. We are not yet at a stage when such certainties (as evidenced in Dale *et al.* 1986) are sustainable.

The professional and moral duty, then, is to make judgements which are as good as possible in the light of available knowledge, which are informed by personal insight and available theory. That onerous task should not be the responsibility alone of those in face-to-face contact with clients. Managers and educators must share the burden.

CHAPTER 8

MULTI-DISCIPLINARY WORK IN CHILD PROTECTION

OLIVE STEVENSON
Professor of Social Work Studies, University of Nottingham

The Cleveland Inquiry has given an additional impetus to this topic. Indeed, to those who have long stressed the importance of multi-disciplinary work in various fields, the emphasis that it is receiving in child sexual abuse is puzzling and requires further analysis. In this chapter, we shall explore some of the difficulties which arise in translating into practice exhortations to communicate and cooperate in multi-disciplinary child-protection work and, specifically, in cases of child sexual abuse.

Preoccupation with child abuse and other aspects of child welfare should not lead us to ignore the fact that there is, in general, much discussion and encouragement of inter-disciplinary work at present. This has been precipitated by a new wave of concern about community care. In particular, the interface between health and social services is rightly perceived as crucial in relation to care of frail old people, those who are intellectually impaired and those who are mentally ill. The trenchant comments of the Audit Commission (1986) stress that there are formidable structural difficulties in the way of working together effectively. We wait to see what will come of the Griffiths Report on Community Care (1988). Sir Roy seeks to improve cooperation in part through clearer definitions of areas of responsibility between agencies and admits to 'ducking' the Audit Commission's suggestion of a 'supremo' who would be in charge locally of plans for particular client groups. As we shall see later, these matters are by no means irrelevant to child-protection work.

Since failure to 'get the act together' often results in inadequate services with consequent suffering to all kinds of clients and patients, why then the particular importance it has been ascribed in child protection? There is, of course, the actual risk to life which results from failure. This has been amply shown in nearly all inquiry reports. Sadly, however, similar failures occur in the case of adults, such as an old person at risk alone or a mentally ill person who commits suicide. The fact that so little publicity attends these is in part an indication of social attitudes towards different groups. In any case, risk to life itself is unusual in cases of child sexual abuse; yet there is none the less intense official preoccupation with the need to work together. It is evident that the level of public concern about abused children, at least as refracted through the media, exceeds that about other vulnerable and dependent people. This makes it extremely difficult for social workers and others involved to maintain a sense of proportion.

Events in Cleveland obviously influenced the decision by DHSS Social Services Inspectorate to conduct a national survey specifically into inter-agency cooperation in child sexual abuse (DHSS 1988a). This is understandable since the breakdown in some relationships in Cleveland was so bitter and so public. Indeed, the intensity of emotion which child sexual abuse generates among lay and professional alike may be one of the reasons why it proves so difficult to achieve harmonious working relationships. It is rare for government circulars to take note of the emotional impact upon staff; one reads with interest (in the Guidance for Senior Nurses, Health Visitors and Midwives) the comment: 'In general, possible or actual child abuse, and particularly sexual abuse, stirs up feelings which can be deeply troubling and may be difficult for professionals to accept. They may unconsciously use various defence mechanisms in order to cope . . .' (DHSS 1988c, p.5).

Such an official acknowledgement of the subtlety and complexity of the processes involved in cooperation is surely to be welcomed. However, the extent of the preoccupation with child sexual abuse and the danger of exaggeration is shown by the statement in the relevant guidance for doctors: 'More than any condition adversely affecting health of children, child sexual abuse requires close coordination and exchange between the services, agencies and different types of professionals who are concerned with the overall well-being of children (DHSS 1988c, p.2).

Why is child sexual abuse thus put above child abuse? And what would parents and teachers of handicapped children have to say about this statement? (It is to be noted that there is no acknowledgement in the guidance that doctors, like senior nurses, need insight into their feelings!)

Elsewhere (Stevenson 1988a) I have outlined a number of dimensions along which exploration of inter-professional and inter-agency cooperation may usefully be examined. In what follows here, these dimensions will again be used but in a different order with some modifications and with an extended discussion. The dimensions here considered are:

- structures and systems
- relative status and perceived power of the parties
- role identifications
- professional and organisational priorities
- the extent to which cooperation is perceived as mutually beneficial and in which ways
- the dynamics of case conferences
- differing attitudes towards, and values concerning, child abuse and the family.

Structures and systems

The significance of structures and systems in ensuring cooperation is now widely accepted and has been stressed in the many documents emanating from the DHSS and local authorities.

Much of the earlier literature on multi-disciplinary work was focused on hospitals (Kane 1975) and concentrated on teams – working groups in which the participants defined roles in relation to each other in the performance of the task. While this is by no means unproblematic and there are important lessons to be learnt from those experiences, most workers in child protection in Britain are in a different position. They do not usually work as a team in the sense in which this is commonly understood. Indeed, it may be that some meet only rarely outside the case conference. The inevitable effect of this is that knowledge and understanding of each others' roles and responsibilities takes longer to acquire, negative experience may go uncorrected and the workers are less aware of the stress which others may be experiencing.

The Cleveland Report 'strongly' recommends the development of Specialist Assessment Teams (SATs), a proposal which is treated cautiously in *Working Together* (DHSS 1988b). Behind such a recommendation lies the recognition that, in Cleveland, when difficulties arose over assessment of individual cases, there were no inter-professional structures to sort them out. The report goes into considerable detail as to the ways in which these should work. They should comprise an experienced doctor, social worker and police officer, drawn from approved lists. 'They should be prepared, at the request of their medical colleagues, social services or the police, to examine a child and participate in a formal multi-disciplinary assessment'. (p.249)

The report suggests that a team 'will have the advantage of building a reservoir of expertise in a difficult area of work. The intention is to foster teamwork and coordination of activity without undermining professional responsibility or agency function' (p.249). However, the individuals in the team would not be engaged in this work full-time. Indeed, the report suggests that 'a special interest reflected in allocated time, complemented with other less demanding work is the most likely arrangement to avoid stress and ensure a balanced perspective' (p.249). Such arrangements would not necessarily lead to the formation of a team who customarily work together. It would depend on the size of the lists, the amount of allocated time, and on how often particular individuals met others for the assessment process. Moreover, as a second-tier structure whose function is solely that of assessment, it leaves untouched the basic need for better mutual understanding at field level and in the ongoing work of monitoring and intervention.

Thus SATs as proposed lie midway between the present structures and a fully-fledged inter-professional specialist team. Furthermore, it is not clear why they are proposed solely for work in child sexual abuse and whether this can be justified.

Two much wider questions remain, concerning the structures which would facilitate more effective cooperation. The first concerns the desirability and feasibility of developing inter-professional child-protection teams within social services departments. The second, raised by Blom-Cooper in the Kimberley Carlile Inquiry, concerns the organisational location of child-protection work, and whether its continued place within social services departments is appropriate.

Inter-professional teams outside hospitals have been slow to develop in social services departments, although community mental handicap teams may offer a partial model. Consideration of their place in child-protection work should draw on this experience. In particular, the issue of leadership in relation to the structures of accountability and professional status is likely to be problematic. In general, however, the concept has much to commend it in a range of fields, from the social care of elderly people to the development of programmes for juvenile delinquency.

There are, of course, wider issues concerning specialisation in general and the merits of specialist teams, whether inter-professional or not. These issues have been explored in some depth elsewhere (Stevenson 1980) and cannot be reiterated here. It is enough to say that in the years following publication, social workers in social services departments have been pulled in different directions, dictated in no small measure by the preference of managers for models of service delivery which give priority to the notion of local community needs and strengths (or those which stress the importance of expertise while concentrating on the needs of particular client groups). This has resulted in a bewildering diversity of patterns across the country. As Challis and Ferlie (1986) show, no one pattern is 'winning', although there are some recent indications that more specialist teams are emerging, especially as a means of counteracting the neglect of client groups which rouse less public concern, yet whose social needs are so urgent. In various parts of the country, therefore, their contribution to programmes of preventive work with families in difficulty could be most significant. We should also consider the part which others could play in complementing social-work skills. In this country we have not used psychologists, clinical or educational, as extensively as do some other countries. There would be merit in such an experiment. In particular, close team-working with health visitors and psychologists might improve the overall level of observation and understanding of children, to which reference was made in the previous chapter.

This suggestion does not lift specialist teams out of the local authority social services department. Nor does it deal with the wider issues raised by Blom-Cooper when he asked, 'who is responsible for child protection in this country?' (Carlile 1987, pp.139ff). His lengthy and rather confusing answer considers, then rejects as 'too radical' (but attractive to him) the idea of establishing 'one statutory child-protection authority' and proposes two possibilities. One, a modification of the single authority:

. . . will not mean all the work involved being carried out by the single authority, but to function well the system will require the full cooperation of the public, and of all relevant professionals and agencies. Case conferences would remain the crucible of the system, and it would continue to be possible to appoint key workers, but these key workers and all involved in the case would have to be answerable to the controlling authority. This authority, if it is to avoid responsibility without power, would need to be empowered to demand action, within their competence, of all contributors to the system. For the purpose of managing the child-protection system, all participants would thus be answerable to the controlling authority. This structure has the advantage of making accountability clear. It has the advantage of being intelligible to the outside world. More conscientious and determined action may also follow if overall responsibility is not diffuse. It has the disadvantage of separating child protection from other areas of child care and child health, unless the one authority is a massive children's agency. It also has the disadvantage of cutting across existing organisations and professional hierarchies, thereby making change unlikely, particularly if the authority were to be placed under local rather than central government. . . .

The second structure requires that overall responsibility for the management of the system is shared, although it would be possible for specific parts of the responsibility to be formally delegated. The multi-disciplinary structure has the advantage of leaving people accountable within their own hierarchies. It has the advantage of sharing an awesome responsibility. It has the disadvantage of inducing ambiguity in accountability and leaves the door open for confusion, conflict and inter-agency hostility to enter if something goes wrong. It has the disadvantage, given the number of agencies involved, of creating a body with many heads, and would need all agencies to be equal in authority while some, in reality, might reckon that he who shares honey with the bear has the least part of it. Accountability could be made clearer, and management possibly more effective, and efficient, if a governing body was appointed by the contributing agencies. This body would need to have executive powers, in contrast to existing Area Review Committees (Carlile 1987, pp.139ff).

The deafening silence which had greeted this part of Blom-Cooper's report suggests that government is not prepared to take on such massive restructuring as the first proposal would entail, nor to grasp the nettle of a 'governing body' to make the second into a reality. As we shall argue later, new Area Child Protection Committees (ACPCs) in place of Area Review Committees (ARCs) will not fundamentally strengthen the structures for cooperation at senior level. The only real change in the second Blom-Cooper 'model' concerns 'government' at that level. It is to this matter that we turn now.

Area child protection committees

Working Together (DHSS 1988a) places upon the new Area Child Protection Committees (which replace Area Review Committees) a major coordinating role.

Each ACPC should establish a programme of work to develop and keep under review local joint policies and procedures. The main areas of activity will be:

a. to establish, maintain and review local inter-agency guidelines on procedures to be followed in individual cases;
b. to review significant issues arising from the handling of cases and reports from inquiries;
c. to review arrangements to provide expert advice and inter-agency liaison;
d. to review progress on work to prevent child abuse;
e. to review work related to inter-agency training (see Part 8). (DHSS 1988a, p.39)

It is suggested, however, that they are 'accountable to the agencies which make up their membership. These agencies are jointly responsible for Area Child Protection Committee actions' (p.38). 'Each agency should accept that it is responsible for monitoring not only the performance of its own representative but also that of the Area Child Protection Committee' (p.39). Their financing will be by these constituent agencies. DHSS recommend that senior officers, who will have 'sufficient authority' and have a considerable measure of delegated authority, should be appointed to the ACPC.

Shades of Cleveland hang over these proposals which are considerably expanded and more precise than those in the draft (1986) circular. The Cleveland Report documents the trials and tribulations of the ARC, subsequently Joint Child Abuse Committee (JCAC), in seeking to resolve the inter-agency and inter-professional problems which arose over child sexual abuse and concludes that they: 'provide for the most part an ineffective mechanism to coordinate the work of the key agencies in the field of child sexual abuse' (Cleveland 1988, p.53). There was, it was suggested:

> . . . some evidence before the Inquiry to suggest that representatives attending may have more concern to protect what they saw as departmental interests than to commit themselves to the prime purpose of establishing an effective coordinating mechanism. The role of the Joint Child Abuse Committee throughout the crisis in Cleveland demonstrates the ambivalence that its constituent members had towards it. The function of the committee was not recognised by the senior management and none sought to use it to resolve the underlying conflicts until early in July. . . .

> The major agencies involved in the committee had no responsibility for it and the representatives did not have the ability to bind their respective agencies to implement the policy approved by the committee. This may be a reason why the JCAC was not to any extent involved in the resolution of the crisis. To be effective, the committee needed its purpose to be defined and agreed between the Chief Officers and Senior Managers of all participating agencies. Representatives had to have sufficient delegated authority to commit their agency. Each agency needs to have formulated the basic principles and framework of its own practice and be committed to the importance of coordinating work with others (p.54).

To be successful, the report suggests, *inter alia*, that:

> The chairmanship should be held by a person of calibre, sufficiently experienced in both practice and policy issues to ensure that problems are properly considered and resolved. One way of ensuring a greater commitment would be for the chairmanship to rotate on a biennial basis between senior staff of the agencies involved reporting direct to each authority (p.54).

This emphasis in recommendation is in some contrast with the cautious DHSS advice that the chair:

> should normally be an officer . . . of the social services department of at least Assistant Director status and should preferably possess knowledge and experience of child-protection work in addition to chairing skills. However, there may be situations where the social services department, with the agreement of the other Committee members, arranges for the

chairmanship to be undertaken on its behalf by a senior officer of one of the other agencies or by an independent person with the requisite knowledge, experience and chairing skills (DHSS 1988b, p.39).

We have little evidence concerning the work of the former ARCs over the country. There has been little comment on their work in previous inquiry reports, presumably because their focus had been on individual cases and therefore on field-work activity which did not throw ARC operations into relief. The Cleveland comments, however, remind us of the Audit Commission's observations (1987) on community care in general. Even with the changes now proposed, the essential problem remains unresolved. Put crudely, what happens when there is trouble in the higher ranks? As long as there is goodwill, mutual trust and confidence, ACPCs can work well. Yet at the very point when such structures are most needed, they may be impotent. Obviously, the seniority and, most importantly, the personality and attitudes of the chair will be significant in resolving difficulties. Yet if (say) an ACPC is chaired by an Assistant Director of Social Services and difficulties arise with other agencies, neither that person (nor, indeed, the Director) has the authority to insist on resolution. Furthermore, as in case conferences (although here there can be appeal to higher authority), a social services chair may not be seen as impartial, representing as he or she does a party in the proceedings which has a powerful interest in its outcome.

It is disappointing, despite Cleveland experiences, that this nettle does not appear to have been grasped. Two particular points would have been worthy of consideration. First, why does the chair have to come from one of the participating agencies? Could not the possibility of appointing as chair, a person in a relevant field of higher education, known and trusted locally, have been considered? Secondly, what is the role of central government when difficulties arise? – a matter not discussed in the Cleveland Report. Should there be a formal structure, mirroring that of the ACPC, available to mediate if relationships break down locally? The proposed structure will prove adequate for most situations. It leaves unresolved problems of authority which will arise when strong and sometimes difficult personalities from different agencies clash over principle, policy or procedures. One notes with anxiety the comment in the Cleveland Report:

. . . The Police tell us that they now accept unequivocally the principle of joint investigation of child sexual abuse together with Cleveland Social Services, and the need for inter-agency cooperation in order to meet a child's on-going needs. We are by no means convinced that the implications are either understood or accepted at all levels throughout the Force. . . . in particular that the question of prosecution may be only one of a number of matters to be faced and that the protection and welfare of the child are important elements in the overall considerations. It appears to us that it was the crisis in 1987 which forced the Police somewhat reluctantly into a multi-disciplinary stance (Cleveland 1988, p.100).

Communication

The new guidance is replete with reference to the need to establish procedures or systems to ensure that relevant information is communicated, records transferred, persons consulted and so on. Each agency has responsibilities for these. Quite onerous duties rest upon 'senior nurses' in the matter, as in others. They are enjoined to:

set up an effective communication system between senior nurses and practitioners and between senior nurses, other disciplines and agencies. This is to ensure that a regular update about staff shortages, emergencies, individual cases and changes in procedures is provided for the various agencies. The operation of the system should be tested and reviewed from time to time (DHSS 1988b, p.9).

(No such action is required of doctors: guidance is focused almost exclusively on the management of individual situations.)

The advice, which is designed to ensure that systems are used to give information about the current staffing situation, is particularly welcome. The inquiry reports frequently mention, sometimes in passing, changes in personnel or absence through sickness with the consequent dislocation of the arrangements for monitoring children at risk. To an extent these are an inescapable feature of our complex structures; but some of the most deprived areas in which children are most at risk suffer particularly badly in this respect. The Kimberley Carlile case is a sad example of this. In earlier inquiries, the effects of reorganisation upon social service provision was also the subject of comment (Auckland 1975; Chapman 1979). This suggests the need for particular care when these changes occur; even local restructuring (such as the development of a patch or specialist team) has a bearing upon the continuity of planning for children and families, a number of whom may be at a particularly stressful point. Effective multi-disciplinary work would seek to ensure that when particular agencies and individuals within them are in difficulty, others move in with a safety net.

Surprisingly, no mention is made in the new guidance of the contribution which modern technology can make to efficient systems and some of the issues which may arise from it. In particular, the use of computers in maintaining and accessing registers is not referred to. This issue was noted in the Tyra Henry case; recommendation F states: 'The use of a computerised system for limited storage and dissemination of important child-care and protection data should be investigated and if feasible implemented as a matter of priority' (Henry 1987, p.167).

Good communication is not simply a product of goodwill and careful planning; nor should its failures be laid at the door of particular individuals who may be overloaded and stressed. In other fields of activity, sophisticated information systems are developed to counter 'human error'. Why is this not stressed in child-protection work? One fears that the answer lies in the reluctance to admit the resource implications which would flow from such a policy.

However, that being said, the 'human factor' needs to be addressed, especially in relation to those in all the organisations involved who are the 'message takers', including doctors' receptionists, school secretaries and so on. It is in detailed attention to their training needs that the safety of children may lie.

Thus it can be seen that structures, systems and administrative procedures affect the policy and practice of inter-professional work in child protection at every level and in complex ways. Proper attention to these matters should lessen the tendency to view failures and tragedies purely in terms of the personal responsibility of individuals.

Yet it has to be recognised that structures for child-protection work cannot and should not be divorced from wider considerations, both those of social services departments as a whole and those of the various agencies concerned in community care, using that term in a broad sense. Structural change has a ripple effect. It is sure to afford examples of the 'unintended consequences of planned change', but there is a heavy responsibility on policy-makers and managers to minimise these by a careful analysis of the ramifications of any specific changes it is desired to make, whether that be the SAT envisaged in the Cleveland report, a specialist inter-professional team for child-protection work or one with a wider remit.

It may be that radical change in terms of the development of full-blown inter-professional teams, whether in or out of social services departments will be rejected. This need not prevent quieter initiatives, which may often be quite local, in bringing together in a team which has a clear identity, a range of profes-sionals at the centre of child-welfare work.

It has to be said, however, that the position of JCACs remains equivocal and that innovations at field level will be dependent on those bodies presenting a more dynamic image of their collabora-tive activity than heretofore. Recent guidance is not reassuring.

Relative status and perceived power of the parties

This is a matter to which I, with Hallett (Hallett and Stevenson 1980) gave attention in a study of case conferences. It is now widely understood that inter-agency and inter-professional work-ing is affected by the ways the parties see each other, although there may be little insight into the dynamics of particular situations. As I have suggested elsewhere (Stevenson 1988a), it is important that the chairs of conferences should be aware of the way that these dynamics affect discussion of the case, both in assessment and in intervention. The Beckford Report affords a recent example.

Louis Blom-Cooper in the Beckford Report remarks cautiously of a health visitor's contribution that: 'We hesitate to conclude that the reason for such dismissal of Miss Knowles' information was the inferior status accorded to health visitors by the doctor' (Beckford 1985, p.82). He continued: 'Where physicians are trained in psychosocial context, medical people are more likely to perceive themselves as coequals and colleagues of nurses, health visitors, social workers and occupational therapists, rather than being top dogs' (p.82). However, Blom-Cooper does not refer to the issue of gender in relation to occupation.

One has only to observe the difficulty many women have in breaking into a formal conversation, even in relation to strength of voice, to see how unhelpful the interaction of gender with occupation may be. Yet, hearing the quiet, even uncertain, voice in a case conference may be critical (Stevenson 1988a, p.7).

However, the conference is only one forum for cooperative activity and one needs also to be aware of the impact such feelings are having on inter-professional work. There are personal factors, such as class, gender and race, but there are also occupational factors which have a particular 'twist' in child-protection work. We are accustomed to the difficulties which may arise between doctors and social workers given the established position of the one in comparison to the other. In this work, however, social workers in social services departments are placed, unequivocally, centre stage in their responsibility and hence their power, albeit within the framework of the law. This is made even more clear in the latest DHSS guidance:

All those likely to be professionally concerned with the protection of children . . . should be aware, in particular, that legislation places the primary responsibility for the care and protection of abused children on local authorities. They *advise* and *assist* 'the local authority in the discharge of its child protection duties' (DHSS 1988b, pp.5 and 6, author's italics).

Despite the clarity of this statement, however, problems remain, in particular in the relationship between doctors and social workers. Take, for example, the role of the paediatrician in this work. A social worker looks to a paediatrician for expertise in child health and physical condition including indications of abuse; he or she may also value associated advice on the child's emotional state. When we move into family functioning and the matter of associated risk to the child, the weight given to the paediatrician's views will be heavily dependent on the respect and confidence which the particular doctor has gained – professional wisdom, perhaps, rather than technical expertise. Doctors are accustomed, however, through training and role, to exercise authority and are often required to be expert across a wide range of matters which have little to do with medicine. At critical points in child protection when decisions must be taken, it may not be easy for them to accept an advisory, less influential, role.

However, too much concentration on the interaction between different professionals, such as doctors and social workers, oversimplifies the reality, which is of complex relationships both within and between the professions and occupations involved, involving status and power of different kinds. In child-protection discussions, some problems arise from power conflicts; but others arise when the observations and views of certain front-line workers – play-group leaders, residential care staff, family aides and so on, are not ascribed due weight because of their perceived lower status, linked perhaps to uncertain self-presentation.

In conference, this may be further confused by uncertainty as to expertise. For example, valuable as the direct observations of a teacher on a general practitioner may be, whether to ask him or her to express a firm opinion on whether a child should be placed on a register may depend upon that individual's general knowledge of child abuse. In short, the contribution that each makes to the discussion of a child-abuse case should be related to their particular area of expertise but is too often inappropriately linked to perceived status. Difficulties may be further compounded when the purpose and status of the conference itself is inadequately understood by those present. The DHSS *Working Together* is unambiguous in its recent guidance:

The result of the discussions are recommendations to individual agencies for action. While the decision to implement the recommendations must rest with the individual agency concerned, any deviation from them should not be made, except in an emergency, without informing other agencies through the key worker (DHSS 1988b, p.28).

Yet it is easy to see (Hallett and Stevenson 1980) that the range and nature of decisions recommended during the case conference, from registration and care proceedings, to minor interventions in the family, may lead to difficulties in the minds of those present about their agency role. In particular, resentment at the perceived and actual power of the social services departments may be felt when the extent of their legal responsibility is not fully grasped and when their personnel appears also to dominate the proceedings numerically. Perhaps it would be more accurate to suggest that there is considerable ambivalence about the role of social services departments, in which relief at not having to carry the ultimate responsibility mingles with anger when decisions appear to be 'fixed' beforehand or when they run counter to the view of those present.

Role identifications

It is commonplace to stress the need for workers to understand each other's roles. Thus we shall better appreciate what it is reasonable to expect another professional to do or not to do. However, that has little bearing on one of the most central difficulties which arises in multi-disciplinary work, namely, the effect which role definition has upon the attitudes and feelings of the workers involved. This has a number of components. First, workers in child protection have had different socialising experiences in training and subsequently with regard to involvement with clients or patients. Barristers 'win some and lose some'; they are trained to present as good a case as possible for their clients, but are not expected to grieve over an unsuccessful outcome (whether they do or not is another matter). This stance, required in the role, and the difficulty it gives rise to in interdisciplinary working, is well illustrated in the Cleveland story. The social services director, Mike Bishop, reported in *Social Work Today* (7 July 1988) his pain and incredulity at learning that the lawyers in the case had a bet on which of them could make a witness say 'hippopotamus' while giving evidence.

Some would argue that a fair measure of professional training of doctors and nurses fosters the denial of involvement rather than its acknowledgement and constructive use. Workers in training in child protection need to confront a paradox: the role requires involvement if appropriate sympathy and empathy is to be offered; yet it also requires detachment if one is not to be sucked into the vortex of the clients' troubles (perhaps drowning with them) or to collude with them through an inappropriate identification.

In work involving close human interaction, the role ascribed takes on an emotional as well as an intellectual significance. In particular, the closer the role is to those in family life, the more emotionally charged it becomes. Hence, for example, the importance of support to nurses on children's wards, apparently lacking in the Cleveland episode. Furthermore, whether through initial personal motivation or the effect of the role definition ascribed, the parties involved may tend to identify with particular family members. The inquiries illustrate this: 'mothering the mother' was an example given in the previous chapter. However, another earlier example relates to the involvement of the Probation Service in child protection. Perhaps many social workers in the Probation Service could just as easily have entered other forms of social work. Yet they are socialised into a proper identification with the needs and problems of the offender. One of the first examples of that leading to difficulties in child-protection work came from the Lisa Godfrey Inquiry (1975) in which the identification of the Probation Officer with the mother apparently led her to ignore the warnings that the mother gave of 'intention to harm' and to take insufficient notice of the child's physical state. More recently in the Tyra Henry case, the role of the Probation Service in protecting Tyra from her violent father seemed weak: aspects of it were sharply criticised in the report. In these examples, the role involves identification with a person in the family.

In the case of the police, the emotional investment may be in the role as investigator of a crime, rather than as a helper. That is perfectly proper and inescapable in police work. However, the role of police investigation in child protection, in particular child sexual abuse, is pushing them in a different direction, in which their pursuit of 'the facts' relating to a crime has to be tempered by a range of other considerations in multi-disciplinary work, above all the well-being of the child. One wonders whether police who specialise in this work will be accorded respect by their peers and what effect it will have on their career prospects.

These are but examples of the conflicts and problems which may arise when workers invest in their roles – which is, in itself, a natural and desirable process, provided the goal is socially acceptable. One aim of multi-disciplinary cooperation and related training is to explore the impact of role on the workers' perception of the family and its problems. It is clear, however, that as important as these differing contributions may be, the protection of a child is paramount, morally and professionally.

The difficulties in working this out are hinted at in the recent

DHSS guidance; however, these passages occur specifically in the guidance on child sexual abuse, whereas many inquiries testify to the need for guidance in child-protection work generally.

Social workers, probation officers, doctors and others engaged in the long-term treatment of disturbed relationships in sexually-abusing families need regular supervision and support. Work with these families makes considerable emotional demands and there is a tendency to over-identify with an individual in the family and to be drawn into the collusive behaviour patterns within it. Arrangements to provide for both professional supervision and personal support for fieldworkers should exist in all agencies.

The social services department will need to assess with the greatest care whether to deploy one or more social workers, and whether one social worker can adequately serve the interests of the child, the alleged abuser and other family members (DHSS 1988b, pp.35–7).

Professional and organisational priorities

One of the most significant differences between those who work together in child protection and those in conventional teams, is the extent of the difference which may exist between them in relation to professional and organisational priorities. However, this requires clarification. It should not be used as a defence for the inexcusable. If a child's life is in danger, or he/she is at risk of serious injury or harm, at that time it is everyone's priority. Therefore, for a general practitioner not to attend an initial case conference or for teachers not to devise adequate systems for internal communication in schools, 'is like saying of the *Herald of Free Enterprise* disaster, the staff had a lot of other things to attend to beside the bow doors' (Stevenson 1988a).

There are, however, two important differences between the child-protection task group and a conventional team. First, those involved vary a great deal in the amount of time which they devote to such work. This obviously has a significant effect on experience and expertise which in turn affects what may be described as 'risk awareness'. That was illustrated in the case of Reuben Carthy

(1985) in which the general practitioner's actions were said 'at the very least to lack the essential urgency which child-abuse identification and referral demands' (Carthy 1985, p.32). It also means that those who come together have very different patterns and pace of work. To a general practitioner, for example, whose average consultation time is less than 10 minutes, some child-protection meetings seem interminable. It also presents logistical difficulties for those whose working day is tightly structured around surgeries, ward rounds or classroom teaching. These events, which involve a significant number of people, are bound in one sense to be accorded priority.

However, it is the interaction of these difficulties with the value which the various parties ascribe to the work which on occasion makes them appear insurmountable. In an intensive-care team, it is highly unlikely that any member seriously questions the value of the tasks which are performed in sustaining life. To that end, information on the patient's state is routinely and freely shared. In child-protection work, even if there is general acceptance of the value of protecting children from harm, workers may differ quite fundamentally on what they consider it important to share. One facet of this, of course, concerns confidentiality; but there appears to be a growing inter-professional consensus in this country that this principle should not be used to withhold knowledge significant in the protection of children. (Christopherson, however, shows how localised this feeling is in Chapter 4.) More important, therefore, may be the knowledge and understanding of the subject which participants bring to inter-professional encounters and in some instances the theoretical framework which they espouse, which affects the weight they give to particular factors. Linked to this is the value ascribed to the act of sharing and discussing. The education and training of the professionals involved has so far placed little priority upon talking to others about the patient or client. Yet it is a matter of common observation (and often some resentment) that most do spend a substantial time on that activity. If that is not counted as 'real work' and the priority accorded to it is low, there is a fundamental problem of cooperation. That is not to suggest that all such time spent is necessary or profitable!

The extent to which cooperation is perceived as mutually beneficial and in what ways

Much of the discussion of cooperation has taken place on the moral high ground, with an underlying assumption that, if we only understood its importance, our concern to protect children will ensure that it happens. This would ensure 'mutual benefit'. One would like to believe that this will be so in specific situations when a child is at grave risk. However, real life is more complex and less direct; judgements have to be made as to the extent of the risk; meetings have to take place to plan and to discuss intervention; the exhortations to cooperate do not relate only to field-level personnel directly involved. The Cleveland Report in particular, because of its focus, lays heavy emphasis on the need for multi-disciplinary work at the higher echelons. It is therefore important to be realistic about the mutual benefits which the workers concerned may derive.

There is an extensive sociological literature on coordination and cooperation between agencies. It has been pointed out that 'mandated cooperation' of the kind we now see in child-protection work arises when voluntary effort is not good enough. Whetten (1982) suggests that critical components of a successful mandated relationship are justification of the linkage to those required to implement it as well as certainty of sufficient resources for this. He argues:

If these conditions are not met and an organisation is forced to establish a large number of coordination linkages that are perceived as having little instrumental value in meeting the organisation's objectives, it has been shown that mandated cooperation creates a negative, fatalistic attitude in the organisation's staff that sharply limits its effectiveness (p.18).

There are serious, even critical, problems for those in the British welfare structure who are thus mandated; paradoxically, at a time when the former condition, of instrumental value, seems more widely accepted than ever before, the straitened resources of the public sector, notably in certain parts of the country, such as London, may lead to despair and cynicism. For greater cooperation to be a reality some increase in resources is a prerequisite. For example, the simple (yet seemingly intractable) problem of adequate secretarial resources for case-conference minutes recurs again and again in the inquiries. At a deeper level, the energy and commitment to multi-disciplinary work, which has innovative and challenging possibilities, will diminish when bombardment and staff shortages grind workers down. Evidence given by NALGO to the Kimberley Carlile Inquiry painted a grimly accurate picture of the state of Greenwich Social Services at the time of the tragedy – a picture which is not fully conveyed in the report itself. Many of the inquiry reports have tended to avoid the contextual information which is vitally important in understanding how a specific situation was handled. One report (on Paul Brown) succeeded in conveying vividly the deplorable conditions under which Wirral Social Services were working.

Motivation to cooperate, therefore, is affected by the morale of workers, in part associated with resourcing. However, it is also important that workers at different levels perceive cooperative initiatives as an activity which is approved of, validated and encouraged by their colleagues and seniors. Such approval needs to be rewarded. For example, it should be a factor taken into account when promotion is considered. The Audit Commission (1986) pointed out that there were few rewards for managers who sought to improve collaboration between health and social services in community care. Indeed, there were even disincentives.

In considering motivation, one should acknowledge the enjoyment, stimulation and challenge which is experienced by some who embark on improved collaborative activity. It is easy to present these matters only as problematic. They are, but they also afford legitimate opportunities for enhanced professional satisfaction.

The dynamics of case conferences

Much of the preceding discussion bears on the dynamics of case conferences and in the last section we shall explore the single most important factor in those dynamics – the attitudes of the participants to family life and to child abuse. However, conferences merit some particular attention in any discussion of multi-disciplinary work. They are the forum in which highly significant encounters take place, in which recommendations and decisions are made which are of crucial importance. Their importance is demonstrated in the scrutiny which they receive when inquiries are held. We cannot reiterate the matters discussed in an earlier publication (Hallett and Stevenson 1980), as the focus here is mainly upon one element – that of chairing conferences. We were among the first to stress the skill needed in chairing them and this is now widely accepted; indeed recent DHSS guidance (1988a) lists 9 duties of the chair, who should be a senior officer in social services or from the NSPCC and without direct involvement in the case (p.29). Thus, the need for a degree of neutrality and objectivity in the role is emphasised. However, it has to be said that such impartiality is not easy to achieve, nor is it easy for others to believe in it. Unlike ACPCs, it would be impracticable to find persons outside the multi-disciplinary work group who could chair them. The difficulties of the role therefore must be explored in training. The literature broadly agrees on the function of case conferences (Hallett and Stevenson 1980; Jones *et al*. 1987; DHSS 1988a). Much emphasis is placed on their instrumental functions, such as 'coordinating intervention'. However, Jones *et al* refer to their function in relief of individual stress; Hallett and Stevenson suggest a similar purpose: 'to share and sometimes to defuse the anxiety which is inevitably felt by those most respon-sible and accountable' (p.64). Important as clarification of profes-sional and administrative purposes is, neglect of the expressive or emotional component in such groups, especially by the chair, can have a negative effect on the process.

One of the issues which has been little discussed is the manner in which the 'feeling component' in conferences should be managed. Observation of conferences suggests that it is rare for that to be explored with any openness, even if it is noted. Clearly, such exploration would only be justified when the primary task of the conference is hindered by the particular feelings which have been aroused. Furthermore, those who chair are not authorised to probe deeply into the personal reactions of members. However, there are occasions when a modest and light acknowledgement by the chair of the strength and nature of feelings which are present in the group is proper and helpful. For example, to comment on the fact that a member does not look pleased, or looks worried following another's remark, may enable a valuable contribution to be made, exposing an important difference of perception or opinion. Similarly, in some cases, such as those involving grosser forms of sexual abuse, it may be a relief to the group, and hence free members to contribute more effectively, if the feelings that this has engendered are acknowledged and legitimated. Training courses for conference chairs are mushrooming; it is to be hoped that this dimension of their work will be given due weight.

Examination of the conference process as described in some of the inquiries suggests that the task of avoiding group collusion is of great importance. It is possible to demonstrate in experimental conditions that in many matters 'several heads are better than one'; a game used in training, for example, will show that a small group reaches more accurate answers to questions on the Highway Code than the individuals alone within it. However, such games do not simulate accurately the case-conference situation, in which anxiety is high, significant decisions have to be made quickly and in which the information to be shared is not all 'hard' or readily checked as correct or incorrect. Essentially, conferences are about making judgements and in this resemble the situation described by Janis (1968) during the events which led up to the Bay of Pigs disaster. In this, it is suggested a group of intelligent, well-informed politicians and military men convinced themselves of the need of a course of action which was to prove disastrous.

Thus it would seem that a chair might have to be most vigilant in situations in which there appeared to be little inter-disciplinary conflict and in which members appeared fired with enthusiasm for a particular course of action. 'Standing apart' is indeed difficult at such times.

The skills of chairing in the next few years will be especially taxed by three issues currently receiving much attention. The first concerns child sexual abuse. It seems to be generally agreed that conferences focused upon this do create particular problems. There are a number of reasons for this. Firstly, the strong feelings aroused by this subject are very difficult to handle. Mechanisms of denial, well recognised in earlier years in matters of physical injury, are once again much in evidence. An element of voyeurism, even excitement, will sometimes also be present, probably accompanied by guilt. Secondly, the evidential aspects of this are more complex than in child abuse generally. Because concrete physical signs are often not available, the process of assessing child and family becomes a minefield, a matter to which we return in the last section. Thirdly, the feelings of men and women in the conference may differ; certainly, strongly-held views about gender roles and male oppression are never far below the surface when child sexual abuse is under discussion in a group of professionals. The strain which this imposes on the chair is considerable.

A second element, currently receiving much attention, concerns the attitudes and feeling aroused when the family under consideration is black. We shall later consider this in more general terms; in the conference, reserve and diffidence, to which we referred earlier and which characterises so much of the discussion about feelings can become almost paralysing. Among the more sophisticated, fears of being racist, of attributing inappropriately certain behaviour to cultural origins can result in tense passivity or what I have described elsewhere as 'white liberal immobilisation' (Stevenson 1988a). The clash between those adopting that stance and those who are less aware of the pitfalls can be painful and difficult to handle. Again, the role of the chair is vital but stressful.

The third matter about which one foresees much debate concerns the presence of parents at conferences. We noted earlier the latest guidance from the DHSS on this matter. The shift of emphasis from the draft guidance will be welcomed by many. Research and accounts of experiments have been reassuring (see, for example, McGloin and Turnbull 1986; Rousiaux 1984). However, there is no doubt that many of those who chair conferences are anxious about the implications of this, perceiving rightly, that most of the responsibility for ensuring that the process works well will fall upon them. There are a number of grounds for concern in the DHSS guidance, which lead one to wonder whether the implications of their recommendation had been properly thought through.

The guidance includes the following point:

A case conference is an inter-professional meeting but on occasion it may wish to invite a non-professional who is working with the child or family, for example, foster parents or volunteer workers. In this event, the key worker or the professional not closely involved with the non-professional should undertake to brief him or her beforehand about the purpose of the conference, the duty of confidentiality and the primacy of the child's interest over that of the parents if a conflict of interest arises. (DHSS 1988b, p.28)

Whatever the merits of this suggestion, there is no doubt that the inclusion of parents at conferences alters the character of the conference. Can it still be regarded as an inter-professional meeting?

On parental attendance, the guidance advises that parents are to be invited to attend 'where practicable' part, or, if appropriate, 'the whole of conferences, unless in the view of the chairman [sic] of the conference their presence will preclude a full and proper consideration of the child's interests' (pp. 29–30). It takes little imagination to predict the difficulties which will arise in making that judgement, especially when the views of the professionals involved on the general principle itself will vary considerably.

It is regrettable that the matter of parental attendance in cases of suspected child sexual abuse is not specifically referred to in the guidance. One cannot ignore the particular difficulties which this raises. For example, the difficulties which a man may have in speaking openly in front of a group of strange people (and his partner) about the details of his alleged sexual activities are likely to be considerable. Indeed, one might go so far as to say that his willingness to speak might be unhealthy, given the social taboos which exist. It is clear that this is not a matter which can be left to a series of ad hoc discussions. It will be an early task of the ACPS to formulate some more detailed guidelines for chairs. As important will be training in the management of actual situations; in the end, this procedure will be judged not on lofty principle but on how all concerned, families and other professionals, feel about the usefulness of the experience. It is all too easy to see how such encounters could be humiliating, painful and frightening for the parents if not handled well. Indeed, even when they are, professionals must expect certain parents to experience them as negative. This is not to suggest that the underlying principle of greater parental participation is not to be warmly welcomed, simply to stress the need for a move from principle to sensitive practice.

In singling out three topical matters, concerning child sexual abuse, race and parental participation, it is not intended to elevate these above other conference matters which require chairing skills, in which, in general, professionals have received little training. It is hard to overestimate the importance of this role; we are only just beginning to devise training programmes which will adequately help to equip those who perform this onerous task.

Family life: attitudes and beliefs

In this concluding section, we come to what many would consider as the nub of successful inter-disciplinary work. The point of the activity is that different knowledge and perspectives of the individual and family functioning should be shared in order to provide a fuller picture on which intervention can be based. The image is of a jigsaw; when the pieces fit, it is satisfying. Unfortunately, the reality of child-protection work is often much less so. Pieces of the jigsaw are missing or apparently do not fit. Sometimes they seem even to have been taken from another jigsaw altogether.

There are two central difficulties, both concerning the nature of child-protection work although they are by no means exclusive to it. Firstly, the amount of 'hard' information (injuries, etc.) which can be shared by the participants is relatively small in comparison with the 'soft' information concerning the family's behaviour and attitudes. This second type of information is processed and filtered by the workers, and often noted in the course of separate encounters with families. It cannot be presented objectively, although efforts may be made to do so. Workers are all affected by values and assumptions as to what constitutes healthy or unhealthy family life. (It should be added, however, that even so-called 'hard' information is subject to such filtering, as Abercombie (1980) showed in a fascinating analysis of medical students' comments on X-rays.)

Secondly, such inter-disciplinary discussion often leads to the question – 'what is to be done with the child?'. Hence, it has an intensity and an urgency; it evokes powerful feelings about what is best for children, which we considered at length in the preceding chapter.

This makes more complex and problematic a process which is anyway not simple. The different professions and occupations, and within these numerous sub-groupings, have been trained to look at individuals or families in particular ways and to lay emphasis on particular facets. Those who do not work in close teams may not even be aware of the reason for the interest which workers show in certain aspects of behaviour.

The extent to which our perceptions of child abuse are affected by our views of family life is strikingly illustrated by research studies cited by Hallett (forthcoming) in a discussion on the knowledge base of research in child abuse. She points out that the impact of social class, ethnicity and gender have been shown to be important in identifying child abuse. For example:

O'Toole, Turbett and Nalepka 1983 used an experimental design to study the influences of socio-economic status, ethnicity and level of injury on physicians' and nurses' recognition and reporting of child abuse in the USA. Physicians' judgements were affected by all three variables while nurses were affected by the level of injury alone and not by socio-economic status or ethnicity.

Dingwall, Eekelaar and Murray 1983 studied these processes at work in three local authorities in England. They found that casualty officers' suspicions of child abuse were based on social assessments of the family rather than the specific nature of the child's injuries.

As many have argued (for example Dingwall *et al.* 1983; Parton 1985a), this process extends into the action taken, certain groups being more readily identified as in need of social surveillance than others.

However, an overreadiness to identify child abuse in some kinds of family and to deny it in others is but part of that difficulty. Whatever the class or ethnic background of the family under consideration, workers have to relate their assessment to their view of what constitutes sound or 'good enough' family life. This is in part derived from personal experience, although it has been suggested that the effect of working experience plays its part too. Giavannoni and Becerra (1979) for example, found that social workers were inclined to accept 'lower' domestic standards than the general public. The cases of Malcolm Page and Lucie Gates, discussed in the previous chapter, both the subject of inquiries, raise that question rather sharply.

Multi-disciplinary work involves discussion of 'the bottom line', below which workers believe a family cannot function without state intervention. There may be sincerely-held differences of opinion in relation to the wide range of behaviours defined as child abuse. (An obvious example concerns corporal punishment of young and school-age children.) Yet it is a matter of fact that everyone has such a 'bottom line'. It is, therefore, of particular importance how these normative values and beliefs are affected by the notion of cultural relativism. This term, which at present is more often related to race, although it is equally significant in social class, suggests that 'all cultures are equally valid ways of formulating relationships between human beings . . .'. One can move from that to say that 'members of one culture have no right to criticise members of another by imparting their own standards of judgement' (Dingwall and Eekelaar 1984, p.82). Thus, although 'moral character is . . . central to decision-making in child abuse . . . it is possible to avoid making direct moral judgements by resorting to cultural relativism' (p.80).

I have suggested elsewhere (Stevenson 1988a) that conflict between professionals over cultural relativism may arise in three ways. Firstly, they may vary in their awareness of the significance of cultural differences. Secondly, they may differ in their views as to the extent to which certain behaviour is normal in a particular culture. Thirdly, they may differ as to what weight should be given to these cultural variations in the decisions that are made. In the first and second of these, much depends on the emphasis given in training and, in particular, whether social factors were perceived as important. Lying between the first and second is the dangerous ground of stereotyping, in which a 'little learning' is indeed dangerous. It is offensive not simply because the attributes may be inappropriately attached to a certain cultural group, but because such generalisations do an injustice to the variation and distinctiveness of particular families within that group. It is like using a telescope when a microscope may be required. An unusual and interesting example of stereotypical assumptions is suggested in the Tyra Henry Report. Tyra's grandmother, an Afro-Carribean, was asked to care for Tyra. The Report, noting the way Mrs Henry was described in the records, comments:

We believe that the assumption that Beatrice Henry would cope in the circumstances we have outlined was rooted in the perception of her as a type rather than as an individual. There is an ever-present danger in social work (and not only there) of believing that the poor are so accustomed to poverty that they can be expected to get by in conditions which no middle class family would be expected to tolerate. There is also a 'positive', but nevertheless false, stereotype in white British society of the Afro-Caribbean mother figure as endlessly resourceful, able to cope in great adversity, essentially unsinkable. In it are both a genuine recognition of the endurance of Afro-Caribbean peoples in conditions of great hardship and an evasive and guilty recognition that disproportionately many such people live in poverty in modern Britain. We do not suppose for a second that anybody concerned with social services in Lambeth would have taken a conscious decision that a lower standard of social support was more appropriate for poor black clients than for others, but we do think that it may have been an unarticulated and unconscious sense that a woman like Beatrice Henry would find a way of coping, no matter what, that underlay the neglect of Area 5 social services to make adequate provision for her taking responsibility for Tyra (Henry 1987, pp.108–9).

This is a more subtle and convincing analysis of the problem than one usually finds.

The third difficulty, the weight to be given to such factors, raises an issue not simply of awareness but of philosophy. The question of the rights of different cultural groups to live as they will has to be addressed and answered by individual workers and their agencies. I have suggested that:

. . . conflict does not usually arise in relation to the actual incidents of child abuse. It is only rarely that the child-rearing practices of a particular group offends fundamentally against the prevailing norms and values of our society to a point when someone believes a child's well-being is seriously endangered. If such situations exist, then it can reasonably be argued that cultural relativism is not an acceptable justification. What is quite common, however, is that aspects of the family functioning, which may be felt to bear on child abuse but are not a direct cause of it, may be unacceptable to some of the participants discussing the case. A frequent example concerns marital roles; in various cultural groups in the country, white or black, there are traditions of female subservience which some regard as oppressive. The extent to which that situation is accepted or to which intervention is designed to change it becomes, therefore, problematic. These related issues may influence the attitudes of professionals in reaching a judgement about the future; for example whether to remove children from the parents or to return them (Stevenson 1988a).

An example which many would find distressing concerns female circumcision, which now is against the law in this country. Even were it not so, it might raise agonising dilemmas for some workers who knew that it was likely to take place. Here, values about gender and race might be in head-on collision.

It would seem impossible for workers in child protection to adopt an extreme stance of 'cultural relativism'; whether social workers in the local authority or other public servants, they implicitly accept that the upbringing and treatment of children has to take place within the broad framework of our social norms and conventions, although these are subject to wide variations: Dingwall and Eekelaar (1984) have expressed this well:

Just as we regard it as acceptable for a liberal state to ban certains forms of sexual or racial discrimination, trading freedom of speech, association, or contract against the rights of certain individuals or groups to enjoy access to the society on equal terms, so it is justifiable to prohibit certain forms of parental behaviour so that their children are not avoidably deprived of physical, moral, or emotional conditions to an extent that would have a permanent adverse effect on their chances.

The practical problem is that of designing social institutions capable of enforcing children's rights under the equality principle without degenerating into a moral tyranny (p.109).

They continue:

. . . the present system is reasonably successful in these terms. Designed in one normative climate, it has adapted to another. Enforcement workers are tied by a set of cultural and organisational checks and balances in such a way as to inhibit their intervention in the absence of strong counter-pressures (p.109).

However, such a position places a very heavy moral and professional responsibility on workers to exercise their 'best judgement' on these matters. In particular, they will need to scrutinise their own individual, cultural and class assumptions about what is good and bad in family life in order to determine what for them can be jettisoned as non-essential and what is, in their view, central to a child's physical, social and emotional health. In the process, much regarded as axiomatic may be challenged. More openness about our normative assumptions is essential and local training initiatives should have this high on the agenda.

We conclude this section with some reflections on the Cleveland episode. Social attitudes to child sexual abuse are ambivalent and confused. Individual workers in this field have had little clarification or support from the society which they serve. That aspect of the inquiry, which may eventually come to be regarded as the most important, concerned the handling of the situation once suspicion was aroused. The blaze of publicity surrounding the key figures in the debacle has left in shadow the numerous social workers, police and others, such as nurses, who were involved at ground level (where were the teachers, by the way?). We know little of their feelings about the events and the actions which they were required to take. It is frighteningly evident that they could not control or even affect the tide of events and it is unclear how far they would have wished to do so. This has been sensitively discussed by John Chant, an assessor to the Inquiry.

Mr Chant acknowledged there was a fundamental problem in people accepting the reality of such abuse. 'You have to ask yourself how social workers could respond by bringing so many children into care without feeling able to challenge the diagnosis. It wasn't just the usual problem of how you say "no" to the consultant. Social workers were concerned to face the reality of sexual abuse having occurred. They sought to deal with this by suspending disbelief – they adopted the view that you could not be sure who was abusing or not. Once they did, they de-skilled themselves.' (*Social Work Today*, 1988)

What is clear is that a group of concerned workers had no wider framework of values, policy or practice to call upon in their hour of need. Central government, professional peers, informed public opinion were not available to offer openly an alternative view to that of the Cleveland management – that children suspected of being sexually abused must be removed forthwith from their families.

Multi-disciplinary work in child protection, therefore, does not take place in a kind of professional vacuum. Workers are vulnerable to the push and pull of external forces, often mediated through employing agencies. The burden is a heavy one; it is therefore of the utmost importance that the support given is practical, sensitive and appropriate. There are three elements in such support: firstly, shared accountability for decisions taken – a point usefully stressed in the guidance to senior nurses (DHSS 1988c); secondly, proper intra-agency arrangements for case discussion, to address the issues raised in this chapter; thirdly, a range of inter-professional training initiatives which will address both child abuse and multi-disciplinary work as related but separate matters and which explore the emotional as well as intellectual aspects of such work. This is a highly skilled enterprise.

The above will seem like windy rhetoric unless there is a national commitment to better resourcing of the public services upon whom this burden falls. Resources alone will not suffice, but they are an indispensable prerequisite.

Bibliography

Abercrombie, M. (1980) *The Anatomy of Judgement*, Harmondsworth: Penguin.

Aitchison, D. (1987) Letter to *The Guardian*, 11 August.

Ambache, J. (1988) 'The very harsh realities of tackling child abuse', *Community Care*, no. 705, March, p.12.

Asogwa, S.E. (1986) 'Sociomedical aspects of child labor in Nigeria', *Journal of Occupational Medicine* 28: pp.46–8.

Association of Directors of Social Services (1987) *Press Release*, ADSS, July.

Association of Directors of Social Work (1988) *Scottish Child Abuse Statistics*, ADSW Social Services Research Group.

Audit Commission (1987) *Making a reality of Community Care*, London: HMSO.

Baher, E., Hyman, C., Jones, C., Jones, R., Kerr, A. and Mitchell, R. (1976) *At Risk: An Account of the Work of the Battered Child Research Department*, London: Routledge and Kegan Paul.

Baker, A.W. and Duncan, S.P. (1985) 'Child sexual abuse: a study of prevalence in Great Britain', *Child Abuse and Neglect* 9, pp.457–67.

Baldwin, J.A. and Oliver, J.E. (1975) 'Epidemiology and family characteristics of severely-abused children', *British Journal of Social and Preventive Medicine* 29, pp.205–21.

Ball, C., Harris, G., Roberts, G. and Vernon, S. (1988) *The Law Report: Teaching and Assessment of Law in Social Work Education*, paper 4.1, London: Central Council, Education and Training in Social Work.

Baneke, J. (1983) 'The Dutch approach to child abuse', in J. Leavitt (ed.) *Child Abuse and Neglect: Research and Innovation*, NATO AS1 Series, The Hague: Martinus Nijhoff.

Barn (1985) *Barnens Ratte Ar I Fara*, Stockholm: Radda Barnen.

BBC (1986a) *Childwatch: A Briefing*, London: BBC.

BBC (1986b) *Who would hurt a child?*, London: BBC.

Blum, J. (1978) *Pseudoscience and Mental Ability: The Origins and Fallacies of the IQ Controversy*, New York: Monthly Review Press.

Bottoms, A.E. (1977) 'Reflections on the renaissance of dangerousness', *Howard Journal of Penology and Crime Prevention*, XVI: 2, pp.70–96.

Bottoms, A.E. (1980) 'An introduction to the coming crisis', in A.E. Bottoms and R.H. Preston (eds.) *The Coming Penal Crisis*, Edinburgh: Scottish Academic Press.

Bradshaw, J. (1972) 'The concept of social need', *New Society* 19, p.496.

British Association of Social Workers (1982) *Child Abuse Inquiries*, Birmingham: BASW.

Caffo, E. (1983) 'The importance of early intervention in child abuse: the Italian experience', in J. Leavitt (ed.) *Child Abuse and Neglect: Research and Innovation*, NATO AS1 series, The Hague: Martinus Nijhoff.

Campbell, B. (1987) 'The skeleton in the family's cupboard', *New Society*, 31 July.

Caplin, S. (1987) Letter to *The Guardian*, 14 August.

Challis, D. and Ferlie, E. (1986) 'Changing patterns of fieldwork organisation: The headquarters view', *British Journal of Social Work*, Vol. 16, No.2.

Childline (1987) *Childline: The First Year*, London: Childline.

Child Migrants Trust (1988), *Annual Report*, Nottingham.

Childwatch (1986) *Unestablished Manuscript*, London: Childwatch.

Christopherson, R.J. (1983) 'Public perception of child abuse and the need for intervention: are professionals seen as abusive?', in *Child Abuse and Neglect* Vol.7, No.4, pp.435–42.

Christopherson, R.J. (1981) 'Two approaches to the handling of child abuse: a comparison of the English and the Dutch Systems', *Child Abuse and Neglect*, Vol.5, No.4, pp.369–73.

Christopherson, R.J. (1986) 'No children's Gulags', *Community Care*.

Christopherson, R.J. (1988) *Intracultural Variations in Perception of Child Abuse and Neglect, an Examination of Public Attitudes in Great Britain and the Netherlands*, Paper to the VII International Congress on Child Abuse and Neglect, Rio de Janeiro.

CIBA Foundation (1984) *Child Sexual Abuse Within the Family*, London: Tavistock Publications.

Cohen, S. (1985) *Visions of Social Control: Crime, Punishment and Classification*, Oxford: Polity Press.

Cohn, A.H. (1983) 'The prevention of child abuse: what do we know about what works?', in J. Leavitt (ed.) *Child Abuse and Neglect: Research and Innovation*, The Hague: Martinus Nijhoff.

Community Care (1982) 'Child death: council wants staff disciplined', *Community Care*, 18 November, p.2.

Corby, B. (1987) *Working with Child Abuse*, Milton Keynes: Open University Press.

Costa, J.J. and Nelson, G.K. (1978) *Child Abuse and Neglect: Legislation, Reporting and Prevention*, Lexington, Mass.: Lexington Books.

Court of Appeal (1988) *R. v. Exeter Juvenile Court ex parte H, R. v. Waltham Forest Juvenile Court ex parte B.* Queens Bench Division, *The Times* Law Report, 19 February.

Court Committee (1976) *Fit for the Future. Report of the Select Committee on Child Health Services*, Cmnd 6684, London: HMSO.

Creighton, S. 'Child abuse research', *Social Services Research*, Vol.16, No.3, pp.1–7, University of Birmingham, Department of Social Administration.

Creighton, S. (1976) 'Child victims of physical abuse', *3rd Report on the Findings of NSPCC Special Unit Registers*. London: NSPCC.

Creighton, S. (1984a) *Trends in Child Abuse*, London: NSPCC.

Creighton, S. (1984b) 'The characteristics of the sexually abused child and its family', *Research Briefing No.2*, London: NSPCC.

Creighton, S. (1984c) 'Incidence of child physical abuse', *Information Briefing No.4*, London: NSPCC.

Creighton, S. (1985a) *Child Abuse in 1983 and 1984: Initial Findings from NSPCC Register Research*, London: NSPCC.

Creighton, S. (1985b) 'Child abuse deaths', *Information Briefing No.5*, London: NSPCC.

Creighton, S. (1986) 'Child Abuse in 1985', *Initial Findings from NSPCC Register Research*, London: NSPCC.

Creighton, S. (1987a) 'Child abuse in 1986', *Initial Findings from NSPCC Register Research*, London: NSPCC.

Creighton, S. (1987b) 'Child Abuse in 1986', *Social Services Research*, Vol.16, No.3, University of Birmingham, Department of Social Administration.

Creighton, S. and Owtram, P. (1977) *Child Victims of Physical Abuse: A Report on the Findings of NSPCC Special Unit Registers*, London: NSPCC.

Croft, J. (1978) 'Research in Criminal Justice', *Home Office Research Study No.44*, London: HMSO.

Dale, P., Davies, M., Morrison, T. and Waters, J. (1986) *Dangerous Families: Assessment and the Treatment of Child Abuse*, London: Tavistock.

Department of Health and Social Security (1968) *Report of the Committee on Local Authority and all the Personal Social Services*, Cmnd 3703, London: HMSO.

Department of Health and Social Security (1970) *The Battered Baby*, London: DHSS.

Department of Health and Social Security (1974) *Non Accidental Injury to Children*, LASSL (74) 13; CMO (74) 8, London: DHSS.

Department of Health and Social Security (1980b) *The Report of the Committee of Inquiry into the Case of Paul Steven Brown*, Cmnd 8107, London: HMSO.

Department of Health and Social Security (1980a) *Child Abuse: Central Register Systems*. LASSL (80) 4, London: HMSO.

Department of Health and Social Security (1980b) *The Report of the Committee of Inquiry into the Case of Paul Steven Brown*, Cmnd 8107, London: HMSO.

Department of Health and Social Security (1982) *Child Abuse: A Study of Inquiry Reports 1973–81*, London: HMSO.

Department of Health and Social Security (1985a) *Child Abuse Inquiries*, London: HMSO.

Department of Health and Social Security (1985b) *Social Work Decisions in Child Care*, London: HMSO.

Department of Health and Social Security (1986) *Child Abuse – Working Together. A Draft Guide to Arrangements for Inter-agency Cooperation for the Protection of Children*, London: HMSO.

Department of Health and Social Security (1987) (Home Office, Lord Chancellor's Department, Department of Education and Science, Welsh Office, Scottish Office) *The Law on Child Care and Family Services*, Cmnd 62, London: HMSO.

Department of Health and Social Security and Welsh Office (1988a and b) *Working Together: A Guide to Inter-agency Cooperation for the Protection of Children from Abuse*, London: HMSO.

Department of Health and Social Security (1988c) *Child Protection Guidance for Senior Nurses, Health Visitors and Midwives*, DHSS, HMSO.

Department of Health and Social Security (1988d) *Diagnosis of Child Sexual Abuse: Guidance for Doctors*, London: HMSO.

Department of Transport (1987) *MV Herald of Free Enterprise: Report of Court No. 8074. A Formal Investigation*, London: HMSO.

Deutsch, E. (1984) 'The medically neglected child (West Germany)' in A. Carmi and H. Zimrin (eds.) *Child Abuse*, Berlin: Springer-Verlag.

Dingwall, R. (1986a) 'The Jasmine Beckford Affair', *Modern Law Review*, Vol.49, No.4, pp.489–507.

Dingwall, R. (1986b) 'Some observations on divorce mediation in Britain and the United States', *Mediation Quarterly* 11, pp.5–24.

Dingwall, R., Eekelaar, J. and Murray, T. (1983) *The Protection of Children: State Intervention and Family Life*, Oxford: Blackwell.

Dingwall, R. and Eekelaar, J. (1984) 'Rethinking child protection', in M. Freeman (ed.) *The State, The Law and The Family*, London: Tavistock.

Doek, J. and Slagter, S. (1979) *Child Care and Protection in the Netherlands*, Utrecht: Werlverbank Integratie Jeugdwelzijnsuerk Nederland.

Eaton, L. (1988) 'Jobs crisis blamed on inquiry', *Social Work Today* 14, 6 January.

Eisikovits, Z. and Sagi, A. (1984) 'Abusing children's development potential. The case of moral development', in A. Carmi and H. Zimrin (eds.) *Child Abuse*, Berlin: Springer-Verlag.

Family Rights Group (1986) *FRG's Response to the DHSS Consultation Paper Child Abuse – Working Together*, London: Family Rights Group.

Finkelhor, D. (1979) *Sexually Victimised Children*, New York: Free Press.

Finkelhor, D. (ed.) (1986) *A Sourcebook on Child Sexual Abuse*, Beverley Hills: Sage.

Finkelhor, D. and Baron (1986) 'High risk children', in D. Finkelhor (ed.), *A Sourcebook on Child Sexual Abuse*, Beverley Hills: Sage.

Fischer, J. (1973) 'Is casework effective?' *Social Work*, Vol.18, pp.5–20.

Fischer, J. (1978) 'Does anything work?', *Journal of Social Science Research*, Vol.1, pp.215–43.

Floud, J. and Young, W. (1981) *Dangerous and Criminal Justice*, London: Heinemann.

Fogelman, K. (ed.) (1983) *Growing Up in Britain*, London: Macmillan.

Franklin, A.W. (ed.) (1975) *Concerning Child Abuse*, Edinburgh: Churchill Livingstone.

Franklin, R. (ed.) (1987) *The Rights of Children*, Oxford: Blackwell.

Franklin, W. *et al.* (1987) 'Severe asthma due to household pets: a form of child abuse or neglect', *New England and Regional Allergy Proceedings* 8, pp.259–61.

Fraser, R. (1982) *Richard Fraser 1972–77. The Report of an Independent Inquiry*, London Borough of Lambeth, Inner London Education Authority and Lambeth, Southwall and Lewisham Health Authority (Teaching).

Fry, A. (1988a), 'Time to dim the blue light of dramatic intervention', *Social Work Today*, Vol.19, No.44, pp.16–17.

Fry, A. (1988b) 'The trial of working through a nightmare', *Social Work Today* Vol.19, No.44, pp.12–13.

Fuller, R. and Stevenson, O. (1983) *Policies, Programmes and Disadvantage*, London: Heinemann.

Gaylin, W. *et al.* (1978) *Doing Good: The Limits of Benevolence*, New York: Pantheon Books.

Gelles, R.J., (1979a) 'Psychopathology as cause: a critique and reformulation', in D.G. Gil (ed.) *Violence Against Children*.

Gelles, R.J. (1979b) 'The social construction of child abuse', in D.G. Gil (ed.) *Child Abuse and Violence*, New York: AMS Press.

Gelles, R.J. (1980) 'Violence in the family: a review of research in the seventies', *Journal of Marriage and the Family* 42, pp.873–8.

Gelles, R.J. and Straus, M.A. (1987) 'Is violence towards children increasing?' *Journal of Interpersonal Violence*, Vol.2, No.2, pp.212–22.

Gershenson, C.P. (1979) 'Child maltreatment in the federal role', in D.G. Gill (ed.) *Violence Against Children*.

Giarretto, H. (1982) 'A comprehensive child sexual abuse treatment programme', *Child Abuse and Neglect* 6, pp.263–78.

Giavannoni, J.M. and Becerra, R.M. (1979) *Defining Child Abuse*, New York: Free Press.

Gil, D.G. (ed.) (1979a) *Violence Against Children*, Cambridge, Mass: Harvard University Press.

Gil, D.G. (1979b) 'Unravelling child abuse', in D.G. Gill (ed.) *Violence Against Children*.

Gil, D.G. and Noble, J.H. (1979) 'Public knowledge, attitudes and opinions about physical abuse in the United States', in D.G. Gil (ed.) *Violence Against Children*.

Goldstein, H. (1973) *Social Practice: A Unitary Approach*, Columbia, SC: University of South Carolina Press.

Goldstein, J., Freud, A., Solnit, A.J. (1980) *Beyond the Best Interests of the Child*, London: Burnett Books.

Gough, D. (1980 and 1982) Variations in Strathclyde Registrations. Unpublished.

Gough, D. (1988) Personal Communication. Unpublished.

Graham, P., Dingwall, R. and Wolkind, S. (1985) 'Research issues in child abuse', *Social Science and Medicine* 21, pp.1217–28.

Greenland, C. (1987) *Preventing CAN deaths*, London: Tavistock Publications.

Greenland, C. (1978) 'The prediction and management of dangerous behaviour: social policy issues', *International Journal of Law and Psychiatry* 1, pp.205–22.

Greenland, C. (1980a) 'Psychiatry and the prediction of dangerousness', *Journal of Psychiatric Treatment and Evaluation* 2, pp.97–103.

Greenland, C. (1980b) 'Lethal family situations: an international comparison of deaths from child abuse', in E.J. Antony and C. Chiland (eds.) *The Child and His Family*, New York: Wiley.

Greenland, C. (1986a) 'Preventing child abuse and neglect deaths: the identification and management of high risk cases', *Health Visitor* C59, 7 July, pp.205–6.

Greenland, C. (1986b) 'Inquiries into child abuse and neglect (CAN) deaths in the United Kingdom', *British Journal of Criminology* 26, 2 April, pp.164–73.

Greenland, C. (1986c) *Preventing Child Abuse and Neglect Deaths: An International Study of Deaths due to Child Abuse and Neglect*, London and New York: Tavistock.

Griffiths Report (1988) *Community Care: Agenda for Action*, London: HMSO.

The Guardian (1987) 7 August, p.1 and p.32.

The Guardian (1987) 31 August, p.4.

Günçe, G. and Konanç-Onur, E. (1983) 'Child abuse in Turkey', in J. Leavitt (ed.) *Child Abuse and Neglect*.

Hallett, C. and Stevenson, O. (1977) *Case Conferences: A Study of Inter-professional Communication Concerning Children at Risk*, Keele: University of Keele.

Hallett, C. and Stevenson, O. (1980) *Child Abuse: Aspects of Inter-professional Cooperation*, London: Allen and Unwin.

Hallett, C. (forthcoming) 'Research in child abuse: some observations on the knowledge base', *Journal of Reproductive and Infant Psychology*.

Hamilton, J.R. and Freeman, H. (eds.) (1982) *Dangerousness: Psychiatry Assessment and Management* London: Gaskell.

Hennessy, P. (1986) *The Great and the Good: An Inquiry into the British Establishment*, London: Policy Studies Institute.

Hinton, J. (ed.) (1981) *Dangerous Problems of Assessment and Prediction*, London: Allen and Unwin.

Hobbes, C.J. and Wynne, J.M. (1986) 'Buggery in childhood – a common syndrome of child abuse', *The Lancet*, 4 October.

Hobbes, C.J. and Wynne, J.M. (1987) 'Child sexual abuse – an increasing rate of diagnosis', *The Lancet* 10 October.

Holman, R. (1975) 'The place of fostering in social work', *British Journal of Social Work*, Vol.5, No.1.

Horne, M. (1987) *Values of Social Work*, Aldershot: Wildwood House.

House of Commons (1977) *Select Committee on Violence in the Family: Violence to Children: Session*, London: House of Commons.

House of Lords (1978) *D. v. NSPCC*, 1 All England Reports.

House of Lords (1988) *D. v. Berkshire County Council and others*, 1 All England Reports, pp.20–45.

Hulsmann, L.H.C. (1978) 'The Dutch criminal justice system from a comparative legal perspective', In D.C. Fokkema *et al.* (eds.) *Introduction to Dutch Law for Foreign Lawyers*, Klewer: Deventer.

Hutchinson, R. (1986) 'The effect of inquiries into cases of child abuse upon the social work profession', *British Journal of Criminology*, Vol.26, No.2, pp. 178–82.

Jampole, L. and Weber, M.K. (1987) 'An assessment of the behaviour of sexually abused and non-sexually abused children with anatomically correct dolls', *Child Abuse and Neglect* 11, p.2.

Janis, I.L. (1968) *Victims of Group Think: A Psychological Study of Foreign Policy Decisions and Fiascos*, Boston, Mass.: Mifflin Houghton.

Jason, J. *et al.* (1982) 'Epidemiologic differences between sexual and physical child abuse', *Journal of American Medical Association* 247, p.24.

Jay, M. and Doganis, S. (1987) *Battered: The Abuse of Children*, London: Weidenfeld and Nicolson.

Jenkins, J. and Gray, O.P. (1987) 'Changing incidence of non-accidental injury to children in South Glamorgan', *British Medical Journal* 294, p.27.

Jones, D., Pickett, J., Oates, M.R., Barbor, P. (1987) *Understanding Child Abuse*, London: Macmillan.

Kalisch, B.J. (1978) *Child Abuse and Neglect: An Annotated Bibliography*, Westport, Conn.: Greenwood Press.

Kane, R.A. (1975) *Interprofessional Teamwork*, Manpower monograph. No.8., Syracuse University, School of Social Work.

Kempe, C.H., Silverman, F.N., Steele, B.F., Droegmueller, W., Silver, H.K. (1962) 'The battered child syndrome', *Journal of the American Medical Association* 181, pp.17–22.

Kempe, C.H. and Helfer, R.E. (eds.) (1980) *The Battered Child*, 3rd edition, Chicago: University of Chicago Press.

Kempe, C.H. (1980) 'Incest and other forms of sexual abuse', in C.H. Kempe and R.E. Helfer, *The Battered Child*.

Kirschner, R.H. and Stein, R.J. (1985) 'The mistaken diagnosis of child abuse: a form of medical abuse', *American Journal of Diseases of Children* 139, pp.873–5.

Kitzinger, J. (1988) 'Defending innocence: ideologies of childhood', *Feminist Review* 28, Spring, pp.77–87.

Kjönstad, A. (1981) 'Child abuse and neglect: viewed in relation to fundamental principles in a Western social and legal system', *Child Abuse and Neglect*, Vol.5, No.4, pp.421–9.

Koers, A. (1981) *Kindermishandeling*, Rotterdam: Donker.

Korf, J. (1987) Personal Communication. Unpublished.

La Fontaine, J. (1988) *Child Sexual Abuse: An ESRC Research Brief-ing*, London: Economic and Social Research Council.

Langan, M. (1985) 'The unitary approach: a feminist critique', in E. Brook and A. Davis (eds.) *Women and the Family and Social Work*, London: Tavistock.

Lavery, G. (1987) 'The rights of children in care', in R. Franklin (ed.) *The Rights of Children*.

Lealman, G.T., Haigh, D., Phillips, J.M., Stone, J. and Ord-Smith, C. (1983) 'Prediction and prevention of child abuse – an empty hope?', *The Lancet*, 25 June, pp.1423–4.

Leavitt, J. (ed.) *Child Abuse and Neglect: Research and Innovation*, NATO AS1 Services, The Hague: Martinus Nijhoff.

Leulliette, P. (1978) *Les Enfants Martyrs*, Paris: Sevil.

Lipsky, M. (1971) 'Street level bureaucracy and the analysis of urban reform' in *Urban Affairs Quarterly*, Vol.6, No.4, pp.391–409.

Local Authority and Allied Personal Social Services (1968) Report of the Committee, Cmnd 3703, London: HMSO.

Lynch, M. (1978) 'Child abuse: the critical path', in C.M. Lee, *Child Abuse: A Reader and Sourcebook*, Milton Keynes: Open University Press – originally published in *Journal of Maternal and Child Health*, July 1976, pp.25–9.

Lynch, M.A. and Roberts, J. (1977) 'Predicting child abuse: signs of bonding failure in the maternity hospital', *British Medical Journal*, pp.624–6.

Lynch, M.A. and Roberts, J. (1978) 'Early alerting signs', in A.W. Franklin (ed.) *Child Abuse: Prediction, Prevention and Follow-up*, Edinburgh: Churchill Livingstone.

Lynch, M.A. and Roberts, J. (1982) *Consequences of Child Abuse*, New York: Academic Press.

Lynch, M.A., Roberts, M. and Gordon, M. (1976) 'Child abuse: early warning in the maternity hospital', *Development Medicine and Child Neurology* 18, pp.759–66.

Lystad, M.H. (1979) 'Violence at home', in D.G. Gil (ed.) *Violence against children*.

McCotter, D. (1981) *Children in Limbo: An investigation of circum-stances and needs of children in long term care in Western Australia*, Western Australia: Department of Community Welfare.

McGloin, P. and Turnbull, A. (1986) *Parent Participation in Child Abuse Conferences*, London Borough of Greenwich, Director of Social Services.

Main, M. *et al.* (1986) 'Review of 125 children of 6 years of age and under who were sexually abused', in *Child Abuse and Neglect* 10, pp.223–9.

Maluccio, A.N. *et al.* (1986) *Permanency Planning for Children: Concept and Methods*, London and New York: Tavistock Publications.

Markowe, H.L.J. (1988) 'The frequency of child sexual abuse in the UK', *Health Trends*, Vol.20, No.1, pp.2–6. London: HMSO.

Mattinson, J. and Sinclair, I. (1979) *Mate and Stalemate*, Oxford: Basil Blackwell.

Mech, E.V. (1983) 'Out of home placement rates', *Social Services Review*, pp.659–67.

Mitchell, J.C. (1983) 'Case and situation analysis', *Sociological Review* 31, pp.187–211.

Mitchell, R.G. (1975) 'The incidence and nature of child abuse', *Developmental Medicine and Child Neurology* 17, pp.641–4.

Monahan, J. (1981) *The Clinical Prediction of Violent Behaviour*, Rockville, MD: US Department of Health and Human Services.

Morley, J. (1905) *Life of Gladstone*, Vol.i, London: Macmillan. Cited in K.C. Whearre (1955) *Government by committee*, Oxford: Clarendon Press.

Mrazek, P., Lynch, M.A. and Bentovim, A. (1983) 'Sexual abuse of children in the U.K.' in *Child Abuse and Neglect* 7, pp.147–53.

Nagi, S.J. (1977) *Child Maltreatment in the U.S.: A Challenge to Social Institutions*, New York: Columbia University Press.

Nash, C.L. and West, D.J. (1985) 'Sexual molestation of young girls', in D.J. West (ed.) *Sexual Victimisation*, Aldershot: Gower.

National Institute for Social Work (1988) *Residential Care: A Positive Choice. Report of the Independent Review of Residential Care, Chaired by Gillian Wagner*, London: HMSO.

Nelson, B.J. (1978) 'Setting the public agenda: the case of child abuse', in J.V. May and A.B. Wildavsky (eds.) *The Policy Cycle*, Beverley Hills: Sage.

Nelson, B.J. (1986) *Making an Issue of Child Abuse: Political Agenda Setting for Social Problems*, Chicago: University of Chicago Press.

Nelson, S. (1982) *Incest: Fact and Myth*, repr. 1987, Edinburgh: Stramullion Cooperative.

Newberger, E.H. and Hyde, J.N. (1979) 'Child abuse: principles and implications on current paediatric practice', in D.G. Gil (ed.) *Violence against Children*.

Newson, J. (1978) *Seven Years Old in the Home Environment*, Harmondsworth: Penguin.

Newson, J. and Newson, E. (1970) *Four Years Old in an Urban Community*, Harmondsworth: Penguin.

Observer, The (1984) 'Spectre of children Gulags haunts Sweden', *The Observer*, 19 August 1984.

Obstetrics (1948) Joint Committee of the Royal College of Obstetricians and Gynaecologists and the Population Investigation Committee, *Maternity in Britain*, Oxford: Oxford University Press.

Oliver, J.E. *et al.* (1974) *Severely Ill-treated Young Children in North East Wiltshire*, Oxford: Oxford Regional Health Authority.

OPCS (1987) *Monitor: Deaths by Causes*, Ref. DH 2 87/3, London: OPCS.

Osborn, A.F., Butler, N.R. and Morris, T.C. (1984) *The Social Life of Britain's Five-Year-Olds*, London: Routledge and Kegan Paul.

O'Toole, R., Turnbetts, P. and Nalepka, C. (1983) 'Theories of professional knowledge, incidence of child abuse', in D.J. Finkelhor *et al.* (eds.) *The Dark Side of Families*, Beverley Hills: Sage.

Ounsted, C., Oppenheimer, R. and Lindsay, J. (1974) 'Aspects of bonding failure: the psychopathology and psychotherapeutic treatment of families of battered children', *Developmental Medicine and Child Neurology* 16, pp.447–56.

Ounsted, C., Oppenheimer, R. and Lindsay, J. (1975) 'The psychopathology and psychotherapy of families: aspects of bonding failure', in A.W. Franklin (ed.) *Concerning Child Abuse*.

Ounsted, C. and Lynch, M. (1976) 'Family pathology as seen in England', in R.E. Helfer and C.H. Kempe (eds.) *Child Abuse and Neglect: The Family and the Community*, Cambridge, Mass.: Ballinger.

Ounsted, C., Roberts, J.C., Gordon, M. and Milligan, B. (1982) 'The fourth goal of perinatal medicine', *British Medical Journal* 284, pp.879–82.

Packman, J. and Randall, J. (1989) 'Decisions about children at risk', in P. Sills (ed.) *Child Abuse: Challenges for Policy and Practice*, Community Care and London Boroughs Training Committee.

Packman, J., Randall, J. and Jacques, N. (1986) *Who Needs Care?*, Oxford: Basil Blackwell.

Parsloe, P. and Stevenson, O. (1978) *Social Service Teams – the Practitioners' View*, London: HMSO.

Parton, C. (1989, forthcoming) 'Women, gender oppression and child abuse', in *The Violence against Children Study Group. Taking Child Abuse Seriously: Contemporary Issues in Child Protection Theory and Practice*, London: Unwin Hyman.

Parton, C. (1989, forthcoming) Feminist Perspectives on Child Abuse, in *The Violence Against Children Study Group. Taking Child Abuse Seriously*, London: Unwin Hyman.

Parton, N. (1979) 'The Natural History of Child Abuse: a study in social-problem definition', *British Journal of Social Work*, 94, pp.431–51.

Parton, N. (1989, forthcoming) 'The Natural History of Child Abuse, in *The Violence against Children Study Group. Taking Child Abuse Seriously'*, London: Unwin Hyman.

Parton, N. (1985a) *The Politics of Child Abuse*, London: Macmillan.

Parton, N. (1985b) 'Children in care: recent changes and debates', *Critical Social Policy* 13, Summer, pp.107–17.

Parton, N. (1986) 'The Beckford Report: a critical appraisal', *British Journal of Social Work* Vol.16, No.5, pp.511–30.

Peters, S.D. *et al.* (1986) 'Prevalence', in D. Finkelhor (ed.) *A Sourcebook on Child Sexual Abuse*, Beverley Hills: Sage.

Pfohl, S.J. (1977) 'The "Discovery" of Child Abuse', *Social Problems* 24, pp.310–23.

Pincus, A. and Minahan, A. (1973) *Social Work Practice Model and Method*, Stasca 16, FE Peacock.

Platt, A.M. (1969) *The Child Savers*, Chicago: University of Chicago Press.

Pless, *et al.* (1987) 'A reappraisal of the frequency of child abuse seen in paediatric emergency rooms', *Child Abuse and Neglect* 11, pp.193–200.

Potts, D. and Herzberg, S. (1979) *Child Abuse: A Cross-Generational Pattern of Child Rearing?* Paper presented at the Annual Meeting of the Midwest Psychological Association, Chicago.

Prescott, J.W. (1979) 'Deprivation of physical affection as a primary process in the development of physical violence: a cross-cultural perspective', in D.G. Gil (ed.) *Violence Against Children*.

Radbill, S.X. (1978) 'Children in a world of violence: a history of child abuse', in C.H. Kempe and R.E. Helfer (eds.) *The Battered Child*.

Regan, J. (1986) *Incidence of Child Sexual Abuse: Information Briefing No 2 (reviewed)*, London: NSPCC.

Rhodes, G.C. (1975) *Committees of Inquiry*, London: Allen and Unwin.

Richards, M. (1974) *Nonaccidental injury to Children in an Ecological Perspective, NAI to Children*, Proceedings of a Conference held at the DHSS, 19 June, London: HMSO.

Roberts, B. (ed.) (1982) *Abuse in Families: Workbook and Readings* Milton Keynes: Open University Press.

Rousiaux, S.T. (1984) *Parental Attendance at Child Abuse Case Conferences*, Coventry: NSPCC, Special Unit.

Roycroft, B. (1987) *Statement of the President of the Association of Directors of Social Services (To the Cleveland Inquiry)*, Newcastle-on-Tyne: ADSS.

Schene, P. (1987) 'Is child abuse decreasing', *Journal of Interpersonal Violence*, p.2.

Schenker, S. (1978) *Personal Communication*.

Schwartz, R.H., Peary, P. and Mistretta, D. (1986) 'Intoxication of young children with marijuana: a form of amusement for "pot-smoking" teenage girls', *American Journal of the Diseases of Children* 140, p.326.

Sgroi, S.A. (1982) *Handbook of Clinical Intervention in Child Sexual Abuse*, Lexington: Lexington Books.

Shearer, A. (1979) 'Tragedies revisited (1), *Social Work Today*, Vol.10, No.19, pp.12–19.

Shilts, R. (1988) *And the Band Played On: Politics, People and the Aids Epidemic*, Harmondsworth: Penguin.

Smith, S. (1975) *The Battered Child Syndrome*, London: Butterworth.

Social Services Insight (1987) 'Greenwich Inquiry may be held in private', *Social Services Insight*, 22 May, p.3.

Society of Local Authority Chief Executives, Royal Institute of Public Administration (1977) *Ad hoc Inquiries in Local Government*, London: RIPA.

Spencer, M.J. and Dunklee, P. (1986) 'Sexual abuse of boys', *Paediatrics* 78, p.1.

Starr, R.H. (1988) 'Physical abuse of children', in V.B. van Hasselt, A.S. Bellack, R.L. Morrison, and M. Hersen (eds.) *Handbook of Family Violence*, New York: Plenum.

Starr, R.H. (1982) 'A research-based approach to the prediction of child abuse', in R.H. Starr (ed.) *Child Abuse Prediction: Policy Implications*, Cambridge, Mass.: Ballinger.

Starr, R.H. (1988) 'Pre- and Perinatal Risk and Physical Abuse', *Journal of Reproductive and Infant Psychology*, 6, pp.125–38.

Steele, B.F. and Pollock, C.B. (1968) 'A psychiatric study of parents who abuse infants and small children', in C.H. Kempe and R.E. Helfer (eds.) *The Battered Child*.

Steiner, G.Y. (1976) *The Children's Cause*, Washington, DC: Brookings Institution.

Stevenson, O., (forthcoming) *Issues Arising from Inquiries*, BASW.

Stevenson, O. (1980) *Specialisation in Social Service Teams*, London: Allen and Unwin.

Stevenson, O. and Smith, J. (1983) *Report on implementation of Section 56 of the Children Act, 1975.*

Stevenson, O. (1986) 'Implications of recent child care research for future organisation of services', in *Creative Social Work with Families*, London: British Association of Social Workers.

Stevenson, O. (1988a) 'Multi-disciplinary work – where next? *Child Abuse Review*, Vol.2, No.1.

Stevenson, O. (1988b) *What does Training Offer to Inter-professional Work?*, London: NSPCC.

Straus, M.A., Gelles, R.J. and Steinmetz, S.K. (1980) *Behind Closed Doors*, Garden City, NY: Anchor/Doubleday.

Tonkin, B. (1988) 'Doing the Lambeth Work!', *Community Care*, 3 March, pp.20–1.

Topper A.B. and Aldridge, D.J. (1981) 'Incest: intake and investigation' in P.B. Mrazek and C.H. Kempe (eds.) *Sexually Abused Children and the Families*, Oxford: Pergamon.

Townsend, P. (1979) *Poverty in the United Kingdom*, Harmondsworth: Penguin.

Townsend, P. and Davidson, N. (1982) *Inequalities in Health*, Harmondsworth: Penguin.

Toynbee, P. (1985) *Lost Children*, London: Hutchinson.

Tribunals of Inquiry (1966) (Royal Commission on) Cmnd 3121, London: HMSO.

Vann, J. (1971) The Child as a Client of the Social Services Department, *in British Journal of Social Work*, Vol.1, No.2.

Vander Hey and Neff, R.L. (1982) 'Adult-child incest: a review of research and treatment', *Adolescence*, Vol.XVLL, No.68, pp.717–35.

Von Hirsch, A. (1985) *Past or Future Crimes: Deservedness and Dangerousness in the Sentencing of Criminals*, Manchester: Manchester University Press.

Walker, N. (1978) 'Dangerous people', *International Journal of Law and Psychiatry* 1, pp.37–49.

Watt, G.E. and Peters, S.D. (1986) Issues in the definition of child sexual abuse in prevalence research, *Child Abuse and Neglect* 10, pp.231–40.

Webb, D. (1981) 'Themes and continuities in radical and traditional social work', *British Journal of Social Work*, Vol. 11, No.3.

Wedge, P. (1973) *Born to Last*, London: Arrow Books.

Whetten, D.A. (1982) in Rodgers, D.L. and Whetten, D.A., *Interorganizational Coordination: Theory, Research and Implementation*, Iowa: Iowa State University Press.

Wolf, S. (1984) 'A multifactoral model of deviant sexuality', *Paper Presented to the Third International Congress of Vicstimology*, November 1984, Lisbon.

Wolff, R. (1975) 'Kindesmisshandlungen unde ihre ursachen', *Arbeitsgruppe kinderschutz gewalt gegen kinder*, Reinbek bei Hamburg: Rowohlt.

Wolock, I. and Horowitz, B. (1984) 'Child maltreatment as a social problem: the neglect of neglect', *American Journal of Orthopsychiatry* 54,4.

Wraith, R.E. and Lamb, G.B. (1971) *Public Inquiries as an Instrument of Government*, London: Allen and Unwin.

Inquiry reports

Published reports into the death by ill-treatment of a specific child are usually referred to by the child's name. Reports are listed in alphabetical order.

AUCKLAND (1975) Report of the committee of inquiry into the provision of services to the family of John George Auckland (London: HMSO).

BAGNALL (1973a) Report of working party of social services committee inquiry into circumstances surrounding the death of Graham Bagnall and the role of the county social services (Salop County Council).

BAGNALL (1973b) Report of a committee of the hospital management committee into the circumstances leading to the death of Graham Bagnall insofar as the hospital authority were concerned (Shrewsbury Group Hospital Management Committee).

BECKFORD (1985) *A Child in Trust*: the report of the panel of inquiry into the circumstances surrounding the death of Jasmine Beckford (London Borough of Brent).

BREWER (1977) Report of the review panel appointed by Somerset Area Review Committee to consider the case of Wayne Brewer (Somerset Area Review Committee).

BROWN (1978) *Paul Brown*: report of an inquiry held at Wallasey (Wirral Borough Council and Wirral Area Health Authority).

BROWN (1979) An inquiry into an inquiry (Birmingham: British Association of Social Workers).

BROWN (1980) The report of the committee of inquiry into the case of Paul Stephen Brown. DHSS Cmnd 8107 (London: HMSO).

CAESAR (1982) Report on the involvement of the social services department in the events preceding the death of Jason Caesar (Cambridge: Cambridgeshire County Council).

CARLILE (1987) *A Child in Mind*: protection of children in a responsible society (London Borough of Greenwich).

CARTHY (1985) Report of the standing inquiry panel into the case of Reuben Carthy (Nottinghamshire County Council).

CHAPMAN (1979) Lester Chapman inquiry report (Berkshire County Council).

CLARK (1975) Report of the committee of inquiry into the considerations given and steps taken towards securing the welfare of Richard Clark by Perth Town and other bodies or persons concerned (Scottish Education Department, Social Work Services Group: HMSO).

CLARKE (1979) The report of the committee of inquiry into the actions of the authorities and agencies relating to Darryn James Clarke. DHSS Cmnd 7739 (London: HMSO).

CLEVELAND (1988) Report of the inquiry into child abuse in Cleveland 1987. Cmnd 412 (London: HMSO).

COLWELL (1974) Report of committee of inquiry into the care and supervision provided in relation to Maria Colwell (London: HMSO).

COLWELL (1975) *Children at Risk*: a study into the problems revealed by the report of the inquiry into the case of Maria Colwell (Lewes: East Sussex County Council).

COLWELL (1976) *Child at Risk*: joint report of the County Secretary and Director of Social Services (Lewes: East Sussex County Council).

GATES (1982) Report of the panel of inquiry into the death of Lucie Gates, Vol.1; Chairman's Report, Vol.2: Report of other panel members (London Borough of Bexley and Bexley Health Authority).

GODFREY (1975) Report of the joint committee of enquiry into non-accidental injury to children with particular reference to Lisa Godfrey (Lambeth, Southwark and Lewisham Health Authority (Teaching); Inner London Probation and After-Care Committee; London Borough of Lambeth).

H FAMILY (1977) *The H Family*: report of an investigation by the Director of Social Services and the Deputy Town Clerk (Surrey County Council).

HADDON (1980) Report of the Director of Social Services on Claire Haddon born 9 December 1978 (City of Birmingham Social Services Department).

HENRY (1987) Report of the public inquiry into the death of Tyra Henry (London Borough of Lambeth).

HOWLETT (1976) Joint inquiry arising from the death of Neil Howlett (City of Birmingham District Council and Birmingham Area Health Authority).

KOSEDA (1986) Report of the review panel into the death of Heidi Koseda (London Borough of Hillingdon).

MEHMEDAGI (1981) Maria Mehmedagi: report of an independent inquiry (London Borough of Southwark; Lambeth, Southwark and Lewisham Area Health Authority (Teaching); Inner London Probation and After-Care Service).

MENHENIOTT (1978) Report of the Social Work Service of the DHSS into certain aspects of the management of the case of Stephen Menheniott (London: HMSO).

MEURS (1975) Report of the review body appointed to inquire into the case of Steven Meurs (Norfolk County Council).

NASEBY (1973) Report of the committee of inquiry set up to inquire into the treatment of baby David Lees Naseby, deceased, at Burton-on-Trent General Hospital from February to May 1973 (Staffordshire Area Health Authority).

O'NEILL (1945) Report by Sir Walter Monckton on the circumstances which led to the boarding-out of Dennis and Terence O'Neill at Bank Farm, Misterley and the steps taken to supervise their welfare. Cmnd 6636 (London: HMSO).

PAGE (1981) Malcolm Page: report of a panel appointed by the Essex Area Review Committee (Essex County Council and Essex Area Health Authority).

PEACOCK (1978) Report of committee of inquiry concerning Simon Peacock (Cambridgeshire County Council; Suffolk County Council; Cambridgeshire Area Health Authority (Teaching); Suffolk Area Health Authority).

PIAZZANI (1974) Report of the joint committee set up to consider coordination of services concerned with non-accidental injury to children (Essex Area Health Authority and Essex County Council).

PINDER/FRANKLAND (1981) Child abuse inquiry sub-committee report concerning Christopher Pinder/Daniel Frankland (born 19 December 1979, died 8 July 1980) (Bradford Area Review Committee).

SPENCER (1978) Karen Spencer (Derbyshire County Council).

TAYLOR (1980) Carly Taylor: report of an independent inquiry (Leicestershire County Council and Leicestershire Area Health Authority (Teaching)).

WOODCOCK (1984) White, R.: Report on the death of Shirley Woodcock (London Borough of Hammersmith and Fulham).

INDEX